I KNOW BETTER NOW

I KNOW BETTER NOW

BETTER

NOW

MY LIFE BEFORE, DURING, AND AFTER THE

RAMONES

RICHIE RAMONE with Peter Aaron

Backbeat
Books

AN IMPRINT OF HAL LEONARD LLC

Published in 2018 by Backbeat Books
An Imprint of Hal Leonard LLC
7777 West Bluemound Road
Milwaukee, WI 53213

Trade Book Division Editorial Offices
33 Plymouth St., Montclair, NJ 07042

All lyrics used by permission of Richie Ramone.

Printed in the United States of America

Book design by Michael Kellner

Library of Congress Cataloging-in-Publication Data is available upon request.

ISBN 978-1-61713-710-5

www.backbeatbooks.com

To my father, Leonard Reinhardt, who left us this year,
and the family that loves him still: my mother, Mary Ann Reinhardt;
my big brother, Lenny; and my wonderful sisters,
Marlene, Christine, and Kathleen

Contents

Foreword

Richie Ramone ain't no footnote.

Richie Ramone is the *lynchpin*. The guy whose frighteningly fast and powerful beat blasted the Ramones back into their rightful place in the rock 'n' roll firmament, when it looked like they were bound to crash and burn on the Bowery from whence they came.

Could the Ramones have found another drummer in their hour of need, back in 1982? Sure. But would it have been someone as kick-ass and as mind-bogglingly awesome a drummer as Richie? Someone who could, besides playing the living *hell* out of the drums, sing for the band—and not only backups but even occasional lead vocals? Someone who, besides doing those things so well—things that certainly aren't easy to do; the Ramones' music is not nearly as easy to play, correctly, as the prevailing perception would have many believe—could also write songs for the group? Songs as great as "Somebody Put Something in My Drink"? Or "Smash You"? Or "(You) Can't Say Anything Nice"? Dream on. You're going to have a very hard time finding another punk-rock drummer with all those qualities press-rolled into one explosive package. The fact that the Ramones and Richie found each other at exactly the time they needed each other is nothing short of miraculous.

But, really, I'm not here to make the case for Richie as a crucial, driving part of the Ramones' music. The three albums he made with them during his five frantic years (four years and nine months, if you want to get technical) in the band—1984's monumental *Too Tough to Die*, 1986's *Animal Boy*, and 1987's *Halfway to Sanity*—along with all the non-album cuts, official and bootleg live recordings, and videos of that unique and powerful lineup that are out there, make the case well enough, thank you. No, I'm here on behalf of Richie Ramone the man. Or the mystery man, as it were, in light of his being such a quiet soul when he was in the Ramones and famously fading from view for so many years after his leaving them in 1987. I'm here to help him tell his tale.

I really think it was fate that brought Richie and me together to work on this book. I ended up in Ohio, and then New York later on, but, like Richie, I'm originally a Jersey boy. We both grew up in the same general area, and we spent our formative years haunting a lot of the same places that northern New Jersey teenagers haunted back in the 1960s and '70s. And, of course, we have our love of music in common—especially when it comes to the music made by Richie and his departed bruddas.

By this point, there have been many books written about the Ramones and the punk scene they initiated, a couple of them by other Ramones. But in each of those books, Richie is barely mentioned, and he's never fully given his due—despite the fact that he, in the words of Joey Ramone himself, "saved the band." Until now, as far as the individual stories of the band members go, only those of Joey (by way of his brother, Mickey Leigh), Dee Dee, Johnny, and Marky have been told; even Monte Melnick, the band's intrepid road manager, has written a book. Richie has been the missing link in the Ramones' story—the link that re-energized the quartet with a rapid-fire renaissance that gave them some of their greatest music, and kept them going long after he was no longer physically present in the band. But with *I Know Better Now*, he's the link that's no longer missing.

Working with Richie on this book has been both a pleasure and an adventure. I certainly learned a lot about him over the course of doing it. And I really think Richie learned a lot about himself as well. Now, though, it's time for *you* to learn what we learned.

I already know you like great rock 'n' roll. It's what brought you here. But I hope you also like wild rides. Because you're holding one in your hands right now. Hang on tight.

—Peter Aaron, 2018

Acknowledgments

To my fallen, but never forgotten, Ramones brothers: Joey, Dee Dee, Johnny, and Tommy.

To Arturo Vega, Mickey Leigh, and Monte Melnick.

To Joe Blaney, Steve Brereton, Larry Chekofsky, Dean Dobbs, Sandra Linden, Matt Lolya, Steve Miller, John Robinson, James Sant'Andrea (Flash), and Eddie Slivka for helping me remember.

To Peter Aaron, the kind of book-writing partner every non-book-writing author hopes to have.

To Lee Sobel, for making the big deals.

To my sponsors: Karen and Chuck Blashaw at Axis percussion, Mike Ciprari at SJC Custom Drums, Dominick Gagliano at Amedia Cymbals, Larry Guay at Los Cabos Drumsticks, Chris Brady at Aquarian Drumheads, and Michael Ciravolo and Anthony Ramirez at Schecter Guitars.

To my label guys, Darron Hemann at DC-Jam Records and Steve Pilace at Outro Records, for their many efforts on my behalf.

To Ben Reagan, for being there and having my back.

To Kevin Albinder, Steve Appleford, Mariano Asch, Donna Balancia, Rodney Bingenheimer, Julieta Bugacoff, Ailiń Gómez Caraballo, Luke Cauldwell, Keith Cooper, Alan Denkenson, Tina

DiGeorge, Donna and Boney, Dominick Fairbanks, Ted Felicetti, Eduardo Focka, Caroline ffrench Blake, Julia Green, Vicky Hamilton, Dave Hedstrom, Rick Johnson, Daniel Noble, Al Jourgensen, Whitey Kirst, Beth Lyden, Hunter McCann, Darren Merinuk, Cathy Miller, John Nikolai, Joe Queer, Ben Reagan, Paul Roessler, Alex Ruffini, Luca Viola, Peter Walsh, Liz Walton, Daniel Watanabe, and Ivan Weingart, for their talents and support.

To my twin nieces and nephews, Jimmy, Jason, Justin, Cori, Christopher, Jesse, Lenny, Nathan, Rich, Brittany, Amanda, and Cassandra, for their general awesomeness.

To Brett Smith, the very definition of a true friend since the day we met.

To Jeff Jones, for his help with this book, and all kinds of things, for the past twenty-five years.

To Roomba the Wunderdog.

And, of course, to Clare.

Finally, to all you crazy Ramones fans out there, who continue to keep this thing alive all around the world.

—Richie, 2018

Thanks to Richie; Lee Sobel; my mother, Marlene Wegele; my sisters, Monique and Shannon, and their lovely families, which include my rockin' nieces, Sasha and Morgan; Jeff Jones; Bernadette Malavarca and everyone at Backbeat; Monte Melnick; Flash; Deneanne Niebergall; and my indispensable cats, Penelope and Frankie.

—Peter, 2018

Introduction

It's May 19, 2017. Joey Ramone's sixty-sixth birthday. Joey's not around anymore, which is really sad. Neither are the other three original Ramones, Dee Dee, Johnny, and Tommy. But I'm a Ramone, too. And I'm still here.

I'm sitting behind the drums, onstage at Webster Hall on the Lower East Side, at the Joey Ramone Birthday Bash. I used to live just a couple of blocks from this place, which used to be called the Ritz. That was almost thirty-five years ago. The whole neighborhood's really different now—totally cleaned-up. It used to be filled with freaks, punks, junkies, and bums. But tonight, outside the club, the sidewalks are full of the NYU kids who live around here now. Walking back from graduation in their gowns, they don't even know what happened here, what it was like. Now it's all nice restaurants and fancy stores, nothing like it was when I lived here.

Inside Webster Hall it's different, though. The room is sold out, packed with Ramones fans. A lot of them have flown in from really far away, just to be here tonight. From Japan, Europe, South America, and all kinds of other places. Some of them are old enough to remember what the city was like back in the day. They used to come see the Ramones play in New York, or in their town, when the band was on tour. And some of these people weren't even born when the Ramones were together—but they still grew up listening to the Ramones, like the band never went away. It's crazy, when I think about it. But it's great, too.

To my left, about five feet from the front of the drum riser, C. J. Ramone—who replaced Dee Dee when he quit the Ramones in 1989, two years after I was out of the band—is playing bass. To my right, playing guitar, is Joey's brother, Mickey Leigh. Mickey organizes this whole thing every year. He's been doing it since Joey died in 2001. It's a benefit show that raises funds for research to help fight lymphoma, the disease that Joey died from. This is the fourth one I've played so far, and it's always great, getting together to honor Joey's memory, and seeing the other people he loved to be around. Like George Tabb, the singer for Furious George; and the Ramones' road manager, Monte Melnick, who's emceeing the show.

Sometimes I laugh and say all I did was spend almost five years staring at Joey Ramone's back from my drum stool. But the truth is that during the time I was in the Ramones, Joey and I were really close. On and offstage, we were inseparable pretty much the whole time. We drank together, got high together, worked on songs together, went bowling together, and laughed together. Joey was a great singer, but he was also a great guy with a really big heart, and we were really good friends. I always think about him every time I'm doing a gig with my own band. And, of course, I'm thinking about him even more tonight. I really miss that guy. A lot.

Twenty-seventeen is also the fortieth anniversary of the second and third Ramones albums, *Leave Home* and *Rocket to Russia*, so this year's bash is celebrating their birthdays, too. Those records have Tommy on drums, and they came out before I was in the band, but I played the songs that are on them literally hundreds of times with the Ramones, and they're all deep, deep, deep in my blood. Tonight, C. J. and Mickey take turns singing lead while we blast out a few of them: "Do You Wanna Dance," "Locket Love," "I Can't Give You Anything," "Suzy Is a Headbanger," "We're a Happy Family." Of course, we can never match the sound of the band with Joey, Johnny, and Dee Dee. I know that because I was there, driving that sound for five insane years. But it's fun anyway. Our trio, which we put together just for tonight, is called the Love Triangle. And, yeah, it's nothing but love—for Joey and the Ramones and the music—that I feel from everyone who's here. Not just the fans in the audience, but the other musicians, too.

C. J. has to split to do a gig with his solo band later tonight in Philly. So the three of us walk off, and I grab a smoke outside—no more smoke-filled New York clubs these days—and a beer backstage, while a couple of local bands play some more Ramones songs. After that, it's time for the main house band, which has Ed Stasium (who produced and engineered some of the Ramones' albums) and Walt Stack from the Bullys on guitars, Andy Shernoff from the Dictators on bass, and Clem Burke from Blondie on drums for a couple of songs—until I take over.

We back up a parade of guest singers from New York's rock royalty—people like Pat DiNizio from the Smithereens, Tish and Snooky and Russell Wolinsky from the Sic F*cks, Philippe Marcade from the Senders, and Miriam Linna from the Cramps and the A-Bones. James Vincent Boland, the actor who played Joey on the HBO series *Vinyl*, sings "I Don't Care" with us—which is pretty surreal. All of them are so totally into it, having an awesome time and getting to sing all these songs they've loved for years and years with an all-star band. The audience is crammed in front of the stage, smiling and going nuts, pogoing up and down and singing along to every word of every song.

We do "Rockaway Beach," "Sheena Is a Punk Rocker," "Cretin Hop," "Pinhead," "Swallow My Pride," "Commando," "California Sun," and about a dozen more.

When we're done, I go out into the club and sign autographs for people, put my arm around them while they take selfies of us together. Everybody's happy, and at the end of the night the whole thing feels really great. It just seems like people will always love the Ramones. Always.

"Ramones forever!" is what they say to me when they shake my hand.

And, like I said, I'm a Ramone, and I'm still here. After all the crazy shit I've been through.

I KNOW BETTER NOW

1

Clean White Shirts and Bow Ties

My parents shot tons and tons of home movies when I was a kid. We'd always watch them when relatives came over, or at Christmas or Thanksgiving or whatever. Even after that, whenever I'd go to visit my parents, they always wanted to watch all these old movies. They had them transferred from Super 8 to VHS back in the 1980s, and then they had them put on DVD.

There's one from when I was about two or three. I'm at a playground somewhere with my big brother Lenny, my big sister Marlene, and a couple of my cousins. It's a sunny day out, and everyone else is smiling and laughing, but I'm just sitting there on the slide, looking at the camera and crying. I was always crying back then, my folks tell me. I don't know why. I guess it's just what I did when I didn't get my way, or I had to do something I didn't want to do. Maybe I just didn't want to go down the slide that day. I was the middle child—Lenny is five years older, Marlene is two years older, and there's my little sisters: Christine, eight years younger, and Kathleen, ten years younger—so I guess I always felt like I had to fight for attention. None of us have a middle name. Mom and Dad kept it simple when it came to birth certificates.

Looking back on it now, I had a great childhood, even though I've always been a pretty dark dude. I've pretty much always done what I wanted to do—and I'll fight really hard whenever somebody says I can't get my way.

A lot of punk musicians come from broken homes, fucked-up backgrounds. Not me. I'm from a close, tight family. Middle class all the way. I was born Richard Reinhardt on August 11, 1956, in Passaic, New Jersey. Later on, because of my hometown and my drumming, Ben Reagan, my good friend and band mate, called me "the Passaic Pounder," which was also the nickname of this famous boxer who was born there, Steve Hamas. I was never a huge boxing fan, but I think that's a cool connection, with the nicknames and all that. My dad, who grew up in Passaic, was Leonard Reinhardt, and his father, Cornelius Reinhardt, was from Den Bemmel, a village in South Holland. My grandfather's real last name was Reinhout, but when he came through Ellis Island in 1910, for some reason the immigration people changed it to Reinhardt, and he just stuck with that.

My mom, whose maiden name was Mary Ann Kubalek, is from Wisconsin, and her side of the family is Slavic. She had dark hair then, and she was really tall and beautiful. All of us kids are tall, and we've all got her high, Eastern European cheekbones—except for Christine, who has more of my dad's rounded face, and was shorter and chubby as a kid. I used to make fun of her for that—I'd call her "Hoss," after Dan Blocker's character on *Bonanza*. Man, she *hated* that. I was a pretty mischievous kid, always pulling the hair out of my sisters' dolls or lighting their dolls' hair on fire. I did a lot of other crazy, destructive stuff, too. But we'll get to that later.

If you don't know Passaic, it's a decent-sized city—about three square miles—and it's around sixteen miles from Manhattan. It's a factory town—textile mills were the main industry for years and years. It has some pretty rough spots, but it also has a lot of nice, pretty typical American suburbs. We lived in one of those: wide streets, little square front yards with narrow driveways, two-story houses with wood siding that were mostly built in the 1920s and '30s. Lenny, Marlene, and I were all born when my folks had a railroad apartment on the second floor of a house at 266 High Street. My mom's mother, who we called Nana, lived there with us. One of the home movies has a cute little scene in the backyard there, where my mom is hanging out the laundry to dry. She'd tie me to the clothesline with a little harness attached to a long rope, so I could crawl around back there, and she didn't have to worry about me wandering off while she was bringing laundry in and out of the house. Taffy, our cocker spaniel, would be out there, too, but she'd just let him run around—*I* was the one she kept tied up. I don't really have any memories of that house, though, because, when I was three, we moved a few blocks over, to Howard Avenue. The family was getting bigger, and my dad's business was growing and making more money, so he moved us into a bigger place.

Like my mom, my dad was really tall—a little over six feet. He ran a landscape gardening company called Leonard Reinhardt, Inc. It's still in business today—my cousin Steve owns it. My dad started the company by himself in 1953, and by the time I was a kid in the '60s, he had twenty employees working for him and about eight or nine trucks, all of them painted bright red with "Leonard Reinhardt, Inc.— Landscaping" in gold-leaf lettering on the sides. They mostly handled commercial and industrial jobs—schools, parks, big office complexes, things like that. He worked six days a week, really long days. He'd go in at six in the morning and wouldn't be home until seven at night. And, when he finally did get home, he was usually really stressed out and tired, and you didn't want to piss him off. If you did, he'd get that look in his eyes, and you just knew what was coming if you didn't cut it out fast. He had these really big, giant hands—and he wouldn't think twice about giving you a swat with one of them. People freak out about that kind of stuff now, but in the '60s, people still hit their kids if they were bad. That's just how it was.

My dad worked really hard to provide for us, but he was really strict and pretty closed-off, emotionally. Later on we could say it to each other, but back then I don't remember him ever saying, "I love you," to any of us. Never played catch with us. He was always working. Doing what he had to. He was definitely one of those "children should be seen and not heard" kind of guys. Sometimes, when my mom knew he'd had a really rough day at work, she'd tell me, Lenny, and Marlene— this was before Christine and Kathy, my folks' late-in-life surprises—to head to our rooms before he got home, so we wouldn't run into him until dinnertime. After work, he'd go in his office and have have his scotch. J&B was what he drank—two before dinner. If he had a third one, that meant dinner was late, and there might be a problem with him getting angry. But that didn't happen a lot.

My mom had to have dinner going by the time he got home, and it had to be hot when she put it on the table. *Boiling* hot. If it wasn't, she'd hear about it. Once, I saw my dad smash a plate by putting his bare hand through it because he was so mad at my mom over something being wrong with dinner. And he was really competitive. Couldn't stand to lose. I remember my brother and me playing miniature golf with him once. When you're an adult and you play a game with little kids, you let them win—make them feel good and all that. But he wasn't winning, and I remember he actually got really upset about that. So I'd say I probably got a lot of my competitive streak from him.

At the same time, though, he had a great sense of humor. His favorite TV show was *The Honeymooners*. He loved, loved, *loved* that show. He saw Jackie Gleason, and thought, hey, he's just like me. Back then, he had a little bar set up in the basement of our house. A lot of families in the '50s and '60s had one of those—the whole cocktail-lounge thing. My folks would have these big parties down there every weekend with our relatives and people they knew from the neighborhood, and he'd always be cracking people up with lines from *The Honeymooners*— "To the moon, Alice!" People always dressed up, and there was lots of dancing. My parents loved entertaining, and I was attracted to that. It definitely made me want to go into the entertainment field myself.

Every Sunday, we'd have T-bone steak for dinner, and it *had* to be grilled. That was the only way my dad liked it. I remember my mom being out in back of the house at the grill in the dead of winter, with two feet of snow on the ground, cooking him his steak. She really loved him, though—that's why she did all that. And he definitely loved her, too. You can see that in the home movies I talked about, the way he looks at her when they're both in the shot, or the way the camera lingers on her when it's him doing the shooting. They were both always really, really supportive of their kids when we got interested in anything creative, and we always had really great birthdays and Christmases. Always big, shiny metal Tonka trucks for me and my brother, and new dolls for my sisters. My parents got married in 1950, and they stayed together until my dad passed in 2018, while I was writing this book. Almost seventy years. That's something, huh?

My mom was the protector. She was the one who was always there and really took care of us and raised us, since my dad was gone so much. Now, of course, it's totally different for most families, but that's how it was back then: the husband worked, and the wife stayed home and took care of the kids. My mom loved putting together birthday parties for us. We'd have friends and cousins over in our wood-paneled basement, me and the other boys with clean white shirts and bow ties and our neat little haircuts with Brylcreem in them, and the girls in those frilly little dresses and saddle shoes. Everybody in their little party hats, blowing their noisemakers. Mom would organize games like bobbing for apples, and pin the tail on the donkey. For Halloween, she'd make us costumes and lead us around the neighborhood, going door-to-door for candy. I remember being dressed up as a clown one year, with clown makeup and a pointy hat, and a shiny red-and-white outfit. Typical postwar suburban stuff, I guess.

My mom was really religious, too. Hard-core Roman Catholic. We went to Saint Nicholas Church on Washington Place every Sunday. Never missed a service—well, at least I didn't until I was in my teens, playing in bands and starting to live the rock 'n' roll lifestyle, which didn't really work with getting up early for church. Once that started happening, I never went back. Religion was never my thing. Never had any interest in it. It just seemed like whatever they were pushing, all the "be good to your fellow man" stuff, was stuff you could do yourself anyway. I hated having to learn the Rosary, and the confession booth really freaked me out:

"Father, I stole some money out of my mother's purse."

"All right, son, you are forgiven. Say thirty Our Fathers and twenty Our Mothers."

What the hell did *that* do? Later on, when I was in the Ramones, I wrote a song about that whole experience, "I'm Not Jesus":

Father, son, and Holy Ghost
Say your prayers—it's your only hope
Twelve apostles can't help you now
I'll be back to stake my ground
I'm not Jesus
I can't heal you
I'm not Jesus
I can't heal you

The one thing I actually did like about church was singing along with the hymns. That was my first real experience with playing music "live." All the hymns were in Latin, so you had to memorize all these lines phonetically, without even knowing what they meant. But I really dug it, the call-and-response structure of a lot of the music.

Another musical memory I have from then is of hearing the theme music from *Lassie* on TV. It had a guy whistling this really—I don't know, I guess you'd call it a bittersweet refrain. For some reason, whenever that came on, it always made feel really sad, maybe because I'd seen the show and was worried about Lassie being in danger. I'd start crying and go and hide in this little space in the kitchen, between the refrigerator and the stove. Weird, huh? But I guess it shows how strongly music affected me, even then.

Besides being really religious, the rest of my family is pretty Republican, too. I think a lot of small-business owners, like my dad was, are Republican because they feel like it's better for them—that whole deal about lower tax rates for businesses that the Republicans are always talking about. But I'm on the other side. I'm like a rat, y'know? The black-sheep liberal Democrat of the family. My dad was Dutch Reformed Protestant, but he never really went to church. Didn't like going. Every night, though, he would kneel down and say his prayers before he went to sleep. This big, tough guy, down on his knees next to my parents' bed. That always weirded me out a little, because it would be the only time I ever saw him really letting his guard down, being humble and vulnerable.

The house on Howard Avenue was right at the intersection of Howard and River Road and close to the Union Street Bridge. It's not there anymore. In the mid-'60s, when the state decided to build a section of Route 21 through that part of the neighborhood, and through River Drive, which runs alongside it, they tore down our house and about three others, and we had to move again, this time to Clifton, the next big town over. But we lived at 24 Howard Avenue for about six or seven years, and I guess those were what you'd call my formative years. That's really when my childhood starts to come into focus.

2

Oh Man, the Rats

As you might guess from the name, River Road follows the edge of a river: the Passaic River. It's still one of the most polluted rivers in America, even though they started cleaning it up around 1972. But before then, it was *really* a mess. This chemical plant in Newark that made Agent Orange for the Vietnam War was dumping all this dioxin in it, plus who knows what else there was in there from the other factories. On one side of River Road was our yard and our neighborhood, which was totally clean and nice. We had a corner lot—after we moved from Howard Avenue, we always had a corner lot—and, since my dad was in the landscaping business, we always had the best yard in the neighborhood. Always. I'm talking award-winning hedges; super-green, really full lawn. All that. People were jealous. And that's a lot of the reason why they ended up hiring my dad to do *their* yards. Our yard was like advertising for him.

Anyway, on the other side of the street there was an open, grassy field, and, past that, the riverbank, which had all kinds of junk and trash just sitting there, piled up: rusty old cars and busted-up appliances;

worn-out tires that got filled up with rainwater, which meant you had mosquitos breeding in there. Every fall, the City of Passaic used to dump all the leaves that had been raked up around the town right there on the riverbank, in these giant piles that got wet and rotted and attracted all kinds of bugs. And rats. Oh, man, the rats. That whole place was just *crawling* with rats. It was crazy.

My parents were always warning my brother Lenny and me, "Stay away from the riverbank." But, of course, what did we do? We were bored kids, and it was right there. That place was like our little adventure land, and me and Lenny and my friends—like Bobby Brown, who was the first friend I had—got into all kinds of wild shit down there. I remember I had a bow and arrow set, and we'd take that there and try to hunt rats. I don't think any of us ever got any, though. They were too fast, and none of us was a good shot. One time, we found this old refrigerator down there, and I had some matches, so I lit it on fire. And it just kept on burning and burning and burning! It must have still had Freon in it, and of course, at the time, none of us knew how flammable that stuff was. After a couple of minutes, the fire had gotten pretty out of hand, so we thought about pushing the whole thing in the river. But it was heavy, and the flames were too big, so we just took off running and left it there. I don't know what happened after that. I thought we'd all get in big trouble, but I guess nothing else caught on fire, so no one ever found out about it. Or, if they did, they just didn't care. But that wasn't the craziest thing I remember happening at the riverbank.

There was this weird guy—I don't remember his name—who owned a bar up the block from our house. He also owned this big old barge that he had anchored right there along the river, near the scuzzy part we used play in. I think he bought it with the idea of fixing it up and making it into one of those fancy floating restaurants. But this was Passaic, not the French Riviera, and the river was all polluted and junky, so I don't know what he was thinking with that. Another thing: for some reason, he also owned a donkey that he kept tied up there, close to where the barge was. It would just stand there all day and eat the grass in the field. Being the juvenile delinquent I was, sometimes I'd fuck with that poor donkey—do stuff to spook it, throw shit at it. Just to get it to react and go, "Hee-haw!" We thought that was really funny at the time. Today, I'm a big animal-rights person, but back then, I could be a cruel, stupid kid.

This barge the old guy had was just falling apart, all rusted out, with big holes in the decks and everywhere else. When I think about it now, I'm amazed the thing could still float. It just looked like it was too far gone to do anything with. But I guess he must've gotten it really cheap, and he had these big dreams for it. Like I said, he was weird. To the kids around the neighborhood, he also had a reputation for being this strange, cranky guy, and we were all afraid of him. But that didn't keep us from sneaking down to his barge in the summer, when we were bored, to vandalize it—kick holes in the thing, burn up the different pieces that were hanging off it. Whenever we were down there and we heard him coming, we'd just take off running.

One day, though, we were down there, climbing all over this barge and busting shit up, and we heard some wood creaking and turned around—and there was the guy standing right there, about three feet behind us. And he was *pissed*. Man, was he pissed. This huge guy with his face all red and his eyes all bloodshot and bulging out, just standing there shaking like he was going to have a heart attack or something. He was screaming at us: "What the *hell* are you guys doing here? Who the hell told you could be on *my* boat? Huh? Huh? Who said you could be on here? Huh?" He was blocking us from this wooden plank that was the only way off the barge.

"Did you do *that*?" he screamed at us, pointing to something we'd obviously just fucked up. "Did you do that? WHY did you do that, huh? Why did you do that? WHY?" He was bent over us, screaming, like, five inches from our faces. He was sweating, and I could smell the beer on his breath. Even now, I can still remember how terrified I was.

Then he grabbed Lenny and started holding his head over the top of this empty oil drum. "You think fire is funny? You think that's *funny*?" he yelled, and then he took out this lighter and acted like he was going to light Lenny's hair on fire. Lenny started wiggling around and got him to let go, but we were still stuck there with this crazy guy, thinking we're all going to die.

He started yelling at us: "Come here! *Now!* Get in there! *Now!*" Then he unlocked a padlock, opened up a door that went to this cabin part of the barge, and pushed everybody inside at once. And he slammed the door shut and fuckin' locked us in there. I heard the lock go "click." And then he just left! Didn't say anything else. Just walked off the boat and kept going.

My heart was beating really fast, and I started to cry. Maybe he was going to go get the cops and turn us in to them, I don't know. But it was pretty scary, being in there as a little kid—I must have been about five or six—not knowing what the hell was happening. It was dark in there, and I remember having to be careful about where I was standing, because the floorboards were mostly missing or rotted out, and there was water rushing underneath—I could've fallen right down into that river, easy.

But the other thing was that, since the entire boat was full of holes, there were also plenty of places that little kids like us could easily fit through. So, after a few minutes, that's what we did—as soon as we figured out that this whacko barge guy wasn't out there waiting for us. We squeezed out through one of the holes, ran down the plank back onto the riverbank, and tore ass straight home.

When we got there, we told my mom about the whole thing. I guess she could tell we were pretty traumatized and that we weren't just making shit up. She got pretty freaked out herself, and she called my dad up at work to tell him what had happened. He came home fast and made Lenny and me tell him the whole story again, while my mom was sitting there, crying. "Thank God, thank God," she kept saying, over and over again, after we talked about how we'd escaped and all that. I guess it took a few minutes for it to sink in with her that her boys could've been kidnapped and molested or killed or who knows what.

My dad just stood there the whole time, shaking his head. I could definitely tell he was mad, but there was something else going on. There was this seriousness there that I'd never seen before. He was thinking really hard about something. Going back over it in my mind now, I see what it was: my dad was out for blood.

"Okay, that's it," he blurted out after a few minutes. "That's it! We're going over there. Right now. Right now. Come on, come on!" And he marched all of us—me, my mom, Lenny, and even Marlene—right out of our front door and up the block in the direction of the bar that Mr. Barge Guy owned. My dad was going to confront this guy, right there in front of his customers. I just walked along, watching him, taking it in, keeping quiet. By that point, nothing was scary anymore—it was more like the next part of a big adventure. When we finally got to the bar, though, it turned out the guy wasn't there. Maybe he'd gone back to the barge, seen we'd escaped, and figured we'd probably do just what we did: go and tell our folks. I don't know. But I do know he was lucky he wasn't around, because my dad would've killed him. I'm not kidding. I saw it in his eyes when we were there: he was yelling at the bartender, asking him where the son of a bitch was. He had a right to be pissed off, too. You don't fuck with a man's kids like that. What Barge Guy did was some real serial-killer shit, when I think back on it. Who knows what would have happened to us if we hadn't gotten off that fuckin' boat, y'know?

Anyway, since the guy pulled a no-show at the bar, we all marched back home. I guess my dad must have called him the next day or something and straightened him out, after he'd calmed down a bit. I don't know. No one really talked about it much after that. But from then on, my brother and I stayed away from that stupid fuckin' barge.

Well, mostly we did.

3

Tons and Tons of Whipped Cream

Neither of my folks were ever into music that much, really. When I was a kid, I sang the hymns with my mom and Lenny and Marlene in church, but that was it, back then. But since they loved throwing parties and dancing, they had to have music for that. So my dad bought a really nice record player, what they called a hi-fi then—one of those low, console things with a wooden cabinet that had built-in speakers, a flip-up hatch to get to the turntable part, and sliding doors in the front to the shelves where you stored the LP records. There weren't a lot of LPs in there, but there was one that grabbed me before I'd ever even heard the music.

On the cover, it had a picture of this beautiful, brown-haired woman, who was just sitting there, totally nude—except for the tons and tons of what looked like thick, white shaving cream covering her from the neck down—against a bright green background. She was looking straight at the camera in this really sexy way, licking her finger. When I first found that record in the hi-fi cabinet, I got the feeling that maybe I wasn't really old enough yet to be looking at the picture. But, for some reason, looking at it made me feel all . . . *enthusiastic*, if you know what I mean. I'd sneak down in the basement sometimes, just to take it out of the hi-fi and stare at it for a few minutes, before putting it back inside and sliding the door shut—quick, if I heard my mom or dad coming down the stairs.

If you grew up around the same time as me, you probably know this record, at least by the cover: *Whipped Cream and Other Delights* by Herb Alpert and the Tijuana Brass, from 1965. When my dad finally trusted me enough to let me use the record player, of course it was the first record I played—and it blew my mind. I wouldn't have known who he was then, but Hal Blaine—one of the greatest drummers of all time, and a guy who's worked with everybody from Sinatra to the Beach Boys—plays on that album. And he just totally, totally swings it. The big hit, "A Taste of Honey," is the first song, and I can still remember hearing that for the first time. It opens with that slow, spooky part where it's just the horns, marimba, and a twangy guitar playing that spaghetti-western thing, before it stops and gets totally quiet. And then Blaine kicks in on the bass drum: *Bumm-bumm-bumm-bumm. Bumm-bumm-bumm-bumm. Bumm-bumm-bumm-bumm.* He starts up a tight roll on the snare that gets faster and faster, and then the horns come in: *Buh-bah BOP! Buh-bah BOP! Bah-bup bup-BAHHH buh-bup bah BAH!* And, man, the whole thing just takes off. I was, like, "Whoa! What's *this* about?!" So I guess maybe that's what first got me interested in becoming a drummer: a hot chick covered in whipped cream.

This was in the mid-1960s. I don't really remember much about JFK getting shot—I was too young then. Years later, though, in '68, when Bobby Kennedy was shot, that I saw happen live, in the film they showed on TV the morning after the assassination. That was intense. They showed him giving the speech at the Ambassador Hotel, then he was just walking out, and—*bam!*—the cameras showed all this screaming, and people running everywhere. And then it was just him lying there on the floor, with blood all around him, and people holding his head up. Even as a little kid, I knew that was it for the guy. Really sad.

I vaguely remember when the Beatles were on *Ed Sullivan* for the first time, but I was only eight years old, so they just didn't really register with me. I watched them, and I kind of liked it, I guess. But I didn't really *get it*, y'know? Not at the time, anyway. Lenny, though, was just the right age—he was about thirteen or fourteen, and he was pretty moved by seeing that. All of a sudden, he and his friends and a lot of the older kids around the neighborhood were really into the Beatles and the whole British thing. So that made me pay a bit more attention, I suppose.

Now that I think of it, maybe there's another reason I couldn't really focus on the Beatles that first time they were on *Ed Sullivan*. That was the same day my sister Christine was born: February 9, 1964. Kathleen came along almost exactly two years later, in March of '66, and by then we'd moved again, to a four-bedroom house at 138 Fairmount Avenue—another corner lot—in Clifton, which is the next town over from Passaic. Actually, Clifton is along the west side of Passaic, and kind of shaped *around* Passaic, like, coincidentally, a big *C*. You can start out driving north on Main Avenue in Clifton, cross over the town line, and follow that straight through downtown Passaic; keep going, and you'll end up back in Clifton. It's kind of weird, how they laid it out like that. Except for the low-income apartments around the corner on Martha Avenue—where my friends the Mongelli brothers, Robert and Lenny, lived—the new neighborhood was a pretty typical, quiet, clean place, just like the one we'd moved there from. But in the '60s and '70s—and long after that, too—the downtown part of Clifton was pretty rough and depressed. Lots of gangs and hookers and drug dealers.

At the same time, though, you also had the Capitol Theatre on Central Avenue and Monroe Street, which was this old vaudeville house that a music promoter named John Scher took over. That was a really big place for concerts. I didn't go to the Capitol as much as Lenny and his friends did—being older, they had a head start—but I still got to see some great shows there. I remember seeing Weather Report there, opening for, if you can believe it, Peter Frampton. I think that was in 1975—somewhere around then. Weather Report were amazing. I also saw Billy Cobham, who back then was one of my favorite drummers, there, around the same time—I think he was with George Duke then.

I'm sure a lot of Ramones fans will be shocked to read that I used to be a really big jazz-fusion head, since that stuff is mainly about jamming, and is pretty much the opposite of punk rock in so many ways. But it's true: I loved a lot of that music back in the day—the stuff with attitude, like Weather Report and the Mahavishnu Orchestra, who Billy Cobham played with early on. I guess it was the combination of sheer skill and confidence that a lot of those fusion guys had that inspired me when I was starting to play professionally. Anyway, the Capitol ended up being torn down in 1989, after John Scher got into doing bigger shows at the arena over in the Meadowlands. Which is a shame, because it was a really beautiful old building, built in 1929, and there was a lot of history in that place. The Stones, Springsteen, the Who—everybody played there. Today, it's just a big parking lot.

So, okay, getting back to the moving thing, Clifton was cool because it didn't really feel like that big of a change, really. For my dad, it was close to the garage where he kept his trucks for work; for my mom, it was close to church; and we pretty much still stayed in touch with the people we knew from the old neighborhood. I still went to Franklin School No. 3 in Passaic. But, man, I hated school. Really hated it. Just being there. It bored the shit out of me. If I had to pick the subject I hated the least, I guess I'd say English. Which is weird, because I never liked reading. Still don't. Somehow, though—and I have no idea how—I still got decent grades in school. Even though I'd fool around a lot and get in trouble in class, and get sent to the principal's office. Like a lot of kids, I had a really short attention span. But I guess it was just long enough for me to get by.

Besides me getting busted for being the class clown all the time, another thing that happened a lot was that I faked being sick so I could get out of school. I'd tell the teacher I wasn't feeling good and act all dazed, and she'd send me down to the nurse's office. Then I'd do the same performance for the nurse, and she'd call my mom up and say little Richie wasn't feeling good, and she was letting him go home early. That worked pretty well. For a while, anyway. Eventually, of course, my mom started to catch on to what I was doing, and she stopped believing me. And, yeah, after a certain point, I'm sure it was pretty obvious I was full of shit. Except for this one time. And that was the time I actually almost fuckin' died because of the scam I was pulling.

I was in class one day—I guess I was about ten, so this would've been around fourth grade—and my stomach started hurting. Bad. Like, really, really bad. Kind of a dull pain that kept getting worse. I also started to feel hot and dizzy, like I had a fever or something. So, like usual, I told the teacher, and she sent me down to the nurse, who sent me home. When I got back to the house, my Aunt Bubbles—

my mom's youngest sister, who lived near us, and whose real name is Janet—happened to be over. My mom and Aunt Bubbles pretty much rolled their eyes when I walked in. They were, like, "Oh, come on, here he is again." I'd bullshitted my way out of school one too many times, and they didn't believe that I was really sick. I was, like, "No, no, really, I don't feel good," and I told them what was going on—but they still didn't believe me. I said I was going to lie down on the couch, so I went and did that.

They started laughing and making fun of me, saying they were going to operate on me. My mom went and got this big carving knife out of the kitchen and came back with this little white towel draped over her arm. She pointed the knife at my stomach, and she and Aunt Bubbles kept giggling, saying it was too late, and they were going to donate my body to science and stuff like that. But I guess after a few more minutes had gone by, I must've started to change color or something, because, all of a sudden, something snapped, and my mom got kind of serious. Then she felt my forehead, which was totally burning up.

My mom and my aunt ended up taking me to the hospital, and the doctors said it was a good thing I got there when I did, because it turned out my appendix was about to blow up. They rushed me right into surgery to take it out. The doc said if they'd waited an hour longer, I would've been dead. Simple as that. I'm sure my mom felt pretty bad for not believing me about being sick, but I can't really blame her. I was pretty much the boy who cried wolf—up until then, anyway.

Getting your appendix out is a weird thing. It's kind of debilitating— you almost have to learn to walk again. So I was at the hospital for a couple of days, recovering, watching TV, eating Jell-O, and generally loving being out of school. The other thing that was weird about all that was that they found these worms in my appendix. Pinworms, I think they're called. Wikipedia says they're spread by eating contaminated food or touching something that's contaminated. I have no idea how or where I got them, and as far as I know, no one else in my family ever had them. Lucky me, huh?

4

Stick Control and Syncopation

I was always tapping. Tapping on the dining room table. Tapping on my desk at school. Tapping on my thighs, my chest. Tap, tap, tap. There were always rhythms playing in my head, and I drove everyone crazy with them: my teachers, my classmates, and, especially, my parents. Thankfully, though, my folks helped me actually do something better with the beats inside my brain.

Like I said, outside of my mom's singing along in church and my dad's spinning Herb Alpert on the hi-fi, they weren't really musical people. But even though they weren't, one thing they really wanted was for each of their kids to learn to play a musical instrument. I guess maybe they wished they'd learned to play themselves, and they figured it would help keep us out of trouble. Maybe they also figured they'd never have to pay a band to play at any of the big parties they loved to throw. So, for Lenny it was the saxophone, for Marlene it was piano; clarinet for Christine, flute for Kathleen; and for me, when I turned eight, the drums.

Or *drum*, I should say. Like any drummer will tell you, you start out with just a snare drum. The snare is the core of everything. Before you're ready to move on to a full kit, you have to master the basic techniques—things like timing, rolls, paradiddles—which you then go on to adapt and apply to the other pieces of the kit, one at a time, as each of those pieces gets mastered and added.

My first snare was a red-sparkle Camco, which I set up on a stand in our basement. My folks found a drum teacher in the phone book who lived in town: Mr. Hendrickson (I never knew his first name), who'd come to the house to give lessons. He was a nice, quiet, serious guy. He wore a bow tie, and he was really patient—you've got to be if you're teaching an instrument, especially drums, since so much of it is about precision and repetition. He'd show up every Monday after I got home from school, with his own sticks and snare, and sit right in front of me for an hour, showing me what to play, breaking it down and having me play it back to him, and then pointing out what I was doing right or wrong, and correcting me when I needed it. He also taught me to read music—who'd ever think a Ramone could read music?—and had me get two books, *Stick Control for the Snare Drummer* by George Lawrence Stone, and *Progressive Steps to Syncopation for the Modern Drummer* by Ted Reed. Both these books are classics that are still in print, and I recommend them to any drummer who's just starting out.

Every day after school, I'd be down in the basement, practicing on my little red snare for hours at a time. The other kids in the neighborhood would be outside playing sports, and, yeah, once in a while, I'd do that stuff with them. But I was never a *joiner*, y'know? Mostly, I was happier being by myself, just practicing, practicing, practicing. Now that I'd gotten a taste, learning to play was pretty much all I thought about. I'd seen the future, and it was me, playing the drums. I've got to hand it to my parents, they put up with so much noise—not just from me but also from Lenny, whose first band would sometimes rehearse down in our basement, too. Like I said, my folks were totally supportive of us playing music, and, once we'd started, they could see that at least a couple of their kids were musically talented, and it was going somewhere.

My mom would take me with her when she went shopping at the Great Eastern Mills store on Route 46 in West Paterson, which had a pretty good record section for a discount department store. That was where I'd buy singles by the bands I liked from AM radio. I remember getting 45s there by the Guess Who, a group I really loved back then—"American Woman," "No Time," "Undun," "No Sugar Tonight," great records. I think I got some singles by the Young Rascals at Great Eastern, too. They were local heroes, since they were from Garfield, which is about ten minutes from Passaic, and I thought Felix Cavaliere had a great voice.

Since it was clear I was serious about the drums, my parents bought me my first set just a few months after I'd started lessons with Mr. Hendrickson: a three-piece, oyster-black, pearl-finish Ludwig Downbeat, just like the one Ringo Starr played when the Beatles first came over in 1964. It was awesome—it had a Speed King bass-drum pedal and everything. I'd have many other kits after that, but, man, that one was just beautiful. When I first joined the Ramones, I used it in the video for "Time Has Come Today." But, unfortunately, it got stolen. More on that later.

Anyway, when I got the Ludwig, I set it up in the basement, and I'd play along to records down there. I'd listen hard and try to figure out what the drummers were doing, stopping and starting the records over and over again to dissect the tunes. By now, it was the late '60s, and my friend Dale Oostdyk, who went on to become a star quarterback at Duke University, got me into what they called "FM" or "underground" rock back then—the stuff that didn't get played as much on Top 40 radio, like certain songs by Cream or Joe Cocker—two acts who instantly became big faves of mine. Some days I'd be down there for five hours, trying to keep up with Ginger Baker or Jim Keltner until it felt like I was getting somewhere.

I also took some drum lessons from Joe Morello, who played with the Dave Brubeck Quartet (that's him on "Take Five"). Morello had actually been a student of George Lawrence Stone, the guy who wrote the *Stick Control* book, so there was an important connection there. He didn't make house calls, though. My dad or my mom would drive me to where he was—I think it was in West Orange, or somewhere around Newark—and pick me up when the lesson was over. Morello ran an ad for drum lessons in the back of *Modern Drummer* for years and taught a lot of drummers who went on to be pretty big, like Max Weinberg from the E Street Band, Gerry Polci from the Four Seasons, and Brian Chase from the Yeah Yeah Yeahs. Even the guy from Phish, Jon Fishman, took lessons from Morello. He'd have me work on being able to simultaneously keep one rhythm going on my kick drum pedal, another on the snare, another on the hi-hat, and a fourth one on the ride cymbal. Man, was that a fuckin' challenge, but I really kept at it, and I eventually got it down.

Another key thing that both Joe Morello and Mr. Hendrickson taught me was that, at first, you have to learn to play whatever it is you're working on *slowly*. If you can't play it slow and learn how it's put together, you won't be able to play it correctly when you try to play it faster. Simple as that. Too many young drummers just want to be the fastest freak on the planet, right off the bat. Sorry, but that ain't the way it works. You've got to be able to play it slow before you can play it fast, or even before you can play it mid-tempo. People say I'm the fastest drummer in punk rock—and I'm definitely the fastest drummer the Ramones ever had, by far—but I didn't take any shortcuts to get here.

I'm telling all you aspiring drummers, right here, right now: work on getting it down slow first. Once you've done that, you can go as fast you as you want.

Lenny and I have always been pretty close as brothers, and I really looked up to him. Especially back then, when I was just figuring out that I wanted to be a musician. When he was around sixteen, he started his first band, the Injections. Eventually, they changed their name to the Exceptions; I guess it was hard getting wedding and bar mitzvah gigs, which paid really well, with a name like the Injections. Even still, they got to be the hit of the neighborhood pretty fast, playing all the grownup parties, because the friends and families of the kids who were in the band would always hire them; from there, word got around about how good they were, and they started getting work in other towns. It was a four-piece band with Lenny on tenor sax, plus a guitar player, a Farfisa organ player, and a drummer—no bass player. They did the hits of the day for the kids—Dylan, the Beatles, the Stones, the Doors— and old dance-band standards for the grownups.

The drummer was a guy named Eddy Dandy. Whenever people ask me who my idols were, I always say I was my own idol. When I was a kid and getting into rock 'n' roll, I never had posters of rock stars on my bedroom walls or any of that stuff, like most kids did. But I guess if I ever *did* have to list any drumming heroes I've had over the years, Eddy Dandy would be the first one. Eddy was the coolest. Not only was he a great drummer, he always looked *sharp*. He had the cool haircut, always wore cool clothes—the mod stuff that the English groups wore. His whole demeanor, the way he moved and talked and carried himself, that combination of swagger and talent . . . he just *had it*, y'know? Eddy even taught me how to hide my pack of cigarettes under a rock and smoke them through a perfumed handkerchief, to keep my folks from figuring out I'd started smoking. So, Eddy really made a big impression on me. And, besides being the drummer of the Exceptions, he had a really good, strong voice, and he was also their lead singer on some of the songs. I took note of that, too.

When people talk about me being a drummer who sings, and how uncommon that is, I just shrug it off and say I've always sung at least a couple of songs in every band I've ever played in. I never really thought about it being anything really unusual. It was always just a natural thing for me. But watching Eddy do it was probably what inspired me to give it a try in the first place. I never took any voice lessons or anything, though. I just kind of figured it out by myself. You learn on your own how to breathe at the right times while you're playing; what lines you can sing when, over what rhythms. Obviously, you've got to have a pretty good feel for just playing the drums—a good foundation—first. But, like anything else, the earlier you start and the more you do it, the more natural it becomes, and everything just kind of works together. I'd go along as a roadie when the Exceptions did gigs, and I'd pay really close attention not only to what Eddy was doing but also to what the band as a whole was doing. That was really key, too: watching and absorbing how a band worked *together*, as a single unit, like a machine. They'd let me sit in on the Surfaris' "Wipeout," and maybe some other tunes, and Eddy would give me drumming tips here and there. Sadly, Eddy ended up dying in his sleep when he was around forty. Some kind of congenital heart condition, I heard.

I think I was about nine the first—and only—time I was ever in a fight. Well, I don't even know if you could even call it a fight. There was this weird kid who lived in one of the low-income apartments on

Martha Avenue. I can't remember his name, but I do remember there was always something kind of off about him. I think he had a lot of problems at home. His parents fought a lot; his dad was a drunk or something like that. I forget exactly what the deal was. But, anyway, I was there in the front yard of the apartment complex with him and a couple of other kids, and I guess he wanted to show off and be a badass, and he started giving me shit. He was a little older, so I guess to him there was a pecking order. Who knows what set him off, but he was shoving me, calling me a sissy or whatever kids say, and then—*bam!*— out of nowhere, he coldcocked me. Right in the temple, which of course kind of paralyzes you for a second. I saw stars, I went down, and he just walked away.

I just stood up, shook the dizziness out, and let him go. I know it'll probably sound crazy, but after the shock of being decked wore off, the only thing running through my mind was, "If you get in a fight and get hurt really bad, you might not be able to play the drums anymore." It's true: that's the first thing I thought of, and it's still how I am today when it comes to fighting. And this is after years and years of playing and hanging out in the toughest bars and craziest punk rock clubs on Earth. I guess some people are a little intimidated when they meet me, because I'm a tall dude who doesn't talk a lot, and the Ramones have this tough-guy image and all that. But the truth is, I'll walk away before I'll ever get in a fight. I'm a musician, not a boxer. I don't want to take the chance of being laid up, wondering if I'll ever be able to play, or at least play as well, again. It just ain't worth it. No way.

See, even back then, I knew: *Protect the hands!*

5

Burning Down the House

When I was ten years old, I almost burned my family's house down. Lenny and I shared a bedroom then, like we did when we lived in Passaic. Don't ask me why, but at the time we had a pair of road cones in our room—those bright orange things they stick around to redirect the traffic when they're working on the street, or to let drivers know there's a pothole there or whatever. I guess one of us, probably me, thought it'd be funny to have them around as some kind of freaky "pop art" décor. Maybe I was riding my bike around one night and figured I'd just, uh, *borrow* a couple of them from the City of Clifton. A lot of kids used to steal stop signs or street signs and hang them on their bedroom walls back then. I don't know—do kids still do that today? Probably not.

So, one winter night, my godfather, who was my dad's best friend, George Liptak, was over visiting my folks. George had brought along his son, Mark, who was the same age as me, and we were hanging out up in my room, listening to records while the grownups were downstairs having their cocktails. "Hey, look what I got," Mark said, reaching into his pocket. He pulled out a little white box of matches, and the top of the box had his name printed on it, in gold-embossed ink. He said his dad had them made for him, and I remember thinking, wow, that's insane! I'd never seen anything like that. Something with the name of someone I actually *knew in real life* professionally printed on it? Other than my dad's company trucks, no. And on a box of matches? At the time it seemed very cool and unusual. And, with me being this little pyromaniac, that just made it even cooler.

Naturally, right away, I got the bright idea of us sticking a half-used candle I'd found in the top of one of the road cones and then using one of Mark's monogrammed matches to light it up. So that's what we did. After a few minutes of watching this candle burn, we got bored, so we left the bedroom and went downstairs to watch TV instead—thinking nothing of leaving a burning candle there unattended. Those road cones, at least back then, were made out of this hard, black rubber, which was covered over with the bright orange reflective paint. You wouldn't really think the tiny flame from a candle would be able to do anything to one of them. But you'd be wrong. Like, really wrong.

After a half hour of *Hogan's Heroes*, we headed back up to my room. Halfway up the stairs, we both noticed this really gross smell. Like, well, burning rubber. Well, actually, smoldering rubber, which is what it turned out to be. But we didn't know that yet. We got to the next floor, and suddenly Mark pointed to the hallway ceiling and said, "Wow, look!" There was this dark smoke floating there, mostly right in front of the door to my room. It was kind of disorienting. We both froze. But then, with Mark behind me, I opened the door.

The whole room was filled with this thick, dirty, just overpoweringly stinky smoke. I mean, it was pretty serious. Like one of those smoke bombs you used to be able to get around the Fourth of July. It started burning my eyes, choking me and making me cough really hard. I kind of freaked, I didn't know what to do. So I just ran out of the room . . . and shut the door behind me.

Mark and I bolted downstairs. The adults were in the living room, which was all the way at the other end of the house. To get there, you had to go through a long hallway. I was more terrified of telling my dad about the fire than I was of the fire itself. Like I said, the one thing you *did not* want to do was get my dad mad. The whole time we were running through the hallway, all I could think about was how my dad was going to totally *kill* me for this. In my mind, I could already see his face getting red when I told him, hear him yelling his head off. Feel his open hand knocking my brains loose. What was I going to do, y'know?

So that's when I got a brilliant idea. I'd tell my mom instead! She'd protect me. And, hearing the news from her, my dad wouldn't get as mad as he would if I straight-out told him. At least not right away. I hoped, anyway.

We finally made it to the living room. My dad was in his easy chair, George was sitting on the sofa, and my mom was on the love seat. Dad was holding court, gesturing with his hands about something. I guess he must've been telling a joke right before Mark and I got there, because George and my mom were laughing a bit. We both stopped when we got in the room, keeping our distance from my dad; we were maybe six or seven feet away, with him facing the other direction. Mom noticed us and smiled at me for a half-second. Then she turned back toward the others and went back to listening to my dad. I started waving at her, trying to get her to come to us. She looked over, smiled again, and waved back. I started jumping up and down, waving both my hands, with my mouth tightly shut and my eyes open really wide. She said something to George, glanced over at me and Mark again, and then turned right back to the conversation. I kept jumping up and down, loudly whispering, "Mom! Mom!" She looked over at us, annoyed, while the men kept talking. At last, she stood up, excused herself, and walked over.

"Boys, don't bother us now," she said, bending over and whispering, while my dad told George another joke. "We're *talking* here."

"But, Mom," I started to say. "But . . . but . . ."

She was getting even more annoyed. "Richard, what *is* it? What do you want?"

"There's, um . . . there's a . . . ." Finally, I blurted it out. "There's a *fire!*"

My dad jumped up. "What?!" he yelled. "Where? What fire?! Where—upstairs?!"

"Yeah, in our room!" I answered.

Immediately, my dad jumped out of his easy chair and tore upstairs, with everybody else running behind him. When we got to the top landing, I could see the smoke coming out even more heavily than before, from the top and sides of the bedroom door. Dad threw the door open. Inside, the smoke was so thick you couldn't make out exactly where it was coming from.

"What's on fire?!" yelled my dad. "What's on fire?! Where is it?! Tell me, tell me! Where is it?! Where is it?!"

I told him about the road cone and he started running around the room, bumping into the sides of our beds and coughing while he tried to wave the smoke out of his face. He picked up this metal wastebasket we had in a corner of the room, dumped it out on the floor, and ran across the hall to the bathroom. While we stood there, watching and trying to stay out of the way, I heard him turn the bathtub faucet on, and then the sound of the rushing water hitting the inside of the wastebasket. He must have only filled it up about halfway, because in a few seconds he was back into the bedroom with it. It was still pretty hard to see in there, because the smoke had gotten even more insane by that point. He bumped into the furniture a couple more times until he found the smoldering cone, and then he dumped the water over it. There was a loud hiss. And then, at last, the smoke stopped coming.

But the bedroom, and the whole upstairs, was still full of it. Dad held his breath and grunted while he went around sliding open all the windows in the room. He came back out in the hall to get away from the lingering smoke, which for some reason didn't seem to be going out the open windows, like it should've been. Then, cursing like crazy, he remembered our bedroom had double-pane windows, so he had to go back in and open the outer panes. After that was figured out and the smoke was clearing, he started right into yelling at me about how I could've burned the whole place down. Luckily, though, George and Mark were there, so he didn't smack me.

Feeling like the worst jerk in the world, I went over and looked at the road cone. It was melted most of the way down into a wet, black, gooey mess. My folks made me get to work right away on cleaning everything up—scrubbing all the soot off the walls with a sponge, dragging the curtains and the blankets and sheets off the beds to go in the washing machine, and getting rid of this stupid, burnt-up road cone. The next day, we found out that the soot from the smoke that actually *did* make it out the windows was all over my parents' and the neighbors' cars and a bunch of other stuff. So I had to clean all that up, too.

Of course, after that I was grounded for a long, long time. Which sucked. The good thing, though, was that my mom let me pick out all new wallpaper for the bedroom, since the old wallpaper got ruined. I went for some of that reflective "wet look" stuff, which was the big thing back then. Lenny and I both thought it looked really cool. But as bad and scary as the whole road cone-fire thing was, it wouldn't be the last time I got in trouble for screwing around with fire-related shit.

6

Holiday Inns

When my dad wasn't working or dealing with my mass destruction, he'd take the family on vacation. We went on trips all the time when I was a kid. Like every other New Jersey family, we'd go to the Jersey Shore in the summer. We'd get a place in Wildwood or Asbury Park or one of those places for the weekend, and maybe split the rent with Aunt Bubbles and her family. I remember the boardwalks in Long Branch and Seaside Heights, with the rides and the saltwater taffy and the cotton candy. We took the longest trips, though, in the winter. Being in the landscaping business, my dad didn't have work in the winter. People don't really need their lawns mowed or their hedges trimmed when everything's covered in snow. So he'd work really long days for the rest of the year, and in the winter we'd often go to Florida.

My folks loved Florida. The whole "country club by the beach" vibe. We'd stay at this place on St. Pete Beach called Gulf Winds, this old-school resort with condos you could rent for the season, which is what we usually did. Gulf Winds is still there today, and, looking at the website, the place really hasn't changed all that much. At Gulf

Winds, Lenny and my sisters and I would have a blast. I loved playing shuffleboard with the old folks who were staying there. Not that they were the toughest opponents, but I pretty much always won. I was pretty good at that game. Hey, whatever, it was something to do. And they didn't have shuffleboard back in Clifton—at least not anywhere I knew about. So, that made it this exotic thing I always looked forward to doing when we got down there—which took about three full days, because my dad refused to drive at night.

We'd pack up the car and leave Jersey before the sun came up, at around four o'clock in the morning, and my dad would drive until sundown. Then we'd have dinner and get a room at a hotel, which was always—*always*—a Holiday Inn. My dad had the drive all planned out, and we'd never stay anywhere else. We'd stay at the same Holiday Inns on the way up and down I-95 every year. And what's weird is that it was the same when I was in the Ramones: wherever we went on tour in the US, we always stayed at Holiday Inns. Always. I think it was mainly because of John—Johnny Ramone, I mean. He never wanted to spend any money if we didn't absolutely have to, so he'd never let the band spring for hotels that were expensive. I think the Ramones were even in the Holiday Inn membership rewards program. Our road manager, the great Monte Melnick, would know for sure.

Besides going to Florida and the Jersey Shore, my family also spent a lot of summer weekends at the Pinecliff Lake Community Club in West Milford, which is in Passaic County, about an hour north of Clifton. My dad bought us a little cabin there, a two-bedroom place with an upstairs loft for the kids to sleep in. We'd usually go up on Friday, after my dad finished work, and then drive back real early on Monday, at 5 a.m., so he could head straight back to work. (I think about that sometimes now, and I wonder how he did it. Even though it was supposedly a little vacation for him, it's not like he got any rest, with all of us kids screaming and running around.)

Like people do with their boats or their vacation houses at the shore, the people at the lake would give their cabins names. We called ours *Just a Little Bit*. I'm not sure who came up with that. Maybe my mom. We had a little wood-burned plaque made with that name on it, to put next to the front door. My sister Marlene, who's a really good painter, painted a picture of the place, which still hangs in my mom's living room today.

Pinecliff Lake was great, especially for kids. We'd go swimming all afternoon, and there were paddleboats and volleyball, tennis and basketball courts. My dad kept a boat there, and he'd take us out fishing, or just to cruise around the lake. And, of course, my folks loved to throw huge parties. They'd have these theme parties, "Italian Day" or "Polish Day," which were these epic things that just went on all day. They'd make Italian or Polish food on the grill, and, I'm serious, *hundreds* of people would come. A lot of them were other families with places at the lake, and there were always people there my dad knew from work or my mom knew from church, or neighbors from Clifton. Everyone would sit at the picnic tables and eat together, then the Exceptions would play and people would dance, and Eddy Dandy always let me play drums with the band while he took a break.

After a couple of summers at *Just a Little Bit*, my dad got us a bigger place on the other side of the lake: a four-bedroom, two-bathroom house we named *More Than Before*. Cute, huh? I guess you could call those summers at Pinecliff Lake the last innocent time for me. After that, things started to get crazy. But they were a really great part of my childhood, and I have a lot of great memories from them. Like, all of us watching the first moon landing on TV there, in July of '69, which definitely felt like a huge deal when it happened. But there was something else that landed that summer that, to me, was even more amazing than a moonshot.

Led Zeppelin's first album came out in January of 1969. Lenny and I didn't get it until we were up at the lake that summer, but, man, once we had it, we jammed out to that thing the *whole* time we were there. I'm not kidding—we played that album morning, noon, night, all the time. "Good Times, Bad Times." "Communication Breakdown." "How Many More Times." "Dazed and Confused." Awesome record, man. And heavier and more intense than Cream or anything else I'd been listening to. The whole band was totally killer: Jimmy Page, Robert Plant, and John Paul Jones were all amazing, but of course it was John Bonham, the drummer, who I was really focusing on the most. I'd never heard anything like him before. *At all.*

Bonham played with so much soul, so much feeling. And he played like he had three hands—his foot was his third hand. The way he syncopated the bass drum was just ridiculous. That was something totally new to me. His timing was flawless, and you could tell he really, really listened to what the rest of the band was doing. The whole time. He never stepped on anything; he played *around* the vocals, rather than on top of them, like a jazz drummer would do with a horn player. Give the other guys some space to do their thing, and you make the whole song better, y'know?

That's something I learned from Bonham that I took with me into all the bands I played in later, including the Ramones. Even though the Ramones' music seems really simple and straight-down-the-line, to play it right there has to be a *balance* between all the instruments. As hard as I would play in the Ramones, I always made sure I wasn't overpowering Joey Ramone's vocals, because I knew they were what most people were really focused on when they listened to the songs. Joey's vocals gave the songs their melody, and the melody is what people tend to listen for first, especially in Ramones songs, even if they don't quite realize it.

Another thing I learned from listening to Bonham was how to play the cymbals properly—which is to say, lighter than you hit the drums. Kids don't do that today—they smash those fuckin' cymbals as hard as they hit the drums. It's overkill. The cymbals don't sound the same when you're hitting them that hard. It's not necessary, and it affects the tone when you do it. They're a different instrument. You have to finesse them, layer the sound with the rest of the kit, or else what's the point of having them? You might as well just get rid of the cymbals and add a couple more drums instead. Listen to Zeppelin's recordings: Bonham doesn't hit his cymbals as hard as he hits the drums. And I never do. Never, ever. The motion is there, yeah, but it's a sideswipe, not a full-on smack.

It's funny, everyone thinks of John Bonham as being the ultimate hard-hitting, hard-rock drummer. You know: this big, tough guy who just pounded those things like a caveman, and didn't think at all about what he was doing. But that's so untrue. He played the drums so fluidly, with such melody and precision. Yeah, there are a lot of Led Zeppelin songs where he plays these awesome solos, but for the rest of the song he doesn't put crazy fills where they don't belong or any of that shit. You could tell he could just play in a room by himself, with just the drums and nothing else, and have it sound totally *musical*. A lot of guys can't do that. But he could, and that's what I've always tried to do.

I got *Led Zeppelin II* when it came out, and, just like with the first record, I totally wore out the grooves on it. Believe it or not, though, even though I had some of Led Zeppelin's later albums and totally loved the band, I never saw them live. I really wish I had. I guess maybe it was timing; by the time I was old enough to really start going to big concerts, I was playing in working bands myself, and because of that I missed a lot of stuff.

I do remember being really sad when Bonham died in 1980. I remember hearing about the way he went, just left alone in bed and choking to death after he'd been partying too much and passed out. I remember thinking that, if someone else had just been there at that moment with him, it wouldn't have happened.

To this day, I hate going out partying by myself, because if you're with somebody, you have a better chance of being saved from an unfortunate incident like that. And, as you'll see, I've had my share of incidents that could have been *really* unfortunate. But before I get into those, let me tell you about an incident that was pretty fortunate, for a typical boy like I was, at least: the first time I saw a nude woman. A real, live one. Not one on a record cover, with whipped cream covering up all the good stuff.

7

Try to Look Innocent

must've been about eleven. For a couple of years, I had a paper route, delivering the *Star-Ledger*, which to this day is still the biggest newspaper in New Jersey. Usually, I'd go out on my bike and do it. Or, if it was winter and there was too much snow in the streets to ride my bike, I'd go out on foot, which really sucked—marching around the neighborhood when it was freezing outside, in the deep snow, with this big, heavy bag of newspapers. God, I hated that.

There were kids with paper routes whose fathers who drove them around to deliver papers in the winter, but my dad sure as hell wouldn't have done that. Being the tough, hard-working guy he was, he would have been, like, "Don't whine to me about the weather. It's work, that's how it goes. Get used to it, kid." But, really, all that did was make me want to try even harder to get *out* of doing anything that felt like work. I guess, looking back on it now, maybe he did me a favor in that way. It made me focus more on what I *really* wanted to do as my job, which was playing the drums. I really don't think that was what he had in mind, though. But, hey, it worked out. I've had some other jobs here and there over the years, but I never had to go work at McDonald's or anything like that.

Sometimes, though, my mom would help me out by driving me around to collect the money for the weekly subscription fees. She wanted to make sure I got paid, and neither of my folks really wanted me running around Clifton like an easy target, with all that cash on me. One day, I was out riding around with my mom, collecting money, and we stopped by this one place, in an apartment complex. There was this lady who lived there—I can't remember if she was married or not. I'd seen her around. She was probably around thirty and really attractive. The Mongelli brothers and some of the other guys I hung out with seemed to agree.

This particular apartment complex had a courtyard with some apartments that didn't face the street, and this lady's place was one of those. So, with my mom waiting in the car, I went around the corner and into the courtyard, walked up the front steps, and knocked on the door. Nobody answered. So I knocked again. And again. And again. Nothing. *Dammit, nobody home*, I thought. And then, even though it was something I'd never done before—honest—I figured, hey, nobody's home, I wonder what I can see if I just open this mail slot a little bit and take a quick peek inside . . .

And that's when I saw her.

This was a small apartment, and the bathroom door was off to the right, about nine or ten feet from the front door, and she came running into view just as I was lifting up the little metal slot door. Totally naked. Her hair was dripping wet, and her whole, amazing body was glistening, like it was one of those old bronze statues in the art museums in Italy and France that I'd seen pictures of. She'd obviously been in the shower, and then hopped out after I'd knocked enough times. My eyes popped right out of my little preteen head, and instantly I got all dizzy and warm. And, like with the Tijuana Brass record cover, very *enthusiastic*.

"Who is it?" she yelled. Amazingly, she didn't seem to notice the slot was open and I was right there.

For a second, I thought about letting the flap shut. But I knew the noise would've totally given me away. So I just stayed really still. Turning my head to one side, so my voice wasn't coming straight in through the little opening, I yelled back, "*Star-Ledger*!"

"Be right there!" she shouted, a little louder this time. I guess she couldn't hear that well, over the sound of the shower. She started running frantically in a circle around the room, looking for something. She picked up a black purse off a chair, opened it, and started digging around inside—bending over and giving me a great view of her ass. I remember thinking, wow, this isn't just one of those pictures in one of my dad's *Esquire* magazines—this is the real thing!

I watched her dig around in her purse a bit more, count out the $2.50 or whatever it was she owed me, and put it down on the chair next to her open purse. "Just a minute!" she yelled, still facing away from the door, before turning and running into another room. I guessed she was getting a bathrobe or something to put on before she came to the front door. The show was over. I figured that was my cue to close the slot—quietly—and try to look innocent.

She opened the door. Her hair was wrapped in a white towel, and she was wearing a robe with a bright paisley psychedelic pattern on it. I also remember she had bare feet, and her finger- and toenails were painted bright red. She looked down, straight into my eyes, and smiled.

"I'm sorry, I was in the shower," she said.

I just stood there, totally stunned. Man, I just couldn't talk. My heart was pumping really fast, and I felt lightheaded. Lady, I thought,

I just saw you *naked*. Like, two seconds ago. I mean, *damn*, y'know? All I could make myself do was nod, looking back up into her eyes and trying not to stare at the exposed, shiny-wet skin just under her neck, where the two sides of her robe came together.

"Here you go," she said, handing me the money. You had this big metal ring with cards for all the customers on it, and you'd punch a hole in their card when they paid you. I stuck the money in my pocket, punched her card on the little key-ring thing, and handed her a paper.

"Thank you!" she said, smiling again, dragging out the "youuuu" in a sing-song-y voice. And then she quickly shut the door in my face.

So now I was just frozen there on the stoop, staring at this closed door. Man, I thought, what the fuck just happened?

After a minute or two, I went back to the car. When I got in, I didn't say a word about it to my mom. But the next day, the other boys in my fifth-grade class got the full story. And, man, were they jealous.

Of course, I'm all grown up now, and I don't do it anymore, but that whole thing kind of got me hooked for a while. When I was a kid, whenever I had a chance to look into someone's apartment, I totally did. And there were definitely some images I took away that afternoon that, let's just say, I returned to in my mind a few times later on.

Meanwhile, Lenny and the Exceptions were getting busier and busier, and I kept tagging along to their gigs and sitting in. But I only played the drums. I didn't sing; the trumpeter, Benny Canazaro, was the Exceptions' main singer, doing all the Great American Songbook standards and pop tunes, and Eddy Dandy sang all the rock stuff.

The first time I actually did sing and play in public with a band was when I was a seventh grader at Christopher Columbus Middle School in Clifton. It was for a battle of the bands, basically; a school talent-show thing. I put together a trio with a couple of other kids for it. The group was me, another guy on guitar and vocals, and this girl on Farfisa piano-organ who was a serious music student and played for the school musicals. I can't remember their names. The band had some kind of typically psychedelic name, the Electric Garden or something goofy like that; I forget what we were called, but I can almost picture the logo I'd painted on the bass drum. Like with a lot of the other early bands I was in, for some reason this one didn't have a bass player. Bass players were harder to find back then, I guess—at least where I was. It seemed like most kids either wanted to play the guitar or just sing, or maybe their parents were making them take piano lessons, and they got into playing the organ through that. So this girl I was in the band with would play the bass parts with her left hand while she played the melodies with her right, like Ray Manzarek did in the Doors.

To get ready for the show, we rehearsed after school on the sun porch of the keyboardist's house, a few days a week for maybe two months—which felt like six years—working up around four or five covers. When the big day came, in the school auditorium, I was pretty nervous. Yeah, I'd played in front of people before with the Exceptions. But those people had mostly been either family members or friends of the family, or people at wedding gigs I didn't know and would never see again. This was going to be in front of my classmates. Kids I saw at school every day. Plus, I was going to be playing songs they all knew really well, and they expected those songs to sound just like they did on the radio. Or, at least, pretty close. Plus, I'd be the *lead singer* on all of them. And, like everybody knows, during that middle-school/junior-high period, when you're thirteen, fourteen years old, kids are *really* cruel to each other. Just heartless, man. It can be tough. So I knew if I fucked up or the band sucked, I'd get made fun of for the rest of my time in middle school—maybe even into high school.

Waiting by the side of the stage, though, I started feeling a little more confident as I watched a couple of the other bands set up and then do shitty versions of Beatles songs. I could see how much tighter our band was, compared to them—and how stiff and weak all the other drummers were. And, when our time finally came, we totally killed it. We opened with Creedence Clearwater Revival's "Fortunate Son" and closed with the Guess Who's "American Woman." I can't remember what else we did. I'm sure we must've done a Beatles song, too. I say that about the other bands doing shitty Beatles covers, but most of the time, if you were in a band back then, you kind of had to do a Beatles song; people pretty much expected it. I really dug "Rocky Raccoon" from the White Album—which Lenny had, and which was a big album for me—but I know we didn't do that one. Anyway, whatever other songs we did, the audience loved us, and we ended up winning the thing! The judges gave us ribbons, and we got our names in the school paper and everything.

The show was during the school day, which meant my family couldn't be there. But they were all really happy and proud of me when I told them about it. So that felt really good. Unfortunately, the trio wasn't anything serious, and we never played again after that. But the whole experience of winning the contest was another thing that told me, hey, maybe I'm onto something with this drumming thing. Not long after that, though, something happened that led to me being *sure* I was—something that also led to me getting into some pretty insane shit along the way. Everything was about to change.

8

You Smoke Pot, Too?

My family moved again, this time to a little community called Pines Lake, which is in Wayne, another decent-sized town in Passaic County. Just like Pinecliff Lake, Pines Lake had been a vacation spot for New York City people before World War II, with a bunch of little log cabins that were built around the lake back in the 1920s. But there were also a lot of really nice modern houses there. The new place we moved into had four bedrooms, a garage, a deck—the whole deal. With my little sisters, Christine and Kathleen, getting to be more of a handful by then, we needed a bigger place. My dad, along with the rest of us, really dug the whole lake lifestyle, and he wanted to make it a year-round thing, instead of us living in Clifton and only being able to get our lake fix on spring and summer weekends.

Pines Lake was great. My dad bought a bigger boat and kept it docked right there on the lake, which had all the fishing you wanted (they stocked it with bass and northern pike), and there were always ducks, swans, and geese around. Of course, we went swimming all the time when it was warm out, and there were also woods with trails there, which were great to be able to explore and play in as a kid. And there was a dam at one end of the lake with a one-lane road running along the top of it, looking down into this park called the Glen. Sometimes we'd ride our bikes up there and drop rocks and bottles and other shit down into it. That was fun. (Another time, when I was seventeen, I was driving home after I'd partied a little too much, and I ran my first car—a 1971 Plymouth Satellite Sebring, which I'd jacked up and put Cragar chrome mags and fat tires on, like a lot of kids did back then— halfway off that road. It got stuck, and my dad wasn't too happy about helping me get it unstuck.) There was a big Fourth of July thing there every year, with a parade for all the little kids, and there was also this big cookout called the Lobster Bash, which the Pines Lake Sailing Club would hold at the end of July. So, basically, it was a pretty cool place to move to. And there were a lot of other kids there, too.

But lake kids were different from Clifton kids. Lake kids—especially the teenage ones—were *bad*. In the summer, at night, it seemed like all they did was hang out on the beach by the lake, with cases of beer that they somehow got, even though they were underage. A lot of them had parents who were pretty well-off, so I guess they didn't really have to work much, which wasn't true for Lenny and me—by the time I was in high school, we were both working long days for our dad's lawn service—and their folks pretty much just let them do whatever they wanted, as long as they stayed out of their hair.

That wasn't how it was for me. My folks were always watching over me, trying their best to keep me out of trouble, even when it came to some pretty innocent activities.

I remember being out one night at the age of thirteen, when I was first discovering girls—and the trouble they can bring. I was near the basketball court back in Pinecliff Lake, making out with this girl against the side of a car. This crazy thunderstorm was blowing through, but we didn't care—we just stayed there, making out in the pouring rain. All of a sudden, just when things were really getting good, a car pulled up and shined its headlights right on the two of us. The driver of that car turned out to be my mom, who'd been all worried, and was out looking for me.

Another time, I got home later than I was supposed to, after I'd been hanging out with some other girl in a rowboat on the lake. I snuck up to the front door, really slowly. Trying not to make any noise, I opened it as quietly as possible, tiptoed into the dark entry room, and then— *bam!* My dad, who'd been waiting up for me, gave me a swat upside the head so hard it made me dizzy.

I'd say that, in their own way, my folks definitely at least tried to keep a handle on shit and keep me out of trouble. But there was only so much they could do. Especially when it came to drugs. Because, *man*, were these lake kids into drugs. This *was* the early '70s, y'know? And, like it was for most people of my generation, marijuana was my introduction to drugs.

The summer we moved to Pines Lake, I was out one afternoon by myself, walking around the lake, totally bored and basically looking for friends. This was before school started, so I hadn't met many other kids yet. I passed this one house that was right there on the water, and I knew that one of the cuter girls I'd seen around lived there. Since it was the summer, all the windows were open, and I could hear loud music—acid-rock stuff—coming from inside. It sounded great, so I walked over toward the house to try and hear it better. As I got closer, though, I noticed this really funny smell. It reminded me of the fresh-cut grass my dad came home smelling like, but with a little bit of skunk mixed in. I was, like, *man*, what's that smell?

I kept walking by the front of the house, listening to the music—Cream, Led Zeppelin, Steppenwolf, and other bands I dug—and trying to figure out what else the people inside were doing, besides playing records. I guess one of the things they were doing was watching me, because after almost a half-hour of me walking back and forth and staring at this place, one of the upstairs screen windows slid up, and this girl stuck her head out.

"Hey, wanna smoke with us?" she called down to me, over the music. "What's happenin'? Come on up here and party with us!"

I looked around. Then I looked back up at this girl.

What, I thought, this hot girl and her friends want to hang out with *me*? She's got to be kidding.

"Come on up!" she said. "Screen door's open! We're upstairs. We *got* some stuff!"

I was a little scared, but I slid the door open and walked in. Inside, the place was kind of dark, but the music was a lot louder—and the weird smell was a lot stronger. Right away, I could tell this girl's parents weren't at home. I saw the stairs, so I walked over to them and started up, slowly. Right at the top, on the left side, was the room where the music and the smell were coming from. The door was about a third of the way open, and it had a black-light poster of a wizard on it.

"Come on in," said a voice from the room. I went in and saw more black-light posters, the girl from the window, and two dudes sitting on the green shag carpeting, next to a stack of albums. The gatefold cover of one of the albums, Jimi Hendrix's *Axis: Bold as Love*, was lying open in front of them, and it had a pile of little, dried-up leaves on it.

Wow, I thought, I think that's *pot*.

The window girl introduced herself—Cindy, I think her name was—and I told her who I was. The guys on the carpet just nodded at me without saying anything. They kept sitting there, totally stoned and bobbing their heads to Led Zeppelin. Cindy and I talked about Zeppelin for a bit, going on about which albums and songs we dug most. Then she held out the lit joint she had in her hand. "Come on, get high with us," she asked. "This is some good shit."

This was when I was fifteen. I'd been drunk on beer a few times before then, but I really didn't have any idea of how pot was supposed to make you feel. I took a drag, then another one, and handed the joint back to Cindy, who passed it to the other guys. And then I waited. A couple of minutes went by. Cindy and I talked about music some more, and the two dudes bobbed along to "Ramble On." I still wasn't feeling anything, so I took another toke when the joint came back my way.

"Good shit . . . right?" said Cindy, grinning at me with her head tilted back and her eyelids drooping.

"Yeah, yeah," I answered, totally faking being high and wondering why I wasn't. After a couple more Zeppelin tunes, I told her thanks, nodded at the carpet dudes, and split—not saying a word about being confused and bummed that I hadn't gotten high.

I didn't know you had to get a "head" for marijuana, and that it takes a few times. Once I found that out, though, I kept it up, and after a few more times I was a total pothead. What was funny was that Lenny and I had both started smoking pot around the same time, but a year went by before either of us knew it—which is weird, considering we shared the same bedroom. We'd both been afraid to talk about it, because we were afraid the news might get back to our folks. One day, I finally mentioned to him that I'd been getting high, and he was, like, "What?! *You* smoke pot, too?"

So that was the beginning of drugs for me, and there'd be a lot more of them from there. But besides being the gateway for me getting into certain substances, moving to Pines Lake was also the gateway to me getting more serious about the drums. And that happened when I met this kid named Eddie Slivka.

Eddie was a grade ahead of me at Wayne Hills High School. He was—and still very much is—an incredible drummer, and without meeting him I wouldn't be half the drummer I am today. We met in my junior year, when we were both trying out for the school jazz band, and he beat me out of the spot. Eddie, who later played for a few years under the name Eddie Shorr, had taken lessons from Joe Morello, like I had, and he actually went on to become the protégé of Buddy Rich—which, if you know anything at all about how important Buddy is to the history of drumming, and how demanding he was as a bandleader, says a hell of a lot. Buddy Rich wouldn't waste his time with *any* musician, unless he thought they were truly exceptional, which Eddie definitely is.

Actually, Buddy Rich's playing was one of the first things Eddie and I bonded over. My dad had a copy of Buddy's 1972 album *Stick It*, a record I was obsessed with. Eddie invited me over to his house to check out his drums, and I was blown away. Not only did he have a gorgeous white marine-pearl Slingerland set, he even had it set up on a little drum riser he'd built in his bedroom. He'd practice in there for, like, six hours a day, even in the summer, when school was out and he was working weekends for his dad's window-washing business.

Like Eddy Dandy, this Eddie also dressed really sharp. In school, he always wore these cool-looking turtlenecks, and he had this really neat gold pendant of a miniature cymbal that, once in a while, he'd wear over them. And, of course, he always had all the hot girls, too.

Seeing all that—how Eddie not only had the talent but also constantly worked at it to make himself even better, while he created this whole persona around being a great drummer—was important.

Yeah, I'd gotten a little bit of that sensibility from Eddy Dandy. But Dandy was a lot older—closer to my brother's age—which made him more distant, and not as relatable. Slivka and I were only a year apart, so we had a lot more in common. We were going through a lot of the same teenage stuff—girls, school, getting into partying, getting in trouble—at the same time. I could see some of myself in him, and although I wouldn't have been conscious of it at the time, I also think maybe what I was doing was absorbing how he dealt with all that stuff and expressed it through his playing. It really made me go, *whoa*, there's something *more* to all this—*I* can do this, too. That inspired me to push myself harder when I practiced, and to really start to believe in myself as a musician.

9

I Think She Played Glockenspiel

Eddie Slivka and I got be very close friends. We hung out all the time, playing along on drum pads to Buddy Rich records at Eddie's house, or shopping for cool clothes at Willowbrook Mall. (Bell-bottoms and platform shoes were the thing then; dickeys, those little polyester-knit collars you'd wear to make it look you had a turtleneck on under your shirt, were kind of my trademark. I had one in every color.) We even dated these two girls who were sisters for a while.

When it came to drumming, Eddie and I had a friendly rivalry. We'd ride around together after school in my Plymouth Satellite, each of us taking turns playing single-stroke rolls with our hands on the dashboard, to see who could go faster. Even today, Eddie will tell you: I always won those little speed contests. Eddie's thing was never really speed, it was his sense of swing. Speed belonged to me. And I was already a pretty fast drummer by the time we met. But we learned from each other. I inspired him to play a little faster, and he made me put a little more swing into what I was doing. He'd show me how to play tricky stuff, like John Von Ohlen's parts on the Stan Kenton big band's version of "Malaguena."

Those dashboard drumming contests with Eddie weren't the only musical competitions I won during my high-school career. I joined the marching band, which I totally loved. It was an awesome experience, being in this big, flashy group who wore cool uniforms and traveled around, performing for big crowds at football games and putting out this sound that was just totally huge. I got the John Philip Sousa Award, which is given to one student musician each year for "superior musicianship, dependability, loyalty, and cooperation"—Count Basie was one of the judges on the award panel—and I made the New Jersey All-State Band when I won All-State First Place Snare.

There was one thing about that whole marching band period that was kind of funny, though. Because I'm tall, the football coach and the football players I knew were always coming up to me after practice, trying to talk me into trying out for the team. But I just wasn't into it at all. All I wanted to do was play the music at the games, and then party after we got done. But a lot of the guys I hung out with were jocks. The jocks liked me for some reason, even though I was this freak musician who wasn't really into sports. I don't know why. I guess they thought I was funny, and maybe they respected me because I was good at playing the drums. That and we all liked getting high and goofing around.

The school conductor, who was also our music teacher, saw Eddie and me as his star students. Each of us carried around a little leather briefcase that we kept our sticks, mallets, brushes, and sheet music in. We were serious, y'know? We'd do concerts together with the school big band—two drummers onstage at the same time. For one of them, Eddie wrote a solo for a tune by the bandleader Don Ellis, where we mirrored each other, playing the same rhythms and crossovers simultaneously. We also worked up this cool routine within that, where we threw our drumsticks back and forth to each other during a break in the song. One of us would catch them, play some licks, and then throw them back to the other guy. And we kept that up for maybe five or ten minutes, just back and forth, back and forth. The audience really loved it. Another time, Eddie wrote a duet for two snare drums, which we played as part of a show by the concert band. That was fun, too.

There was one concert I goofed at, but it wasn't anything to do with my playing—it was more about the performance part. I was going to sing "Hey Jude" as a solo vocalist, and I wanted to look extra-cool, so I borrowed the white tuxedo my brother wore when he did formal gigs—which was way too big for me. I almost looked like David Byrne would fifteen years later, with his baggy suit in that Talking Heads concert movie, *Stop Making Sense*. When I walked out onstage, people just laughed their asses off.

Another thing about that show: I can't remember what the hell I was thinking, but for some reason I decided to sing the second verse of "Hey Jude" in Spanish, even though I didn't, and still don't, speak the language. I guess I felt like I knew it because my dad had some Puerto Rican guys working for him at the time, and I'd been around them enough to think I'd somehow picked it up, which of course is crazy. But, hey, I wasn't going to let a little detail like *that* stop me. So, when I did the verse, what came out was fake Spanish—"*Se enta quanto . . . .*" Whatever that was supposed to mean. None of it made any sense, but I thought it sounded good at the time. Like the baggy white tux, it ended up getting some laughs I wasn't really looking for. But even after that, I still liked the attention that came with being onstage. That taste of being in the spotlight, part of the glamor.

Just because I was busy with the school band doesn't mean I was a little angel or anything. Eddie and I would go crazy on the weekends, getting wasted and then doing donuts or patching out on people's lawns in our cars. Besides drinking a lot of beer and smoking tons of pot, we were discovering all kinds of other fun ways to get fucked up—speed, LSD, angel dust. Man, I *loved* angel dust. It made me feel like fuckin' Superman and all spaced-out at the same time. In New Jersey back in the '70s, that shit was everywhere, and it was really cheap. Usually, I'd sprinkle it on the weed when I was rolling a joint, and then smoke it, which will *really* fuck you up. Sometimes, I'd let the other kids take a few hits off one of my "wet" joints and tell them the taste from the PCP was just my "mint rolling papers"—then I'd sit back and watch them try to figure out what was going on when the dust kicked in.

When it came to drugs, I could be sneaky like that, with the practical jokes. I still do that kind of stuff once in a while, too. At the 2017 Joey Ramone Birthday Bash, which I talked about in the introduction to this book, I was going to slip Clem Burke one of my pot-infused chocolates before he went on, just let him think it was regular candy. But at the last minute I figured maybe it wasn't such a good idea. Clem might have been pissed off at me later, if he didn't like it and found out I was the one who dosed him. Then again, maybe it would've made the show even more interesting . . .

I've definitely had some bad trips. Oh, man. Once, me and my friend Rich Lachocki ate some mescaline on a couple of pizza slices. Then we went walking around Pines Lake, just talking about the usual stuff and waiting for something to happen. After a while, I started to feel it coming on. Then things got weird. Really weird. I'd start to think of something I was about to say, and then Rich would say the *exact same* thing I was thinking, just when I was just about to say it. At first, I thought, wow, gee, that's really interesting. But then he kept doing it.

Over and over, with every thought that came into my head. I was, like, Jesus Christ, how the hell is he *doing* that? I started to get pretty freaked out. I grabbed him by the throat and yelled straight in his face, "Man, fuckin' cut that shit out!" But, of course, he had no control over what was going in my brain, which was just totally fried. We almost got in a fight about it, but he talked me down. I remember looking at Rich at one point during that trip, and both of his eye sockets were empty and had smoke coming out of them. Holy shit, y'know? Me and mescaline weren't always such a good match.

Booze became a bigger thing. I kept a bottle of Southern Comfort in my locker, and I'd take nips off that between classes. And, of course, I was getting high and getting hammered every chance I got with Eddie, Rich, and some of the other guys. Naturally, my grades started slipping. And, even though it didn't happen a lot, there were a couple of times when the wild shit I was doing messed up the school-band stuff a little. At one of the rehearsals with the concert band, when I'd been out late partying the night before, I was playing tympani, and I actually fell asleep behind the drums. The band director had to wake me up. But maybe my craziest bit of band debauchery in high school happened in the bus, on a long drive back from a marching band competition.

There was this cute girl, Jeanie something. I think she played the glockenspiel. We kind of had the hots for each other, and we used to flirt a lot at practice and when we saw each other in the hall, between classes. On the way back from this game, which was in South Jersey somewhere, we were sitting together way in the middle of the bus, making out. After a little while, it started getting pretty hot and heavy. One thing led to another, and soon enough one of her hands was down the front of my uniform pants and holding my cock, which felt like it was going to explode. This was in the fall, so it was dark by the time we were riding back from the meet, and since everyone sitting close to us was quiet, I figured they were all dozing, after a long day on the field. Or at least that's what I kept telling myself.

Before long, this girl was bent over my lap, giving me a blowjob, right there on the bus. Since it was a long ride, she'd brought along a pillow, and I put that over her head, trying to hide what was going on, while I tried to stay quiet—which, if you're a guy and you've ever gotten your dick sucked, you know isn't exactly easy to do. So, yeah, that didn't really work too well. When I came, I bit my lower lip and did my best to keep my heavy breathing and moaning at a low level. But everyone around us had seen this white pillow bobbing up and down, and they knew what was going on, even though they didn't say anything at the time.

I was never sure what happened to Jeanie, but I ended up getting in big trouble the next day. It wasn't as bad as it could've been, though, because I was the band director's star student, and my family was really good friends with him; he'd come over to the house in the summer to swim in our pool and hang out with my folks. He didn't report anything to the school authorities, thankfully, but he did end up telling my parents about my little bus incident. I always kind of wondered how awkward that conversation must have been. Anyway, my dad gave me a little "What the hell is wrong with you?" talk, but I don't recall getting hit with any kind of big, horrible punishment over it. So I got off easy on that one. So to speak.

10

Black Turtlenecks

Remember a couple of chapters back, when I said how messing around with fire would get me in trouble again? For my folks, the final straw with my high-school mayhem came right before my junior year, when my friend Steve Marut and I decided we were going to burn down our school's football bleachers.

Steve was this freaky, long-haired dude who played guitar and grew pot in his closet. Me, Steve, and a bass player named Dean Dobbs actually had a band for a bit back then called Moriah; I sang everything, and we did Hendrix's "Little Wing," Derek and the Dominos' "Why Does Love Got to Be So Sad," and some Allman Brothers tunes. Steve also made acid from morning glory seeds, and, believe it or not, years later, he studied to be a professional chemist and actually became one. He taught me the best way to take acid: set your alarm for two hours before you're supposed to wake up for school; get up when the alarm goes off and drop the acid; go back to bed; and then get up at the normal time, just as the stuff is kicking in, so you'll be high at school all day.

I don't know why we wanted to burn down the bleachers. I'm trying to remember which one of us came up with that idea. I think it was Steve, and I just went along with it, me being such a pyromaniac. I guess we were just bored kids who wanted some excitement. Why else do kids get into vandalism? I figured the bleachers were out in the middle of this big, empty field, not close to any houses or anything, so there was no way anybody could get hurt.

So Steve and I had it all planned out. Well, sort of. He got together a couple of cans of gasoline, and I got some matches. We put on black turtlenecks, met up a few blocks from the school, and smeared dirt on our faces to darken ourselves up, like the good guys did on *Hogan's Heroes* when they were on a night mission to blow up some Nazi warehouse or something. We decided to do this thing on a weekend night, because we figured there was less of a chance that anyone else would be around the school grounds then. We were just going to douse as many of the bleacher benches in gas as we could, drop a couple of matches on them, and then run away.

That was pretty much the plan. But there wasn't any part in the plan about us making sure we didn't leave any evidence behind. Or about us promising each other not to tell *anyone* else about the whole thing. Or about us coming up with an airtight cover story that we would get straight between us, when our parents and the cops started asking questions—which I figured was guaranteed to happen. Marching up to the football field, all of these little points started hitting me at once. And I started getting nervous.

"This is gonna be so fuckin' cool!" said Steve, laughing like he was nuts. The day we thought the whole thing up, I was laughing too, and thinking, ha-ha, yeah, it *is* going to be really cool. But now I wasn't so sure. Something didn't feel right.

The bleachers ran in a closed oval around the football field. We went through one of the entryways and straight across the field to the middle of the grandstand on the other side. Steve unscrewed the cap on one of the gas cans and just started dumping gas on the very bottom bleacher, walking along the length of the row, pouring it out as he went. He kept going until he'd emptied the entire can, and then he walked back to me. "Come on, man, let's go," he whispered loudly. "You got the matches? Let's go, let's go!"

I froze. Yeah, I had the matches. But I was scared. Suddenly, I could see myself getting in huge trouble for this shit. Definitely getting expelled. Maybe even going to jail—where I wouldn't be able to bring my drums with me.

"Oh, man, I forgot 'em," I said, even though they were right there in my pocket. "I think I, uh, left 'em at home."

"You *left 'em at home*?!" said Steve, really pissed off.

"Yeah, I think so—wait here, I'll go get 'em," I told him. And then I took off and just left him there.

An hour later, Steve called my house from a payphone outside the school—this was way before cell phones—looking for me. But I wasn't there. I was hiding out down the street, listening for sirens, because I figured he'd just find some matches somewhere else and finish the job without me, and I wanted to watch the action when he did. But I guess he got cold feet, too, because thankfully he didn't go through with it. When he called the house, though, my mom answered, and, like a mom will do, she somehow got the whole story out of him. So, when I got home that night, she and my dad were waiting up for me. And even though I didn't actually burn anything down, they told me this was it: the kids I was hanging out with were a bad influence on me, and they were sending me to military school.

I freaked. Having to cut my hair short, get yelled at by some asshole drill sergeant, go to bed super-early, and then get up super-early? And, on top of all that, not being able to play the drums in a band, which was all I wanted to do? No way. I started bawling. I literally begged on my hands and knees, promising and promising I'd straighten out and be good.

I guess they could see I was pretty shook-up about the idea—I knew they didn't necessarily *want* to send me away, especially my mom—so they said they'd hold off, since summer would be over soon, and I was already enrolled at Wayne Hills for the fall. But they also said they'd be watching me, to see how it went during the year, so I'd better stay in line. The place they'd been thinking of sending me was Staunton Military Academy in Virginia, which I later found out is where Johnny Ramone had gone, just a few years before all this happened.

The false alarm with the bleachers had been the last straw with my folks, but there were also some other incidents not long before that that hadn't helped my case, mainly with me getting high. My mom and some other parents from the neighborhood went to this "Is *Your* Teenager Using Drugs?" seminar at the police station. The cops showed them a movie at this thing that told you how to tell if someone was high—how your eyes look if you're stoned, what kind of behavior to watch for, blah blah blah. So, pretty soon, my mom was checking my eyes every time I came home at night.

Once I'd started driving, in my senior year, she'd go out to my car while I was getting ready for school in the morning, look through the ashtray, take out all the roaches she found, and leave them on the seat— just to let me know she was keeping an eye on me. She and my dad started getting on my case about all the partying I was doing with Eddie Slivka, saying he was "leading me down a bad road." And, after the whole bleacher-fire thing, they *really* didn't like Steve Marut, who actually went on to have a pretty horrible life: his mother murdered his father, set their family's house on fire, and hung herself. Then, years later, *he* hung himself.

I get it now, how my parents were cracking down on me out of love, and how they were just worried because they were seeing all this stuff in the news about kids getting really fucked up and OD'ing and all that. But I didn't want to hear it at the time. (Incidentally, even though I hung around a lot of intravenous drug users before, during, and after the Ramones, I never shot heroin—needles have always freaked me out. I did chase the dragon—smoke it off tin foil—a couple of times. Thankfully, though, I didn't like it enough to get hooked.)

I was fifteen when I lost my virginity. It was at a party at Pines Lake; some kid's parents were out of town, and they'd left him alone in the house for the weekend. Always a good idea, right? While everyone was downstairs, getting drunk on Budweiser, passing joints around, breaking shit, and blasting the Stones and Zep on the stereo, I was upstairs in one of the bedrooms with this blonde chick who'd been making eyes at me about a half-hour before. We started making out and ended up on the bed, and the whole thing went by pretty fast. I got the feeling she'd done it before. I remember it felt really good to come and all that, but after we got done I just felt really dirty. Like I'd done something really shameful and bad. But that feeling didn't last too long, and, after that night, getting laid was the main thing for me—next to playing the drums and getting fucked up, of course. I don't remember that girl's name. She was from another town, and I don't think we ever saw each other again. Oh well.

My first real girlfriend—the first one I brought home to meet my folks, when I was a senior—was a girl named Sandi Linden. Sandi was a brunette the same age as me who liked to walk around barefoot all the time. Her biological mom was mentally ill and had ended up in Greystone Psychiatric Hospital, so she lived with her stepmom, a political lobbyist. I thought that whole situation was kind of funny, since even though Sandi was a "good girl" who didn't do drugs, she was also really into rock 'n' roll, like me, and her mom was this Nixon-loving conservative who was always going to Republican fundraisers and leaving us alone at the house to do who knows what.

Sometimes, Sandi would hang out with me in Eddie Slivka's basement, where she'd watch us smoke pot and listen to us jam along to records. But even though I'd already lost my virginity by the time we were dating, Sandi still had hers, and she wasn't in any hurry to lose it, even with me. Years later, she told me she'd actually been a little afraid of me back then. I was never violent with her or anything, but I guess me being this moody guy who did drugs and liked to bang on the drums was a little scary for a well-behaved girl like her. Anyway, after us being together almost a year, I'd had enough of her whole good-girl thing, and we broke up. We ended up getting back together for a while after graduation, though, after I'd messed around with a few other girls, and we finally took things to the next level then. Like they say, good things come to those who wait.

11

Triple Nipple

There are three things most Ramones fans ought to be pretty surprised to know about me. The first: I was born with three nipples (the extra one is about two inches below my left one), which puts me in the same club as Mark Wahlburg, Tilda Swinton, and Carrie Underwood. The second: I'm among the two percent of the people in the world who were born with a rare version of a gene called ABCC11, which keeps my armpits from having any kind of smell. So, even though I sweat like everyone else, I have *no* body odor. None. I can play a gig, sweat my ass off, and after that, I'm good—I don't stink. You wouldn't know I was sweating at all, if you weren't looking at me. Of course, I still feel all grimy and want to take a shower when I sweat a lot, but at least no one's holding their nose and telling me to take one.

The third thing, and maybe the most shocking thing to a lot of people, is this: Before I was in the Ramones, the most famous punk rock band in the world, I played polka and disco music. I'll get to the disco in a bit. First the polka. Remember when I told you about how, when I was really little, I'd sit in with my brother's band, the Exceptions, when they played at our big family parties at Pinecliff Lake? Well, since my mom and her side of the family were Slovak, they'd all grown up with polka music, and, being these older Slavs, that was what they really loved to dance to. So, to make them happy, the band would throw in some polkas once in a while—"Too Fat Polka," stuff like that—and sometimes I'd play on those songs. Once in a while, my cousin Steve would sit in on accordion, and whenever we got some other horn players to join in alongside Lenny, it was just this huge sound.

Believe it or not, playing polkas when I was learning the drums really helped prepare me for playing in the Ramones. How? Well, doing it made me really learn about *always* keeping a dance tempo. I'd watch the dancers, concentrate on matching what they were doing, and then work to keep that up, making sure to always stay steady and give them what they wanted. The polka beat, which is pretty much the same in every song—like it is in a lot of Ramones songs—is a really simple beat. But, because it's so simple, you have to do it well, or people will notice; if you're not doing it right, you'll throw their dancing off. And I learned to do it well, snapping that snare on the offbeat, keeping the hi-hat going, and just being totally unwavering. So that mindset was something I still had when I was in the Ramones. With the Ramones, there was *definitely* no wavering. Just like in a polka band, whatever beat a song started with stayed the same until the song finished. Period.

People like to say that one of the things that made the Ramones different was that the drums were locked in with the guitar, instead of the bass, like they are in other rock bands. But the only person I was ever locked in with was myself. It was Dee Dee counting off, "One-two-three-four!" and then, inside my head, it was, "Let's go—come on, catch me!" If I tried anything even a little fancy, the music would have fallen apart. Like, if I'd thrown a triplet into one of the songs, it would've totally thrown John off. Of course, playing something like that would've been totally wrong for the Ramones anyway—I always knew that. Anyway, think about all this the next time you're at a wedding, and the band is playing polka tunes. Maybe you'll have a new appreciation for the music.

My first real, serious band was a duo called Tapestry: me and Jim Wynne, this organ player who used to jam with Lenny's band. We wore these matching "hippie" vests my mom made for us out of upholstery fabric. Both of us sang, and we did the typical stuff that was big at the time, or had been big a few years earlier: Cream, the Young Rascals, the Doors, Santana, probably some Beatles and Stones. This was in early 1972, before I was old enough to drive. Jim, who was about six years older than me, would pick me up in his '69 Camaro—I took the bottom heads off my drums so they'd stack together in the back seat, next to my cymbals and hardware; Jim's compact organ and amp fit in the trunk—and we'd go play these little dive bars in towns like Hoboken or Newark or Greenwood Lake, a vacation spot right on the border of New Jersey and Orange County, New York. I was underage (fifteen), but I had an ABC card from the state, which allowed me to perform in bars as a minor.

Playing in bars like that, I was around a lot of really wild shit— stuff that most other kids in my class definitely weren't seeing. There were tons of fights and, of course, *lots* of people who were just really, really fucked up. And, since it was North Jersey, of course there were a lot of mafia dudes around, too. I remember we played some VFW- or Knights of Columbus–type community hall once, and the next day my dad asked me the name of the place we'd played at. "The Hall for Hire!" I told him. Hey, that's what it said on the little marquee sign out front, so fifteen-year-old me just figured that was what the place was called.

Anyway, Tapestry was a good first band, because, since it was a duo, I had to learn to fill out a lot of the music on my own. That made playing in larger bands later on a lot easier, because then I really felt freed-up to really get into it and just focus on keeping a good, solid beat. Plus, Jim was a good guy. He ended up marrying my sister Marlene. They're still together and have three sons.

On top of Tapestry, I was also playing part-time with Lenny in the Exceptions, subbing for the drummer they had after Eddy Dandy had left. Besides doing weddings and bar mitzvahs, we'd play all these Borscht Belt resorts in the Catskills, backing up stage dancers, magicians, old big-band singers, and comedians. (I got really good at rim shots—*bah-dump-bum!*) The Catskills gigs were great because usually we'd work the whole weekend, doing sets from the afternoon to late at night, and we'd get free rooms and meals at these places, get to hang out at the pool and all that. And let's just say the bartenders weren't too worried about an underage drummer having a few cocktails now and then. For a lot of the gigs, though, Lenny and I wouldn't stay over; we'd drive back to New Jersey and get home at the crack of dawn and sleep in. After a while, my mom just totally gave up on trying to get us up for church. Between playing in both bands, working for my dad, and not having to pay rent, I had pretty good pocket money for a high-school kid.

By 1974, I was seventeen, and I was growing as a musician. I wanted to move on and try different stuff, so I left Tapestry and joined Windfall, an eight-piece horn band led by my friend John Robinson, who was the singer. Besides the regular guitar/bass/keyboard/drums setup, we had a couple of guys on saxophones and trumpets. I really dug that big, brassy horn-band sound: Three Dog Night; Chicago; Blood, Sweat, and Tears. I guess it felt familiar because that was what my big brother had been into. I mean, if Lenny had been in the MC5 or something, I probably would've been in bands doing stuff like that instead.

Along with the horn-band stuff, we covered songs by Joe Cocker, David Bowie, Boz Scaggs, and Van Morrison. Most of the clubs we played weren't fancy. I remember this scuzzy, little dump in Asbury Park called the Roman Arches. It was just down the street from the Stone Pony, where Bruce Springsteen and Southside Johnny and the Asbury Jukes were starting out, around the same time. Around then, Lenny was also playing in a funk band called Tuff Duck—he was the only white guy in the band; the other members were all black guys from Passaic—and I'd watch them rehearse and pick up drumming tips. I loved playing that music, and doing it made me a more versatile drummer than I would've been if I'd only ever played rock.

Besides introducing me to the concept of romantic patience—or trying to, anyway—Sandi Linden also introduced me to the drummer in one of the coolest bands of the time: Neal Smith, from the original Alice Cooper band. Sandi's dad lived in Germany, and on the plane back from visiting him she met this model named Babette, who was Neal's girlfriend at the time. The two of them hit it off, and she invited Sandi and me up to his place in Connecticut, to hang out. So, one rainy Saturday afternoon, we took the train up there. Neal, wearing green mirrored shades, picked us up at the station in his '60s Bentley, and drove us back to this big, old, amazing house he and Babette were living in. Neal was a super-friendly guy. While the girls had drinks and talked in the living room, he showed me the basement room where he kept his drums. That was amazing. He must've had, like, twenty-five or thirty drum sets down there, everything from the mirrored Premier kit he played with Alice to vintage 1930s sets. They were all neatly stacked along the walls of this huge room, along with all kinds of other gear, and road cases with "Alice Cooper" stenciled on them.

The whole thing was just so insane. This was my first time meeting a real rock star, and the Alice Cooper band was huge back then. I tried to act cool and not come off as starstruck, but it wasn't easy. Neal and I talked about drums for a while, and then, out of nowhere, he said, "Hey! It's time to feed the fish! You wanna help?" It seemed really random and weird, but I said, "Sure." I was a little scared, thinking, wow, he plays with Alice Cooper, so he probably has piranhas—I hope I don't get my fingers bitten off or anything.

He led me back upstairs to the garage, where he grabbed a shovel off a hook on the wall and a bucket off the floor. Then we went out through a sliding door in the living room and walked past a swimming pool and over to the backyard, where he started digging around until he'd found maybe six or seven worms. He shoveled the worms into the bucket, and led me back into the living room, where there was this big aquarium filled with exotic fish, and we took turns dropping worms in the tank and watching the fish go after them. Then we had some drinks and went out to eat with the girls, and Neal dropped me and Sandi back off at the train station after that. The other kids at school couldn't believe it when I told them all about it. Neither could I. But it really happened.

12

Newfoundland Steak

Along with Neal Smith, another drummer who really left an impression on me back then was Nigel Olsson, Elton John's drummer.

In 1974, I went to see Elton at Madison Square Garden. I remember that, as soon as the lights went down and the band was about to go on, it was like the whole room immediately filled up with pot smoke. It was overpowering, like the whole audience had lit up. But, besides that, I remember being totally fixated on Nigel, hunched over his drums with his long black hair. He just played; he didn't shake his head or do any "dancing" behind the kit. No flash. Just him, sitting there and playing his ass off, while the band blasted out "The Bitch Is Back," "Saturday Night's Alright for Fighting," "Crocodile Rock," and all those other great songs.

I take that image with me today, whenever I go onstage. I really hate it when drummers dance, shake their heads, twirl their sticks, or do any of that stupid stuff. *Just fucking play*. Let your drumming take over. Because, with all those twirls, you could be playing something else—like, the actual music, for a start. Drummers and keyboard players should just worry about playing their instruments. Let the singers and guitar players add the flash to the stage.

At that point, even though I'd been playing for a while with all these bands—the Exceptions, Tapestry, Windfall—I still wasn't 100 percent sure if I had what it takes, as far as becoming a professional drummer. As much as I hated getting up early to go mow lawns and prune hedges, I could've just given in and gone that route; kept playing with local bands on nights and weekends, and eventually taken over the family business when my dad retired. But seeing Nigel Olsson play, and getting to hang out with Neal Smith not long after that, really inspired me: *this* was what I wanted to do with my life. And, as long as I could help it, there was no way I was ever going to do anything else.

So I just kept on doing it, practicing every day and playing out every night I could with Windfall. By this time, I didn't think Richie Reinhardt sounded cool enough, so I was using the name Richie Rainbow—this was when the glitter-rock thing was big, and if I was going to be a rock star, I needed a flashy name. But then Richie Blackmore from Deep Purple came out with his band Richie Blackmore's Rainbow, and that was too similar-sounding. So I started using Beau—kind of a shortened version of "Rainbow"—as my last name. Windfall kept going into 1976, but after two years of playing the same small Jersey clubs and making the same small Jersey money, I was feeling like I wanted a change—one that would let me see some different places, and hopefully pay a little better.

I answered a "Drummer Needed" classified ad in the *Aquarian*, which was kind of like the New Jersey version of the *Village Voice*, for a band called Madison. I auditioned, and I easily got the gig. The first job—a residency in Florida, at a club right on Cocoa Beach—started right away. We were down there for a couple of months, doing funk and

TRUE LOVE WAYS: My parents, Mary Ann and Leonard Reinhardt, 1950. *Courtesy Reinhardt Family Archive*

GENESIS: Five-year-old Richie gets ready for his first year of school, 1961. *Courtesy Reinhardt Family Archive*

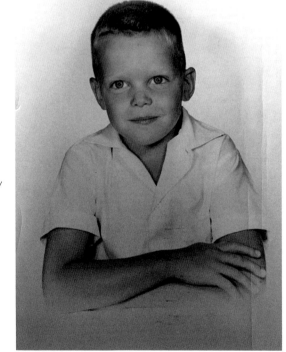

AND THE LIVIN' IS EASY: Lots of family gathered at Lake Hi-De-Hi in New Jersey, 1960. (That's me—bottom row, third from right.) *Courtesy Reinhardt Family Archive*

ALL ATTITUDE, ALREADY: New Jersey Summer, 1963. *Courtesy Reinhardt Family Archive*

BASS MAN STANDING: My very first large mouth. Pinecliff Lake, West Milford, New Jersey, 1965. *Courtesy Reinhardt Family Archive*

NOT SO ROCK 'N' ROLL HIGH SCHOOL: Wayne Hills High School Concert Band, Wayne, New Jersey, 1973. (Not sure what's up with the tongue.) *Courtesy Reinhardt Family Archive*

WILD IS THE WINDFALL: The funky bunch of dudes that comprised the band Windfall, summer 1974. (Me, topless. Can you see my third nipple?) *Courtesy Reinhardt Family Archive*

OH, CANADA: Madison, photographed In Newfoundland, Canada, 1977. These were some wild boys. (I'm second from left, with the Robin Hood beard.) *Photo by Steve Brereton*

DEEP THOUGHTS: Promo shot for Whiteboys, 1979. *Photo © Cathy Miller 2018*

BASEMENT TAPES: Whiteboys rehearsal, 1979. *Photo © Cathy Miller 2018*

WHITEBOYS LIVE: Showtime in New Jersey, 1979, with Steve William (Miller). *Photo © Cathy Miller 2018*

REMOD: An eclectic mix comes together in New York City, 1980. (And I might have a mullet.) *Photo © Cathy Miller 2018*

MAX EFFORT: Onstage with Remod at the legendary Max's Kansas City, New York City, 1980. *Photo © Cathy Miller 2018*

BUT, WHERE?: That's me and Dee Dee. We might be in a storage unit somewhere, or maybe the New York Yankees' locker room, 1983. *Photo by Larry Chekofsky*

**LIFE IN THE
BACKSTAGE:**
Fishing for smokes,
somewhere in Boston,
Massachusetts, 1983.
Photo © Peter Walsh

FORM A LINE, YOUSE:
Looking like a gang
outside of Tower Records
on Fisherman's Wharf in
San Francisco after an
in-store appearance, April
29, 1983. We played the
Kabuki Theater that night.
Photo by Chester Simpson

PUTTIN' ON THE RITZ: Live onstage at New York City's iconic club the Ritz, 1985.

NOW IN STORES: Meet and greet with the Ramones. Comet Record Store, Chatham Street, Dublin, Ireland, June 25, 1985. *Photo by Luke Cauldwell*

DUTCH MASTERS: Dee Dee and me at the Melkweg in Amsterdam, 1987. *Photo © Mike Leach*

disco for the tourists. I mean, c'mon—sand, sun, partying, and girls in bikinis? And I'm this nineteen-year-old Jersey kid? It was awesome.

So this is where the disco comes in. Well, I say disco, but it was really more like light funk. Madison was a six-piece band. We played at supper clubs and hotel lounges—the places that paid the best, where people want to dance to songs by Lou Rawls, Barry White, Kool and the Gang, and Earth, Wind, and Fire. We dressed like one of those prom bands you see in old high-school yearbooks from the 1970s. I had to look the part, but, because my arms were so long, it was hard for me to find ruffled shirts that fit me right. So I'd buy regular-size shirts, and my mom would sew a three-inch extension in the middle of each of the sleeves, making them long enough for the ruffled cuffs to stick out of my jacket sleeves.

Madison's booking agency next got us a run of gigs in Canada, mostly in the dead of winter. We played six nights a week. It was steady work, but it was insanely cold—definitely a big change from Cocoa Beach. And the money part was tough, because we didn't get paid until after the entire run was over. I remember the whole band having to live on, like, $49 a week. At one place we were working at, in Newfoundland, the management wouldn't give us free meals, and the rooms they put us up in didn't even have refrigerators. So all of us chipped in and bought a loaf of bologna, tied a string to it, and left it in a frozen pond behind the hotel. Whenever one of us got hungry, we'd go back there with a knife we stole from the kitchen, pull the bologna out of the pond, and cut off a couple of slices for a sandwich.

What was enjoyable, though, were the drugs—mainly weed or hash oil–laced cigarettes—the booze, and the girls. It was ridiculous. We'd be up there onstage, doing "Jungle Boogie" or whatever, in front of these Canadian families having their vacation dinners, and a lot of the time we'd all be just *loaded*. We hid it well enough, though, I guess; we never got fired for being drunk or anything like that.

By that time, even when I wasn't on coke or speed or anything, I was still fast as fuck on the drums. Thinking back on it now, I'd say that time with Madison made me even more of a solid, high-speed drummer than I was before. Not because we were playing super-fast music—this was way before speed metal or hardcore, and, being a lounge band, we wouldn't have played that stuff, anyway—but because I really developed my level of endurance. Playing a few sets a night will do that for you. It gets to be like riding a bike. Having that level of pacing and endurance already in place made it easier to play faster and longer, when the situation called for it—which, of course, playing in the Ramones would do.

When the other Madison guys and I weren't playing or getting smashed—once again, no one at the bar was exactly studying my ID closely—we were partying in our rooms with the teenage daughters of these vacationing Canadian families, or the townie maids and waitresses who were working at the hotels. I've never been much of a pickup artist—that's not my style. I'm shy. I always prefer it when a woman approaches me, instead of the other way around. And these women were just throwing themselves at us. I don't know why. I guess maybe because they saw us as these exotic American "outlaw" musicians. Plus, like us, they were just horny kids, and they were probably drunk or high, too. Whatever the attraction was, I wasn't complaining.

The year I went from Windfall to Madison, 1976, was the same year punk rock was blowing up in New York and London. I guess I could say here how, when that was happening, I immediately ditched the funk and disco and started following that whole scene, hanging out with Blondie and Johnny Thunders at Max's Kansas City and CBGB's and all that. But I'd be bullshitting you if I did. I was a few years younger than most of the people in those bands, plus I was still focused on being a working musician, trying to make a living playing covers in hotels and bars. And, mostly, the places I was playing were nowhere close to where all the early punk stuff was going on.

Musically, all I was really paying attention to then was what was on the radio at the time, and what I was playing for the people in the lounges who wanted something to dance to—which definitely wasn't punk rock. I was still just a typical suburban New Jersey kid—I didn't know about Andy Warhol or that whole crazy downtown New York thing. When the Ramones were playing their big first British show, at the Roundhouse in London on the Fourth of July, I was camping out and drinking beer next to the George Washington Bridge with John Robinson from Windfall, watching the Bicentennial fireworks and listening to Led Zeppelin on WPLJ.

But even though I wasn't a punk rocker yet—and, of course, I didn't have the slightest clue I'd be in the band someday—I actually saw the Ramones play live that year, pretty much by chance. They were booked at this club in New Jersey called the Showplace (Monte Melnick's book, *On the Road with the Ramones*, lists the date as September 19, 1976). By then, their first album had come out, and there was a little bit of a buzz about it. I think it was John Robinson who said we should go check out the show.

The Showplace was a dark, dingy place with a high stage on Salem Street in Dover that probably held about three or four hundred people legally, but on a lot of nights they packed in way more than that. T. Roth and Another Pretty Face, this New York glam band that I really loved (and who later worked with Ed Stasium, who produced the Ramones) used to play there, and there'd be, like, eight hundred people crammed in. The club first opened as a go-go bar (which is what it ended up becoming again, with a recording studio in the back half), but then they made it into a disco, with live acts like the Trammps and Gloria Gaynor playing between DJs. In '76, the owners noticed they were selling more beer during rock shows, so they switched over to rock full time. The Ramones show was part of their new booking direction, and on that night I was there with John and some other guys from school.

When the band came out, I was standing next to the soundman's booth, which is where I liked to hang out, because of course that's where the sound is the best. Right away, before they'd even played the first note, I could tell the show was going to be way different than anything I'd seen before. They looked and acted serious and mean, like they were some kind of street gang or something. The leather jackets and jeans, and the way Johnny and Dee Dee wore their guitars really low, was nothing like the makeup and glam-y, Bowie-wannabe stuff that I saw a few months before, when T. Roth and Another Pretty Face played there. Joey was the first guy in a band I'd seen who was taller than me, and I remember thinking he actually seemed kind of scary— not at all like the sweet, quiet guy I'd get to know really well when I joined the band.

The soundman turned down the between-bands music that the club was playing over the PA. Joey grabbed the mic and leaned forward. "Good evening, we're the Ramones," he shouted. "And you're a loudmouth, baby—you better shut it up!" Dee Dee counted off, "One-two-three-four!" and they kicked into "Loudmouth." It was like getting run over by a fuckin' wall. The sound was overpowering and just filled the whole room, which couldn't have been much more than half capacity. I don't remember ever seeing a band that loud in such a small place before that night. After "Loudmouth," they went straight into "Beat on the Brat," and then just kept on going, one song right after another—"Blitzkrieg Bop," "I Remember You," "Glad to See You Go," "Gimme Gimme Shock Treatment" . . .

Since I was already a pretty serious drummer, I could see that Tommy probably couldn't really play any busy fills or rolls even if he'd wanted to. But I also remember thinking how cool it was that he was keeping it really, really simple, not trying to do anything that would've been out of place in the songs. "I Wanna Be Your Boyfriend" was one that really stood out to me, just the way the melody was so simple and catchy. I heard some '60s girl-group melodies in that one. I'd liked that music when I was younger, and I still liked hearing it on the oldies stations—even though I wouldn't have admitted that to my friends, who were all about "serious" stuff like prog-rock and fusion. To them, the Ronettes and the Shirelles were little kids' music.

Fifteen minutes into the Ramones' set, I was digging them more and more. I looked over at John Robinson with my eyes all lit up. I was hooked. But the other guys weren't. I could tell John wasn't really into it, and the dudes we came with were saying shit like, "What the hell is *this*?!" and, "Where's the guitar solos?" and, "Can we go now?" I wanted to stay, but, unfortunately, I wasn't the one driving. Before the show even ended, I'd been dragged out to the car. Someone popped in an 8-track tape, "Roundabout" by Yes started playing, and we pealed out of the parking lot, headed back toward Route 46. The whole ride home, my buddies made fun of me for actually liking "that stupid band who can't even play their instruments."

13

A Dog Named Tooey

As much as I dug the Ramones that first time I saw them, I wasn't ready to jump out of my comfort zone and straight into playing punk rock just yet.

The Madison thing started to get old somewhere around the middle of 1977, so I quit and joined a touring cover band called Open Road. Open Road had me on drums plus a guitarist, a bassist, a keyboardist, and a female singer. We did a little theatrical shtick between songs and for some of the sets, I'd leave the drum stool to come out front and sing Elvis songs, and the older ladies in the audience would throw their underwear at me. It was crazy.

I bought a '75 Mazda hatchback to carry my drums around in, and I went out with Open Road for about a year, doing three-week stints at Sheraton Inn lounges east of the Mississippi. We did *five* sets a night, and all the guys in the band had matching, velvet-lapelled suits in different pastel colors; we changed into a different color for each set. Pretty cheesy, but that's how it was. The years with Madison and Open Road were my first time being so far away from home—on my own and with a band. With Open Road, there was more booze and drugs—*lots* of coke and quaaludes—and, like in Madison, lots of partying with girls in our hotel rooms. The money was steadier, but it still wasn't that much better than it was in the bands I was in before. But I loved the whole adventure of it anyway. And I wanted more.

I wasn't going to get much more of it with Open Road, though. One night, when were at the Sheraton Inn Harrisburg or somewhere, I started messing around in my room with the singer—I wish I could remember her name—who was the girlfriend of the bass player and bandleader, this guy with an Afro named George something. I guess since she was with him, she didn't feel too good about fucking me, so, instead, just gave me head. Somehow, word of this got back to George, and of course then there was this awkward vibe in the band. It wasn't long before I was out of there. So that was the end of Open Road. For me, at least.

I answered another ad looking for a drummer, this time in the *Village Voice*, for a New York band called Tiffany in Time. Tiffany was an older hippie woman—it seemed like everyone I played with was older than me back then; now it's the other way around—who sounded just like Janis Joplin. Seriously. She had this really bluesy, really powerful voice. I wonder what ever became of her. I don't know why she never made it. But she was great. She lived on the Upper East Side, and I'd ride the bus in from Jersey a couple of times a week to rehearse with her band.

Looking back on it now, it never dawned on me that Tiffany was gay. She never really hung out with any other guys, and the main place we always played at was this bar in the West Village called the Goddess, where the only people ever there were women. I've never cared about what someone's sexuality is, but it's interesting how it's so obvious to me now that I was playing in a lesbian bar, and at the time I had no clue about that. This was the first time I'd been around that particular scene. Funny how, when you're a kid, you just don't pick up on certain things.

Tiffany and a lot of the women who came to see her play were really into amyl nitrate—"poppers," as people in the gay clubs used to call them. I'd be playing and look out at the room, and all these women would be sitting there together at their tables, sniffing this stuff right there in the bar. The whole scene was really weird. Since it was a small band—just me, acoustic guitar, bass, and a keyboardist—in a really small place, the PA was basically just for the vocals, and, besides playing the drums, the other part of my job was running the sound from a little mixing board next to my stool. Even though Tiffany was a great singer, for me, as a drummer, her music wasn't really fulfilling. She mostly did blues and folk-rock covers—good songs, but not challenging enough when you're a kid who loves to play fast and loud, y'know? And, again, it's not like the money was great, either. After six months, I was ready to move on.

While I was between bands, I was still stuck back in Wayne, working for my dad during the day and living at my folks' place. That all changed, though, not long after I met Francine Valli.

Francine was the daughter of Frankie Valli—yeah, *that* Frankie Valli, the singer from the Four Seasons. She grew up in Nutley, which is about fifteen minutes from my parents' house, and was an aspiring singer herself, with an amazing, five-octave voice. I met Francine when she was singing with Meridian, one of Lenny's bands, and we started dating pretty much right away. I was twenty and she was eighteen, a drop-dead-gorgeous brunette with the whole sexy Jersey-Italian thing going on. Her dad was always away on tour when she was a kid, and her mom, Mary Valli, was pretty fucked up—her folks got divorced when she was eleven—so she was a pretty wild chick, really into getting high and doing crazy shit. Which was just fine with me. She was living in an apartment with Mary, and when she asked me if I wanted to move into her room there, I totally jumped at the chance to get out of my folks' house.

Their place was in a really rough part of town, pure slums—I mean, we're talkin' Newark in the '70s: hookers and dealers all over the block. The dealers really got to know Mary, who, like Francine and me, was really into cibas and codeine—a ciba pill and a codeine pill, which you'd take mixed together. You could buy them on the street like that, already mixed. So you'd take this stuff, and the way you got off was, you threw up, and then you'd be high through the roof for about an hour, until you threw up and got high again. People say it's a lot like a methadone high—you feel totally euphoric at first, and then mellow and relaxed, but it lasts a lot longer.

Mary didn't have a job. She just lived off the money she got a couple of times a month from Frankie as part of their alimony settlement. She'd just kind of sit around the house and wait until the check came, which was every two weeks. When she got the check, she'd go cash it, and then we'd all get high—man, the whole neighborhood would get high. There'd be, like, ten people in the house, waiting in line for the bathroom, to go in there and throw up after they took their cibas and codeine. It was fuckin' crazy.

Another drug we really loved back then were Tuinals—*tooeys*, we used to call them. Actually, Francine and I had a little dog we even named Tooey, because we dug those things so much. I don't think anyone ever walked that dog at all. We'd come home, high, and there'd be, like, a hundred dog shits all around the house. We'd just step around them until we got to the mattress on the floor that we slept on, and then just crash out.

Tuinals were a very unusual drug. Those things would make me into a fuckin' *monster*. You'd feel like you had superhuman strength, like you were the Incredible Hulk and could lift six hundred pounds like it was nothing. Francine and I would drive into the city to get them. You could score them down in Tompkins Square Park or down by Union Square. The dealers would always try to push Seconals on us instead, which they got cheaper and weren't as good, but we knew the difference. So the three of us—me, Francine, and Francine's mom—would all get high on tooeys and then sit at the kitchen table and play cards together. That was ridiculous, because everything was so blurry that you couldn't even see your hand.

My old high-school friend Rich Lachocki—the one I got freaked out by when we did mescaline together—had started a catering truck business, and I went to work for him, driving one of his trucks from Newark to Wayne every morning to sell coffee and hot meals at construction sites. I'd get up at four, usually pretty hungover from partying really late the night before, stop at a couple of places along the way to pick up the food and supplies, and then work until around ten. Then I'd park the truck and go hit a bar until a little before noon, and then go back to these same places for the lunchtime run. After that, I was done for the day, ready to go back home and get high with Francine and Mary, or rehearse with one of the cover bands I was sitting in with here and there until something better came along. I had a coin belt, and I learned to keep all my bills in order in my pocket to make change fast—which also made it easier for me to skim some off for myself. Sorry about that, Rich, if you're reading this.

By then, I'd been doing the cover-band thing for five or six years, and something was starting to hit me: I was never going to make a name for myself as a drummer if all I ever did was play covers in bars and hotel lounges. Punk and new wave were getting people excited about playing original music, and I was one of those people. The thing was, though, the money for playing covers was steady, and it wasn't for bands that did original stuff. But even though that's how it was, I still wanted to make my mark. I started keeping my eyes open for a band who wrote and played their own stuff.

In early 1978, I saw an ad in the *Aquarian* for an originals-only band in the Bloomfield/Montclair area called Whiteboys, who were looking for a drummer, and I went to try out. Most of their songs were written by Steve Miller, who sang lead and played guitar and went by the stage name Steve William, so people wouldn't think he was the "Fly Like an Eagle" Steve Miller. Steve was a cool guy; we're still friends today. The group already had a single out, but their drummer had switched to second guitar, which is why they were holding auditions. I liked the sound of the band. It was snotty and punky and had a little hard rock to it, maybe some Alice Cooper or Thin Lizzy. And it felt good to be playing something really raw for a change, instead of more fusion or Earth, Wind, and Fire covers. They dug my playing, and I was in, although the other guitar player ended up leaving not long after I joined, making us a three-piece.

Other than one gig at a decent place on Hudson Street called Heat, we mostly played crappy New York clubs whose names I don't remember. The good New York clubs, like Max's Kansas City, were hard to get booked in to, if you weren't a known band or didn't have connections. And in Jersey or Connecticut? Forget it. We did play some hole-in-the-wall spots in those places, but back then there was hardly *anywhere* to play if you weren't a cover band. Plus, we kept losing bass players, which didn't help either.

In that band I had a double bass-drum setup. I got the idea from watching Ed Shaugnessy, another great New Jersey drummer, who I saw play double bass in Doc Severinson's band on the Johnny Carson show. But it was too much of a hassle, dragging an extra twenty-six-inch bass drum around, and I didn't have one of those double-beater pedals that let you play both drums at once, just one pedal for each; I still had to play my hi-hat, too, and of course I only have two feet. So that didn't last long.

Neither did Whiteboys. After about a year, Steve gave up on that band and decided to start a new one, a power-pop trio called Ambulance. He asked me to be in it. I thought about that for a bit. "Thanks, but no," I told him. I said I'd be into recording and maybe a gig once in a while, but nothing beyond that. (Ambulance cut a single that's really collectible now, but I'm not on it; two songs I did record with them, though, are on a CD that came out in 2012 called *Planet You*.)

I told Steve I didn't want to start a band from scratch. Instead, I said, I wanted to find one that was already established, within the next five years—and, if I didn't do that, I'd quit music altogether. I even called this idea my "five-year plan." And, hey, y'know what? It turns out that plan worked out pretty well. But there were a few more twists and turns before it did . . .

14

Car Crash

In the spring of '78, Francine and I got some money together and got our own place in Montclair, a cute, small, slow town that you can see the New York skyline from. This was during the time I was playing in Whiteboys and Ambulance, so part of the reason we moved was to be closer to where Steve Miller lived, and where I rehearsed with his bands. But, more than that, it was just to be on our own as a couple, and get away from Francine's mom.

Even though Francine and I were still getting high all the time ourselves, it was just getting too crazy over there, with Mary letting freaks from the neighborhood in all the time to party with her, and Tooey's shit all over the floor. But she was still Francine's mom, and Francine needed to be close to her, and Montclair is right next to Newark. Just because Francine and I got out of the crazy scene with her mom, though, doesn't mean we didn't get into some of our own. And there was one I'm just remembering now that almost got both of us killed. Or at least put in jail.

Back then I had a '67 Volkswagen Microbus, one of those Type 2's with the split-screen windshield and the little four-cylinder engine in the back. Cool-looking van. Plus, it was great for hauling drums and gear around in. I loved that thing. Anyway, one night that summer, Francine and I drove it into the city to score some Tuinals down on the Lower East Side. We bought four of them from some guy in Tompkins Square and headed back uptown to the Lincoln Tunnel—a trip we did a couple of times a month back then. Francine pretty much always popped one as soon as we scored, and she'd be flyin' before we even hit the tunnel. Usually, I'd be a good boy and wait until we were at least back in Jersey. But for some reason, on this particular night, I said, "Fuck it, I don't feel like waiting," and took one at the same time she did.

Dumb move. The thing with tooeys is that, after making you high for a while, they make you really sleepy, and you end up nodding out. I'd been up early, doing the catering-truck job, so I was already pretty tired, and we were both also taking hits off the airplane bottle of Southern Comfort I'd brought along to wash the pills down with. But I figured, hey, we'll pretty much be home before I really start feelin' it . . . right?

Wrong. It turned out there was some kind of roadwork happening in the tunnel, and there was only one lane open. Traffic was backed up and moving really slowly. The Tuinal started kicking in while we were stuck halfway through. By the time we got out, I was pretty fuckin' out of it— sometimes, tooeys make you feel like you're drunk. And, besides that, I was also getting dizzy. Really dizzy. And really . . . really . . . sleepy.

"Richie! Hey! Richie!"

Francine was yelling at me. I opened my eyes wide, like I'd been hit with an electric shock, and sat up straight.

"Are you okay?" she said, grabbing my shoulder. "Richie! Hey! Are you fallin' asleep?"

"No!" I heard myself say. "No. I ain't fuckin' *fallin' asleep*! I'm fine. Don't fuckin' worry about it, all right?"

We were on Route 3, coming up on the exit for Route 46. I remember getting off on 46 and being in the fast lane and going through Clifton, passing the Tick Tock Diner (which is still there today, or at least it was when I was writing this). The sign for the Tick Tock is in big orange neon letters with a clock on it. I'd seen that sign a million times before. But, this time, it was just an orange blur. I felt like I was underwater.

I shook my head and blinked my eyes a couple of times. But it didn't do any good. Everything was still a blur. And, like before, I started feeling really, really sleepy . . .

I woke up to Francine's voice again. Only this time it was her screaming voice, not her yelling voice. And it was right in my ear.

"Richie! Richie, you okay? You okay? Richie? Richie! Get off-a me!"

She was still in her seat, but I was out of mine—and lying sideways on top of her. Actually, the *whole van* was sideways. We were sitting there, passenger side down, on the shoulder of Route 46. Everything was quiet. Except for the cars going by a few feet away.

"Yeah, I'm okay," I groaned. I shook my head again. If I was in pain, I wasn't feeling it. Yet, at least. "You all right?"

Francine seemed like she was fine, so that was a relief. It was a soft flip. The windshield was cracked, a couple of the windows were broken, and the gear I had in the back had been thrown all over the place. There wasn't any smoke, though, and I didn't smell any gas leaks. But the engine was still running, and even though I was really frazzled, I was together enough to know it wasn't a good idea to leave it running. I reached up—instead of over, like normal—and turned the ignition off.

I guess we both must have been lying there for a couple of minutes before we came to. My head was still foggy, and my eyelids were getting heavy again. I heard sirens somewhere down the highway. They were getting louder. And closer.

"Shit! The tooeys!" I yelled at Francine. "The cops! Shit, shit, shit. We gotta get rid of the fuckin' tooeys! Now, now! What'd you do with 'em?!"

"Uhhh," she moaned. "I got 'em in my purse . . . "

"Give 'em to me!" I yelled. "Now! Fast! Give 'em to me! NOW! NOW!"

She dug around in her purse until she found the little ball of tinfoil the two Tuinals were wrapped up in and shoved it into my hand. I figured the foil would be way too easy for the cops to spot, so I unwrapped the pills really fast and dropped them out of the side window that was just behind Francine's seat—right when the police car pulled up behind us, with its siren and flashing lights going full blast. I figured the pills would be on the ground underneath the van, where nobody would see them. Plus, maybe Francine and I could even come back and look for them later.

I told the cop I'd been working all day and I'd fallen asleep, which, y'know, wasn't a *total* lie. I was really scared because I was thinking it was obvious we were high, and that he'd see through my bullshit right away. But, if he did, he didn't take things any further. I don't know why. I guess maybe it was because no one got hurt, and the only thing that got damaged was my van, and the police had more important things to do.

The paramedics showed up and said we were both fine, so the cop sat us in the back of a police car to fill out an accident report—and then he let us go! I called Steve from Ambulance—that's funny, that I was playing with a band called Ambulance when all this happened—from a payphone, and he gave me and Francine a ride to Montclair. When we got home, the two of us smoked a joint together and passed out.

The next morning, the phone rang. It was the cops.

"Good morning, Mr. Reinhardt? This is Officer So-and-So from the Wayne Police Department."

I freaked. Somehow, they must have figured us out. They probably found the pills when they were cleaning up after we left. I was sure we were busted. *Shit.*

Thankfully, I was wrong.

"We towed your vehicle last night to the impound lot over here. Please retrieve it as soon as possible. If the vehicle is inoperable, please make arrangements to have it towed to a junkyard. If the vehicle *is* operable, you're free to drive it away."

So that's what happened. Francine and I got a cab down there, the van started right up, and we drove it straight back to Montclair. We parked in front of our place and started cleaning it up, going through the stuff that got tossed around when it flipped over. And, while we were doing that, we came across something we didn't expect to see: the Tuinals. Both of them were sitting right there on the floor, just behind the passenger seat.

It turned out the window I thought I'd thrown them out of wasn't open, like I thought it was. So they'd just bounced off the glass and landed back inside the van—where the cops never even noticed them.

Francine and I just looked at each other and started laughing like crazy. And you can probably guess what we ended up doing for the next couple of hours.

In December 1979, I was still on my five-year plan, making my way as a musician. Trying to get in a band that was going somewhere. The *Village Voice* would come out every Wednesday, and I'd get it and open it from the back, flip past all the ads for call girls and massage parlors, and turn straight to the musicians' listings in the classifieds, looking for ads that said "DRUMMER WANTED." I hit on one for a band in New York called Remod.

Remod was a four-piece glam band that was kind of getting into punk—a Ramones-style setup, actually, with a standalone lead singer, a guitar player, a bass player, and a drum spot that I took over that month after I blew away all the other guys who were also auditioning at a little rehearsal studio on East Twelfth Street. The music was mostly written by the singer—an Irish-American guy from Westchester who called himself Tak Deluks—and the guitar player, James Sant'Andrea. The bass player was a guy named Devan Carter. Their stuff was pretty fast—and, of course, it got way faster when I joined the band. The newer songs reminded me of the English bands from that time that I was really digging, like the Buzzcocks and Generation X—hooky and poppy, with tight breaks. I remember the Clash's *London Calling* had just come out that month, and I was really into that album, too.

Tak was the first singer I had ever been in a band with who was a real, classic rock 'n' roll front man—this wiry, androgynous guy, like Mick Jagger or David Johansen. His voice was kind of quirky and weird, but in a way that was cool, not annoying. And he was always *on*, all the time—even when he wasn't onstage. Just, like, total high-energy, y'know? Maybe some of it was from speed or coke. I was never really sure, because it seemed like he was just naturally like that. Whatever it was, he was a really good entertainer, and the audiences at the gigs totally loved him—which of course was good for the band, too.

After a couple of months, James showed up at rehearsal in a red leather jacket with his previously shaggy, dark hair now bleached blond and cut short and spiky, like Billy Idol from Generation X. I made a joke that he looked more like the Flash, the DC Comics superhero, than Billy Idol; by the end of the night, the whole band was calling him "Flash." We played every New York club we could: CBGB's, Max's Kansas City, Danceteria, the Peppermint Lounge, My Father's Place out on Long Island. Whoever would book us.

Since I wasn't playing funk or fusion, which were more about the rhythm, anymore, this was the time I started to really become more aware of the vocals, and play to support them, rather than do anything that might step on them. The music I was getting into—super-simple, bare-bones rock 'n' roll—was more about holding it down and keeping it *tasty* with your fills, instead of always trying to impress the Buddy Rich wannabes. (That doesn't mean I ever stopped loving Buddy's playing, it's just different music.) So I started to focus less on the accents and fills and more on keeping beats that were solid and always in time. When I wasn't taking the bus into the city for rehearsals and gigs or crashing at Flash's place on the Lower East Side, I was basically training myself to be a human bpm meter.

Remod recorded two songs for a single we put out ourselves, "Life of the Party" and "Gaygirls Dance." "Life of the Party" came out sounding good, I thought. It really shows how much I was keying into the idea of always having a constant, nonstop beat that was *impossible* to ignore for anyone who heard me play. It sucked that the record hardly got any attention and no one really heard it. (If you can find a copy today, it's worth some money.) But I was finally in a cool band that was part of the New York scene. And I was starting to have the time of my life.

15

Francine

Flash and I really hit it off. We were like musical twins. We dressed alike, had identical mod haircuts. We shared an offbeat sense of humor, and we even shared girlfriends later on. Everyone thought we were brothers. He lived with his single mom, Alice, in a big apartment at 43 Fifth Avenue, right near the corner of East Eleventh Street. Marlon Brando had lived there in the '50s, when he first came to New York to study acting. They let me move in in February of 1980, since Remod were rehearsing and playing a lot, and for me taking the bus back and forth to Jersey so much—there was no way I was going to deal with driving in and out and parking and all that—was getting to be a pain. I was still in a relationship with Francine, and we'd get together a couple of times a month. She'd come out for dinner, or I'd go out there for a night or two, and we'd talk on the phone almost every day.

Living at Flash and his mom's place was another crazy scene. But I'm talking crazy in a great way. Alice was a really cool mom. She let us live there rent free, and she pretty much let Flash do whatever he wanted, growing up. She was also an ex-hippie and a practicing witch, which was definitely something I'd never been around before. Flash and I would come home late at night from playing or hitting the bars, and she'd be in the kitchen, mixing up some kind of potion, or having a séance around the table with some of her witch friends. That was pretty interesting to a kid who grew up in Jersey, like me. Flash slept in this loft they'd built above the part where I was crashing, and some nights he'd be up there, bangin' some girl he picked up at one of the clubs. He'd be doing that or getting high or whatever, and Alice didn't give a shit. Definitely a very liberal lady.

Their place was right in the middle of everything that was cool in New York—the perfect spot to be in. The coolest big club in town, the Ritz, was just around the corner. Irving Plaza, which was almost as cool and almost as big, was five or six blocks away, and so was the Palladium, where the Clash were playing when the *London Calling* cover photo was taken. (I went to see them at Bond's, up in Times Square, in 1981, which was amazing.) Flash and I saw so many awesome shows at those places back around that time—the Psychedelic Furs, the Romantics, Gary Numan, and I don't know how many others. NYU, which had the best radio station in New York back then, WNYU, was right on Washington Square. Parsons School of Design, where all the foxy fashion students were, was right up on Thirteenth Street, and so was the Lone Star Café, where I saw James Brown play. Keith Richards had a place over somewhere around East Fifteenth Street, so I'd see him and Mick Jagger walking around all the time. Plus, now I was, like, three blocks away from Union Square and all the tooeys I could cop. It was awesome.

And then there was Trude Heller's, on Ninth Street and Sixth Avenue. Man, Trude's was our hang. It was this really small club that opened back in the early '60s, as a place with go-go dancers where people came to do the twist. Joey Dee and the Starlighters played there around then, with Peter Criss in the band, long before he was in KISS. That's what I heard, anyway. Otis Redding and bands like the Blues Magoos and the Allman Joys—one of Duane and Gregg Allman's first bands—played there, too, and celebrities like Salvador Dali and the Andy Warhol people had hung out there. Trude, the owner, was a real character, this older lesbian who always wanted the place to be loud and rockin', and it pretty much always was. Gang War, a band that Wayne Kramer from the MC5 and Johnny Thunders had going for a little while, played there in December '79, right around the time I joined Remod. The Bad Brains did one of their first New York shows at Trude's, and the Beastie Boys played there when they were still just a bunch of little kids playing hardcore, before they got into doing rap. Flash and I would be at Trude's almost every night until closing time, even when Remod weren't playing there, which we did as the Monday-night house band for a couple of months.

I got a day job as a security guard at a vintage clothing store in the West Village called Reminiscence. It didn't pay much, but all I really had to do was just show up. It was the perfect job for someone like me, who was always hungover—sometimes even a little wasted, still—from the night before. All I really had to do was stay awake and stand next to the front door all day to make sure people didn't steal anything.

Getting that job was another move that put me in the right place at the right time. Reminiscence was on MacDougal Street right next door to Bleecker Bob's, which was the first record store in America to carry punk records when they started coming out in 1975 and '76. By now, the music was changing over from the old-school, straight-ahead punk sound into what they now call post-punk; getting artier and crossing punk energy with funk, dub reggae, and psychedelic rock from the '60s. On record, a lot of this stuff had heavier bass, and the whole rhythm section was more up front in the mix, with bigger studio production than the more garage-y sound of the Sex Pistols and the other early punk stuff, which made it sound really layered and huge when you heard it over the big sound systems in the clubs. Coming from a funk background, I totally got that angle—it felt really natural to me. It was cool to be part of this musical change that was happening in New York—even though a lot of that music was coming from *outside* of New York.

Most of the big bands Flash and I were into that were part of the whole new post-punk wave were from England. Not a lot of their records were released in America yet, only in the UK, which meant you had to get them as imports. So, on my break and after work, I'd wander into Bleecker Bob's and flip through the import bins for the latest British stuff, looking for bands I'd heard on *The New Afternoon Show* on WNYU, or maybe on a 12-inch that one of the DJs at Danceteria or the Peppermint Lounge or the Mudd Club was playing at the time. Pretty soon, I was bringing home dozens of albums by bands like Gang of Four, Killing Joke, XTC, Echo and the Bunnymen, the Cure, the Psychedelic Furs, and Public Image Ltd. *A Different Kind of Tension* by the Buzzcocks was one we really loved from around that time.

Flash and I played those records constantly, and right away we changed our playing style to be more like the new UK sound. I'd sit him down and make him listen to the drumbeats and explain the rhythmic structure of all the songs to him. After doing that for a while, I told him, "Now go play your guitar like it's a drum set, and you'll be the best rhythm guitarist out there." He did, and I was right: his rhythms got better and better, and more complex and steadier. At gigs, if he wasn't showing off to the audience for a solo or something, he started hanging back by the drum kit, always keeping eye contact with me and making sure his guitar downstrokes were right on time with my snare and bass drum. And I pushed him to *always* play downstrokes, just like Johnny Ramone always played—"If I ever see you playing an up-and-down stroke instead of a straight downstroke, I'll throw a stick at you," I joked.

Man, Flash and I got to where we were so locked in it was ridiculous. When we played, it was like we were two halves of the same machine. By the summer of 1980, we really *were* musical twins. I also taught the band a lot about arranging. They were good at coming up with riffs, but putting them together—that was a different kind of skill. Before I even met them, I'd already spent, like, ten years playing covers. So I knew how hit songs were put together.

Even though things were going really great with me in New York with my playing, they weren't going so well for Francine back in Jersey. And they were about to get really, really bad.

Early in the morning on August 13, I was lying in bed and heard the phone ring. Flash's mom answered and said it was for me. *Ah, shit,* I figured, it's Reminiscence, wanting me to come in early, because someone called in sick. They'd pulled that shit before.

I got up to take the call, and right away I almost fell back into bed—I was still buzzed from hanging out with Flash at Trude's until 4 a.m. It was Mary Valli, Francine's mom, on the other end. She was crying and screaming and having a meltdown.

"Richie! Something's wrong with Francine! Something's wrong with Francine!" she said. "They took her to the hospital. She's not waking up. Something's really, really wrong. I don't know what's going on."

This hot feeling went through me, and I got really lightheaded. All of a sudden, I felt like I was going to throw up. It was mostly from shock, but the six screwdrivers I'd had a couple of hours before weren't helping. I told Mary I was on my way, and I'd see her at the hospital.

I took a cab up to Port Authority and got the bus to Jersey. The whole way out was hell. I actually hadn't been in touch with Francine for a few days, and I'd been starting to wonder what was up with her. Her dad had put her in rehab for a while, and—and this was unbelievably fucked up—her stepsister Celia (Frankie's stepdaughter with his second wife) had died about six months before, after falling off a fire escape when she'd locked herself out of her apartment and was trying to get in through a back window. And, on top of that, her grandfather, Frankie's dad, had just had a stroke.

I sat all the way in the back of the bus, trying not to freak out on the Garden State Parkway. When I got to the hospital, Mary was already in the room, sitting next to the bed. Francine was lying there with her eyes closed. There were breathing tubes in her nose and mouth, and more tubes and wires in her arms, chest, and neck. Mary and I went back outside, and she told me the doctors said Francine had OD'ed from mixing quaaludes and alcohol, and she was in a coma. I felt like I was going to faint. I sat down hard on one of the waiting room couches. Mixing 'ludes and booze was something Francine and I had both done way more than once.

I stayed there at the hospital with Francine, right next to her bed, around the clock for the next three days. But she never woke up.

She was twenty years old when she died on August 16, five days after my twenty-fourth birthday.

I went back to New York to get a suit to wear to the funeral, and Flash and Alice took the bus back out with me for the wake. The next day, I rode in the limo to the funeral with Frankie and Mary and some of the other family members. Man, Frankie looked like he was just totally destroyed. I don't know how he even got through it all. I hear that the story about Francine dying is a big scene in the Broadway musical *Jersey Boys*, and the movie that came out of that, the one Clint Eastwood directed. But I haven't been able to bring myself to see either of those.

Sorry if I sound kind of depressed, telling you all this stuff about Francine. It's just so sad, y'know? Everyone, including me, figured we were going to get married. Even now, almost forty years later, it's still really hard for me to talk about it. On YouTube, there are some recordings of her singing, beautifully, with Lenny and Meridian at a club in New Jersey, only a couple of months before she died. Sometimes I listen to those and think that if I'd been around her more, instead of being off in New York trying to make it as drummer, then maybe I could have done something to stop things from turning out like they did. But then I think about how, besides me being kind of a mess myself back then, she was a musician, just like me—she totally got what I was trying to do. And not for one second would she have wanted to keep me from doing any of it. Just like I wouldn't have kept her from doing the same.

16

Enter the Dragon

When Francine died, I tried to deal with it in the way I knew best: by playing music. But that doesn't mean I didn't go off the deep end for a while, too, with the girls and the partying and all that.

When it came to women, I pretty much became a tramp. Flash and I were East Village crazies. We'd be each other's wingmen whenever we went out to cruise the clubs. With our long bangs and our black trench coats, we looked like we were in Echo and the Bunnymen or some other cool English band, which made picking up girls really easy. I was getting laid, like, every weekend. Sometimes more than that. And, back then, nobody used protection or anything; AIDS wasn't really something most people were worried about yet. You didn't really start hearing about AIDS until the mid-1980s, and that was still a couple of years off. So I just went wild, and it was, like, this great release.

I remember one thing that happened back then that was really crazy. There was a Blimpie's sandwich shop over on Second Avenue that stayed open really late and actually served beer—I don't know if they're even allowed to do that anymore, sell beer. I can't think of any other Blimpie's I was ever in that had beer, but this one did. And, since it was right near our place and it was open until, like, four in the morning, Flash and I would always hit it on the way home from the clubs, go grab some beers and keep the party going.

So, one night we were coming back from one of the free "Mod Monday" DJ nights at the Ritz we used to love going to, and we had these two girls with us that we'd met at the club. Flash and his lady for the night were inside this Blimpie's, at a table, talking and drinking, and I was out in front, making out with mine. Things started getting hot, and she just reached down, unzipped my jeans, took out my cock, and started blowing me, right there on Eleventh Street. I've never been one to turn down a blowjob from a pretty girl—and, this time, there weren't any marching-band or color-guard kids to rat me out about getting one in public. I don't remember there being anyone else around. Or, maybe there were a few people around, and I was just too wasted to remember or care. Like I told you, I was a tramp then.

Speaking of tramps, that reminds me of another neighborhood club Flash and I would hang out at a lot back then: this place called Tramps, a little blues bar on East Fifteenth, near Irving Plaza. A lot of these old blues and soul people would play there, like Sam and Dave, and Big Mama Thornton. But we mostly went there to buy weed from these Jamaican dudes who worked there. They wouldn't sell to everyone, but once they figured out I wasn't a narc, they started liking me and trusting me. We'd also buy quaaludes from this sleazy dentist who had his office right across the street. Sometimes, we'd grind up the 'ludes, sprinkle the powder from that in a joint, and then smoke it. I think I showed Flash how to do that. At first, he thought I was nuts, but then he got to like it—a lot. We also used to grind up those black beauties—

the speed the doctors sold as "diet pills" back then—so we could snort them. Crazy stuff.

But maybe the most insane thing I can think of from back then was this party that all of Remod went to one night. Some guy we met at one of our gigs invited us to it. We bought some beers from a deli and took the train all the way up to his place, which was on, like, 172nd Street or someplace. Somewhere way the fuck up in Washington Heights, up around there. And it took *forever* to get there; none us ever went up to that part of town for anything. Going all the way up there from the Lower East Side was pretty much like going to another planet. But the guy said he had tons of blow, and he told us these girls were going to be there who *really* wanted to meet us—so, y'know, we were definitely interested. When we finally got to the address, we took the elevator up, found the apartment, and knocked. The dude who invited us answered the door and let us in. And what we walked into was a full-blown coke orgy.

There were probably about fifteen or twenty people in the living room of this place; I'd say it was a two-bedroom apartment. The lights were low, it smelled like weed, and the B-52's' first album was playing on the stereo. People were talking loud, and there was the sound of girls giggling—which, if you're a single straight guy out on the prowl, always gets your attention. Along one wall there was a table with a bunch of glasses and open bottles on it: Smirnoff, Jack Daniels, tequila, some cheap red wine. In the middle of the room, between a black-leather couch and a couple of easy chairs, there was a glass coffee table with a fuckin' *mountain* of coke on it. I mean, it must have been, like, five or six inches tall, this thing. I'd never seen so much coke at once before. Two guys and two girls were sitting there around it, bent over and taking turns snorting away at it. Over in one corner of the room, there were these two guys standing next to each other with their pants down, getting blown by these two girls, and through an open bedroom door I could see a guy's bare ass going up and down while he was fucking someone on a bed.

We all sat down and did a line. I guess the whole scene, with all the public sex, was too much for Devan, our bass player, and he ended up leaving after a few minutes. But Flash, Tak, and I were up for a little adventure, and we decided to stick around. I can't remember what Flash got into, but I do remember getting a blowjob in the bathroom from a chick with bleach-blonde hair. Tak, though, man—Tak was out of control, like always. I walked out of the bathroom, and there he was, literally fucking this girl in the ass, right there on the couch. As I was passing by, he called me over and started talking to me about how much he dug the arrangement of one of our new songs.

"Hey man, I *really* like how Flash and Devan lay out after the second chorus, and then it's just you and me, and then there's that quick break, and then the whole band just kicks back in and—*pow!*" he said, speeding his brains out and looking over his shoulder at me while he and this chick were going at it. She didn't seem to mind at all.

"Uh . . . yeah, man . . . it sounds cool," was all I could say. The whole thing was weird. But then it all got even weirder. And scary.

There was some loud, hard banging on the apartment door, and all this yelling coming from out in the hall. I looked through the peephole, and there were maybe, like, eight or nine really tough-looking Chinese guys standing there, looking *really* pissed off. I backed away from the door, really quick, and they started banging and yelling again. They totally looked like some kind of local gang. But no one at the party seemed to know what they wanted. Or, if they did, they wouldn't tell us. All of the yelling these guys were doing was in Chinese, so we had no idea what they were yelling about. One of the girls at the party was Asian, so Flash figured maybe one of them was a jealous boyfriend or something. It also could have been something to do with the coke; maybe the guy having the party owed them money for it. But I did know that the three of us were pretty paranoid, and we thought these guys were going to come in and fuckin' kill us—and everybody else—if they got past the door. We didn't know or care what the other people at this thing were going to do, but Flash, Tak, and I all knew we had to get out of there. Fast.

"Let's just take the fire escape," was Tak's idea, but I told him no way. This place was on, like, the sixteenth floor or something. And, as fucked up as I was, I was together enough to know that *all* of us were too high to take a chance on doing that—the thought of Celia Valli falling off her fire escape was still fresh in my mind. We knew the guy whose place we were in wasn't going to call the cops, not with all that blow in there. And the neighbors weren't going to call 'em, either—unless they wanted to get a visit from the same gang later on. Flash was saying we should just spend the night and wait it out; there was food there, and we could crash out on the floor or something. But I didn't like that idea, either. Sooner or later, these guys were going to find a battering ram or something and get in. Or, maybe they'd just burn down the building with everyone in it. That kind of stuff happened all the time back then. Gang guys didn't care. Whatever they did, though, I sure as fuck didn't want to be around when they did it.

Finally, after about a half-hour, the yelling and banging stopped. It seemed like these guys had given up and left. Tak took a peek out in the hall and said the coast was clear. He was all ready to jump on the elevator and head down. "Are you fucking kidding?! Man, that's the oldest trick in the book," Flash said, and he was right. These dudes weren't *that* dumb. Guaranteed, they were just waiting right outside the elevator down in the lobby, having a smoke and getting ready to beat the shit out of us when we walked out. So, what were we going to do?

"Back stairs," I said. That was risky, too. But at least we wouldn't be stuck in an elevator if the doors opened and there they were. We took off down the stairs as fast as we could, trying not to trip as we made all the turns in this really old stairwell. It took something like fifteen minutes to get all the way down, and, when we got there, all of us were totally out of breath—but we couldn't stop yet. We had to get to the subway, and who knew if we'd run into these guys down there.

We took off out of the exit door and sprinted all the way to the subway, which was maybe six or seven blocks, jumped the turnstiles, and got on the "A" train just as the doors were shutting. It was late, and the car was empty. If the gangbangers were in the station, they'd let us go. We sure didn't stop to look.

The three of us fell on our asses on the subway car seats, laughing like we were out of our minds while we tried to catch our breath. When we got back down to the Village, we hit the Veselka diner on Avenue A for breakfast, laughed some more about our insane night, and went home and crashed. We told Devan about it at the next rehearsal, but it seemed like he didn't believe us. I think he thought we were all just paranoid and high and dreamed the whole thing up, or maybe we just wanted to make him feel like he'd missed out on all the excitement by splitting early.

But even though I was having a wild time with Remod, after two years of playing mostly weeknights in small clubs, without a record deal, it was clear that the band had hit the wall. I need to make a move. So it was back to the *Village Voice* again, looking for something better. And, after a few weeks of checking the ads and jamming with some shitty bands, I found it.

17

Back to Square Two

Velveteen was a newer band started by a bass player named Sal Maida and his wife, a singer named Lisa Burns. Sal had a pretty awesome track record. He'd been in Roxy Music, Sparks, and Milk 'n' Cookies, this glam-y power-pop band from Long Island who were big at Max's Kansas City right before punk started happening. (Way later, in the 2000s, he was in Cracker.) So that was some big-time stuff. Lisa had made an album for MCA in 1978 that was very '60s-girl-group-sounding and was produced by Craig Leon, who also produced the Ramones' first album. I don't think I knew that until later, though. But I did know who Sal was, so I answered their ad in the *Voice* immediately when I came across it. I auditioned, and it went great.

Because Sal was in the band and Lisa was a good singer and pretty cute—this was 1981, when MTV was starting up, so image was getting even more important—there was already some major-label interest in Velveteen, even though the band had only played a few shows at that point. A lot of that was also because they were managed by Jonathan Blank, who also managed David Lee Roth and some other big acts.

Anyway, they offered me the gig, and I was psyched. At last, I was thinking, I'm in a band that does original stuff *and* also looks like it's really going somewhere. Two years in, and my five-year plan was working out pretty well.

Velveteen's style was what people were calling "dance rock." It crossed a little bit of the punk vibe and look with the dance music that was big in the clubs then: slick and very modern, and, like they say, "radio-friendly." The original guitar player, Jimmy McCallister, left after a few months—I can't remember why—and the band started looking for a replacement. Of course, right away, I thought of my buddy Flash, and I really wanted to get him in the band. But Sal and Lisa were calling the shots, and since there was a big buzz about Velveteen, they started getting all these calls from hot-shit guitarists who were looking to try out. They wanted to audition each guy by bringing him in cold, without having learned the tunes beforehand; the idea was to take whichever one looked the part and picked up the music the fastest.

Flash looked cool (like I said, we were pretty much twins), and he was a great player, so there was no problem with that stuff, but of course he didn't really know the songs. I wanted to make sure he got in, though. So, sneaky me, I secretly made him a tape of three of the songs, and he proceeded to totally get them down tight by practicing along to the tape the week before he auditioned. When he came down to the rehearsal space to try out, he totally nailed the tunes and got hired—he couldn't play 'em *too* well, though, or else Sal and Lisa would catch on to our little scam. After a few weeks, I think they probably figured out what Flash and I had pulled. But, hey, by that time, it was too late: he was in the band, and we were sounding great.

Thanks to Sal and Jonathan's connections, Velveteen got to be one of the hottest New York club bands pretty quickly. We headlined decent-sized places—Danceteria, Trax, the Peppermint Lounge, the Electric Circus; the Malibu on Long Island; Hitsville out in Jersey— and they'd be packed. People loved to dance to our stuff, especially girls, which of course always brings the guys in, too. We also got on a lot of good opening slots for big-name bands. At the Ritz, we opened for the Rockats, who were this big-deal rockabilly band at the time, and Huey Lewis and the News. We even headlined at CBGB's on New Year's Eve, which of course was really cool.

Lisa's best friend was Annie Golden. Annie was the lead singer of the Shirts, one of the original CBGB's bands. She was also an actress. She'd been in the 1977 Broadway revival of *Hair*—and the 1979 movie version, too—and she had some TV parts on *Cheers* and *Miami Vice* not long after I met her. (She was in a bunch of other movies and TV shows later, and she played Norma Romano on the Netflix show *Orange Is the New Black*.) Annie was really sweet, and we kind of fell for each other and started dating. After we'd been going out for a little while, I moved out of Flash and his mom's place and into Annie's place over in Brooklyn. I was twenty-four, I was in one of the most happening new bands in New York, and I was living with a movie star. Not bad, right?

Annie came from a real old-school Brooklyn family. Her mom and dad weren't around anymore, but she had a place on Eighteenth Avenue and Ocean Parkway in Kensington, and the two of us lived there, on the sixth floor. The rent was really cheap—$172 a month, which Annie, sweet person that she was, usually paid. I was putting some of the money I was making from my day jobs at Reminiscence and with Flash's dad's trade-show production company into 14-percent CDs. I'd cash those in every few months if I really needed money, but that didn't happen a lot, since it wasn't like I had any big expenses or anything. So I wasn't loaded, but financially, I was in decent shape.

The Shirts had a rehearsal and recording space in a three-story building in Prospect Park. Some of their roadies and other people they knew from the scene, like this big guy named Sven who worked as a bouncer at Danceteria, lived there. Man, that place was open 24/7. It was, like, this crazy rock 'n' roll clubhouse. There'd be all kinds of people from the scene dropping by after the clubs closed, to hang out and jam and get high in the basement den until the sun came up. There was also a neighborhood bar right across the street, which definitely came in handy. I hung out at the Shirts' place almost every night when I lived in Brooklyn. Back then, Prospect Park was a pretty rough area— now it's all rich couples pushing baby strollers around.

I did some gigs sitting in with the Shirts when they lost their drummer and were looking for a new one. Even though they were part of the early punk scene in New York, most of their music wasn't really what you'd call punk rock; it was more straight-up, pop/rock stuff, with a lot of piano by Artie Lamonica, their main songwriter and rhythm guitarist. It was all right for what it was, but it wasn't really my thing. But of course I wanted to help Annie out, so I played with them for a bit while I stuck with Velveteen, who seemed to be getting closer and closer to a major record deal. There was a minute there, though, when it looked like I might be getting an even better gig than the one with Velveteen.

Billy Idol's first band, Generation X, had broken up, and he'd moved from London to New York, right around the time he had his first big solo hit with "Dancing with Myself," a remix of Generation X's last single. Billy was putting together a new band in New York with Steve Stevens on guitar, and they were looking for a drummer. His manager saw Velveteen when we were opening for somebody at the Ritz, and backstage after the set he asked me if I'd want to audition for Billy's band. Right away I said sure—keeping it a secret, of course, from Sal and Lisa. (I did tell Flash, but he was rooting for me, and I knew I could trust him.)

I went up to some place in Midtown a couple of weeks later to try out, playing a couple of Generation X songs with Steve and a bass player and Billy. I knew the tunes pretty well, and I thought we sounded really good, but nothing came of it. I don't know why they didn't take me. Looking back, I think maybe it was 'cause I was too tall. Billy Idol's five foot nine, and Steve Stevens is even shorter, only five foot six—and I'm six foot three. Again, this was when MTV was coming in, and image was key. They ended up going with Gregg Gerson, another Jersey guy, who's a few inches shorter than Billy. But, hey, Gregg's a good drummer, and it obviously worked out well for Billy and the band, so no hard feelings there.

And, back with Velveteen, it looked like things were working out well for us, too. Jonathan Blank got us a deal with Atlantic to do an EP. It was almost unbelievable to me—I was in band that was actually on the same label as Led Zeppelin! I couldn't wait to tell Eddie Slivka and my other old friends back in Jersey, the next time I was out visiting my folks.

In the summer of '82, we went into Secret Sound, Todd Rundgren's old studio on Twenty-Fourth Street, to cut six songs, with Sal and Lisa co-producing. When we got done doing the basic tracks, I heard some rough mixes, and I thought they sounded great. I was proud of my playing, and I was really looking forward to the record—which was going to be called *After Hours*—coming out. But all those good feelings went right out the window when I saw the final artwork.

Sal and Lisa were the only band members in the picture on the cover. Flash and I were nowhere to be seen, even though we'd been in the band for more than a year. Not only that, but I was only on *one* song, a tune called "Wild Rain." The rest of the songs all had electronic drums, and Flash's guitar parts had been replaced with parts played by session guys—and, of course, neither of us got any publishing credits.

Flash and I had a fuckin' fit. We asked Sal what the hell was up, and he just told us to talk to Jonathan Blank about it. So we did. And Jonathan basically said, hey, sorry, that was just how it was: Sal and Lisa had the rights to the Velveteen name, and *they* were the band.

Flash was beyond pissed, and he quit right away. I wavered about what I should do, trying to figure out if I should just suck it up and stay. Maybe if the band hits it big, I thought, Sal and Lisa will see how important I am to the sound, and cut me in at the level I deserve. But the more and more I thought about the way they'd gone about everything, the more insulted and pissed off I got. Jonathan was right: Velveteen was *their* thing, and Flash and I and whoever else they got in the band would always just be hired guns. Plus, Flash was my bud, and I didn't feel good about deserting him by choosing Sal and Lisa over him, after all we'd been through together. So, two or three days after Flash left, I said, "Fuck this shit," and I quit, too.

Great. Now what was I going to do? It was the fall of 1982, and I was coming up on the fourth year of my five-year plan. Time was running out. And here I was, not only without a band but also totally feeling like shit, because only a few days before, everything—a major label, MTV, big tours, hit records, all that—seemed like it was *right fuckin' there*. Instead of smelling like groupies and limos, the future was starting to smell a lot like the stale grass clippings and lawnmower oil back at my dad's landscaping company. Forever. Until I was fuckin' *dead*. Shit.

18

You Ready?

So now it was January 1983. I was hanging out in the bar downstairs at the Shirts' place one Sunday afternoon, getting slowly wasted, and seriously thinking about quitting the whole music thing. It was a new year. The last year of the five years I'd given myself to make it as a musician. I figured I'd better just get it over with the next time I was back in Jersey, and hit my dad up for a job. It was making me feel physically sick, just thinking about doing that. Besides me and the bartender, there were, like, five or six other people in the bar; all old-timers from the neighborhood. It was pretty fuckin' bleak.

Larry Chekofsky, the Shirts' drum tech, who everyone just called Larry Chek, came in. He looked around, saw me at the bar, and came straight over to the stool next to mine and sat down. Larry was one of the guys who lived upstairs. He also worked for a few other bands. One of them happened to be the Ramones. He seemed really excited about something.

"Hey Richard!" he said. I was going by Richard Beau then. "I been lookin' all over for you, man. Hey, Annie told me about the Velveteen thing. That sucks, man."

"Yeah," I said. I couldn't even look up from my beer. "It does." I liked Larry, but I was wishing he'd leave me alone. I was here because I was trying to *forget* about Velveteen. I tried to tune him out. Hopefully he'd get the message and get lost.

"Ahh, fuck Velveteen—listen, man, I might have somethin' for you," he said. "But you gotta promise me you won't say *anything* about it to *anyone*. Okay?"

"What?" I kept staring down into my beer.

"The Ramones are gonna fire Marky."

My head went right up. I looked straight at Larry. All of a sudden I was paying attention.

"Oh yeah?" I asked, trying not to sound too excited.

"Yeah, definitely," he said. He went on to tell me how Marky had become a total drunk and was fucking up really bad. The band had to cancel a gig in Virginia Beach on the last tour because of him. He was still stuck in Ohio, where they'd played a couple of days before, and he was too out of it to make it down to Virginia Beach. He'd missed his plane and everything. The other guys were still really pissed off at him about that, plus they'd just had all kinds of problems with him when they were making their new record. He'd been sneaking booze into the studio the whole time and arguing with the producer about stuff. He was out of there, according to Larry.

Wow, I thought. The Ramones. I'd dug them that one time I saw them, at the Showplace, back in 1976. But I really hadn't thought about them too much since then. I knew they were still around, though, putting out records and touring. They still had the reputation as the band who pretty much started punk rock. Even though I'd never really followed them, it seemed like everybody I knew loved the Ramones. So I knew that it would be a big-time gig.

"Think you can get me an audition?" I asked.

"I think so, yeah," Larry said. "I already told 'em about you. Joey said, 'Okay, if you think he can play.' Dee Dee just said to go ahead and set it up. I still gotta see what John thinks. The thing is, they gotta find somebody really fast, 'cause they start the tour for the new record in a couple of weeks, and they have a buncha other stuff comin' up before that. So they're gonna be doing auditions this week. I can let 'em know—if you're *sure* you wanna do it."

Wow. The Ramones. A *national* act. Yeah, I was sure I wanted to do that. I told him to put the word in, and I'd be there.

Talk about timing, right? Here I was, all bummed out about what happened with Velveteen, figuring I was going to have to hang it up and go back to cutting lawns for my dad—and then this thing comes my way.

I had a couple more beers with Larry, and then I hit the deli for a pack of cigarettes and went home.

The little red light on Annie's cassette answering machine was flashing to show that someone had called and left a message. I pushed the button to play it back.

"Hey, I'm calling for Richard." The caller had a Queens accent. "This is Monte Melnick. I work with the Ramones." I didn't know yet that Monte was the Ramones' road manager. "Larry Chekofsky gave me your number. He said you wanna audition for the band. Please give me a call as soon as you can." He left his number. (I saved the tape with Monte's message on it; I still have it today.)

I was nervous, but I didn't waste any time. I called the number right then, and Monte answered. I told him who I was.

"Hey, Richard," he said. "Thanks for callin'. So Larry says you wanna try out, is that right?"

"Yeah," I answered, right away. "Yes. Definitely."

"Okay, cool. Larry said you were in the Shirts?"

"Yeah. The Shirts, Velveteen, a bunch of other bands. I've been playin' a long time. Since I was kid."

"Okay, cool. Larry says you're really good. You know their stuff, right?"

"Yeah, sure," I lied. Sort of. I mean, yeah, I knew *some* of their songs just from hearing them. But it wasn't like I'd been in any bands that played any of them.

"Okay, good," said Monte. "We're starting auditions on Tuesday. Pick out three songs you wanna do, and I'll give you a call tomorrow, after we figure out which day we wanna bring you in. Okay?"

"Okay. Yeah, yeah. Just lemme know where it is and when you want me. I'll be there."

"Great," he said. "I'll call ya tomorrow." He hung up.

Wow. It was happening. I was going to audition for the Ramones.

There was just one problem, though. I didn't own any Ramones records. Not even one. The only records I really had were the ones I'd been buying at Bleecker Bob's, by all the newer British bands. I knew Flash had a couple, though, so I called him right then. The three Ramones songs I knew the best at that time, just from hearing them played by the DJs in the club, and, once in a while, on the radio, were the same ones most people—even people who barely know about the Ramones—would probably think of first, if they had to name their biggest songs: "Blitzkrieg Bop," "Sheena Is a Punk Rocker," and "I Wanna Be Sedated." For that reason, I figured those were the ones the band would most want to hear me on first, to get a good idea of how well I could do the job.

After telling Flash not to blow it for me by telling anyone else the news, I had him make me a tape of just those three songs. And, the next day, I spent the whole afternoon down in the basement of the Shirts' place, playing along to the tape. I listened hard and paid super-close attention to every little thing Tommy and Marky did on each of those songs, rewinding the tape again and again and going over every part change, every little cymbal accent. Then I focused on Joey's singing, always keeping the melody in my head while I played through the songs, trying to *reinforce* what he was doing, not distract from it. I concentrated on making sure I physically felt the way Johnny's guitar and Dee Dee's bass moved along with what the drums were doing on the songs, or maybe I should say I pictured in my mind how it would feel to be doing that. I tried to mentally put myself in between the sound that each of them was putting out, and to always keep what I was doing *even* with those sounds. Neck and neck, at the right dynamic level.

People think it's easy to do all that, since to them the Ramones' music just sounds like it's all really, really simple stuff. But it ain't. You've got to focus on hitting *every single beat* with the same exact weight and tempo—not too soft, not too hard; not too slow, not too fast—or else it just doesn't work right. And, for Ramones songs, it's not like you can keep your muscles from tightening up and give them a rest by putting in parts that have loose, open rolls or fills. It's too tightly written for that kind of stuff. Too precise, y'know? There *is* something, though, that the Ramones would always do before shows to keep from cramping up when they played. But I'll you about that later. Right here, instead, I'll tell you about another trick that helps with playing.

For years, I'd been building up my speed and the strength and control in my arms by practicing on pillows. Practicing on a rubber drum pad is something you do when you're first starting out, but in the long run it's kind of useless, because your stick just rebounds, and after a while you just sort of get stuck at the same level, and you don't really get any stronger or faster. But a pillow has *no* rebound, so when you practice on a pillow, your wrists have to work harder to raise the stick and push it back down equally. Instead of just working the muscles that control the downstroke, like you do with a pad, with a pillow you're also working the muscles that control the upstroke, and building them up equally. So, after doing that for so long, my right hand, especially, was just *solid*. I could hit sixteenth notes on the hi-hat just flawlessly, all through a song, without wavering at all—which is something you absolutely *had* to be able to do in the Ramones.

When you're a drummer, you find your voice. Just like a singer, Frank Sinatra or whoever, finds their voice. And, by the time I was about to audition for the Ramones, after playing funk and fusion and straight-up rock—and, yeah, even polka and disco—on the road for so long in all kinds of bands and situations, I'd definitely found mine. But with the Ramones, I could see I'd have to change it a bit. My voice needed to be all about *forward motion*—totally consistent, totally flawless, totally unbroken, forward motion.

I already played that way a lot; think back to what I was saying before, about loving how Nigel Olsson played when I saw him with Elton John, really locked down and mostly playing just the beat, with no unnecessary bullshit. But now it had to be even *more* like that. With the Ramones, I was going to be a freight train. That was the way I looked at it. Just an unstoppable freight train, coming straight down the tracks. It was going to take extra concentration, and even more physical strengthening, to keep that up. But I knew I could do it. And I could see hundred-dollar bills in my pocket. Hit songs. World tours. Huge crowds. Parties. Beautiful women. I was ready.

Monte called again the next day, at noon on the dot. The auditions were being held at the Ramones' rehearsal space, which was this place called Daily Planet, on West Thirtieth Street and between Seventh and Eighth avenues in Manhattan. I'd heard of it. I think somebody told me Richard Hell and the Voidiods—who Marky, funnily enough, had played with, before he was in the Ramones—also used to rehearse there. Anyway, Monte said they wanted me there that Wednesday at four. Later on, I heard from Matt Lolya, the Ramones' guitar tech—the band just called him Little Matt; they'd had another road guy named Matt who was taller, so that's how that started—that he had to lie to Marky and tell him rehearsals were canceled that week, to keep him away while all this was going on. Kind of sneaky, I guess. But that's how it goes.

I told Monte I'd see him there.

Wednesday came. I grabbed my stick bag, cymbals, and snare, and got on the train into Manhattan, took it to Penn Station, got off, and walked down Seventh Avenue toward Thirtieth Street. I'm not gonna lie and say I wasn't a bagful of nerves. Sure I was. But, at the same time, like I said before, I felt like I was ready. I had the songs down, and I knew I was good. So I was kind of a cocky motherfucker, y'know? I also knew when and when not to push that, though.

I got to Daily Planet about twenty minutes early and met Monte, a pretty regular-looking guy with a big nose and a moustache—not really the rock 'n' roll–looking dude I was expecting—and Little Matt, who was skinny and had long hair, and looked the part a little more. They seemed cool. We hung out in the hallway a little bit and talked. It was sort of muffled, but I could hear what I figured was the

Ramones and another drummer playing, down the hall. Even with all the soundproofing in the building, I could tell it was really fuckin' loud in that room. Monte asked me where I was from, and I said Passaic, originally, which started a whole conversation between the three of us about the shows we'd all seen at the Capitol Theatre back in the day. Turned out we'd all been at a lot of the same ones, which was kind of cool.

After about ten minutes, this guy wearing a leather jacket and carrying a stick bag and some other drummer gear—obviously the guy I'd just heard auditioning for the band—came walking around the corner to where Monte was sitting. The guy looked kind of dazed. He was trying hard to smile, but he wasn't kidding anyone. I could tell things hadn't gone well for him.

"Okay, man," said Monte, making a mark on his clipboard. "We'll give you a call. Thanks a lot for coming down."

Monte looked at me.

"Okay . . . Richard," he said. "You ready?"

I picked up my gear.

"Yeah."

19

Sweaty Palms

Monte led me down the hall, which I remember seeming really long. We got to the end, in front of a door with a sign that said "Studio A," which I guess was Daily Planet's biggest room. "Okay, man," he said. "Here we are." He opened the door and walked straight in. I could see the lights were low inside. It was kind of dark, just some regular floor lamps, so it was a sudden change after being under the bright fluorescents out in the hall for twenty minutes. Man, I hate fluorescent lights.

I followed Monte in. We got about six feet into the room and stopped. Straight in front of us, all the way against the back wall, was a black Tama drum kit set up on a low riser. Standing to the left of it was Johnny Ramone. He didn't have the giant Marshall stack you saw him using at shows; instead, it was some smaller amp. (Later, I found out it was the same Mike Matthews Freedom amp he used back in the early CBGB's days—very rare.) Dee Dee was on the right, next to a big Ampeg SVT bass cabinet. I didn't see Joey anywhere. Johnny and Dee Dee were wearing T-shirts, jeans, and sneakers—no leather jackets. In my head, I'd pictured them having the leather jackets on, like they always did in all the photos. So the no-leather thing, and Joey not being there, kind of threw me for a loop. Just for a second, though. The smell of weed was in the air, but no one offered me anything.

"Hey, you guys," said Monte. "This is Richard Beau, the guy Larry was telling us about. From the Shirts and . . . who else did you say?" He turned and looked at me.

"Velveteen," I answered.

"Oh yeah, right. And Velveteen. Sorry, I forgot. Anyway. So, yeah, Richard, this is Johnny and Dee Dee."

They both said "hey" and nodded. It was cordial, but neither of them came over to shake my hand or anything. Dee Dee looked at me and smiled, but Johnny was pretty stone-faced. Later on, I heard they'd only tried out two other guys, but at the time I assumed they'd been there all day, auditioning drummers.

I asked where Joey was.

"Oh, Joey couldn't make it," Monte said, heading out. "We'll worry about Joey later." Before he closed the door behind him, he told Johnny and Dee Dee that the next guy was due there in forty-five minutes. They both groaned.

Johnny turned toward me. "So, yeah, this is the kit we keep in here," he said. "You got your snare and everything?"

I told him yeah, and I went over to the riser to get set up. I was actually kind of glad nobody wanted to shake my hand: my palms were pretty sweaty, I realized, when I went to adjust the drum stool. At least they couldn't smell me sweating, though, thanks to my not having any body odor. That comes in handy sometimes.

I got everything set up and dialed in. Then I tested the kick-drum and hi-hat pedals and hit the snare a couple of times, to see how loud it sounded in the room. It sounded good. A nice, thick, crunchy smack. I looked over at Johnny. He'd barely said a thing, but somehow he still gave off a vibe that showed he was in charge.

"Okay, great," he said. "So what song ya wanna do?"

"Uh . . . how about 'Blitzkrieg Bop'?" I answered.

He nodded and got into that stance he always did: low, with his legs spread really far apart. He turned the volume knob up on his guitar, the famous white Mosrite.

Dee Dee turned so he was facing me a little more.

"Are you ready?" he asked.

I nodded.

"Okay," he said. "One! Two! Three! Four!"

We blasted into it. The room instantly felt like, I don't know . . . it's hard to describe. Like a fuckin' hurricane or something. Actually, no, not a hurricane. The feel was exactly like what I was going for when I was practicing and getting myself ready: a freight train. With me in the middle, and these big walls of raw noise on both sides, all of it just flying straight ahead. I could have gone faster if I'd wanted to, but I didn't. I kept it just fast enough, with just the right amount of *give* in the rhythm, so the riffs didn't blur together and make the melody get lost. And I hit all those crash-cymbal parts—the ones that mark off the measures on the verses—totally dead on. I've heard a lot of bands do "Blitzkrieg Bop" over the years, and a lot times the drummer forgets to play those cymbal crashes. Anyway, we got to the ending part—that last chorus of, "Hey, ho! Let's go!"—and I stopped it right on a dime at the very end, locked right in with Johnny and Dee Dee. Since Joey wasn't there, Dee Dee was singing, but, other than that, it sounded just like the record. I mean, seriously, it really did.

"Wow, man, that was good," Dee Dee said, smiling again. He

sounded like a cartoon character, the way he talked. A cartoon character from Queens.

Johnny didn't show any emotion. Just kept his same poker face. But I got the feeling he dug it, too.

"Yeah, not bad," he finally said, after a couple of seconds, keeping his tone really dry. "What else you wanna do?"

"'Sheena Is a Punk Rocker'?"

"Okay, good choice," he said, getting back into his stance. Dee Dee counted off again, and we went into it.

Same thing as with "Blitzkrieg." We blew through "Sheena," and everything they could have wanted from me was *right there*. With "Sheena," especially, the *one* beat on the snare really has to be super, super-tight, and I nailed it all the way. Totally precise.

We did "Sedated" next, and I killed that one, too. Again, it sounded just like the record. Man, the room just roared when we were playing. It was loud and it was *hard*. If there were any cockroaches in the walls of that place—which of course there would have been, 'cause it was New York—they were all dead now, just from the three of us shaking the walls so goddamn hard. It felt good. Really good.

I definitely got the sense Dee Dee thought so, too. Johnny was harder to figure.

"Okay," he said at last, still sounding very detached. "Pretty good. That was pretty good."

It was hard to tell how much he meant it and how much was him just being professional. At least it was something, though. And at least he wasn't saying I sucked or anything. But, as subdued as Johnny was, when you're a musician playing with other musicians, and it sounds good, you just *know*. And all of us knew it sounded way better than "pretty good."

I figured we'd run through the same songs again, but no one said anything about that. It was weird. I was just about to ask it they wanted to play them again when Monte knocked on the door, stuck his head in, and asked if it went all right.

Johnny nodded. "Yeah," he said. "Good, good."

Johnny was Mr. Business. He wasn't going to say what he *really* thought. Not with me in the room, anyway.

"Great," said Monte. "The next one's here. So, hey, Richard, we'll give you a call really soon, okay? We're still figurin' stuff out here. But we'll let you know. Thanks a lot for comin' down."

I packed up my stuff, told them all thanks, said it was great meeting them, and walked out.

Heading back up to Grand Central to get the train home to Brooklyn, I felt confident. I knew it had gone well. I knew the songs and I'd played them well. That's all you can do, y'know?

I also think the fact that, being honest, I wasn't a Ramones fan myself—yet—helped me out a lot, too. Sure, I was a little nervous going in, because I knew the Ramones were a big-name band with eight or nine albums out and all that. But, like I said before, I didn't own any of those albums or follow the band. I wasn't some starstruck, Ramones-obsessed kid, falling all over himself saying, "Oh, it's such a huge honor to be in the same room as you guys," or any of that stuff. If I'd been trying out for Led Zeppelin or some other band I grew up listening to, well, maybe then I would've acted differently. At that point, though, getting in the Ramones—and I'm being honest here—was a survival thing for me, pure and simple. I just wanted to keep playing music, make okay money doing it, and not *ever* have to pull the starter cord on a lawnmower again just to pay my bills. My five-year plan was winding down—and I knew this was my best shot.

It seemed like Dee Dee was happy enough that he and I just played together well. But I got the feeling with Johnny that he really appreciated how I acted professionally and just played the songs well and didn't get all antsy. Like the saying goes, I kept my head down, and I didn't ask too many questions. And I could tell he admired that I was really fast and really solid as a drummer. I hadn't met Joey yet, but it seemed like Johnny was the guy I had to impress first, and I felt like I'd done that.

The next day, Monte called again. They wanted me to come back for another audition. And, this time, Joey would be there. Obviously, that was a really good sign: they wouldn't be bringing him in unless they were getting close to picking a drummer. So I was almost there. I could do this.

To this day, I don't know who I was up against. Someone told me they'd played with Jerry Nolan from the New York Dolls and the Heartbreakers but he wasn't cutting it, so they didn't take him. For this book, I asked Monte and Little Matt about that, and neither of them remembered that happening. I don't think it did. Yeah, Jerry was an amazing drummer, but he was also a big junkie. Everybody knew that. And Johnny, who was really down on junkies, would never have considered hiring one. No matter how good a musician he was, or how famous he was. By then, they'd already dealt with enough junkie bullshit, with Dee Dee being on and off heroin for years. I think the Jerry Nolan story started because the Ramones got Billy Rogers to play drums on "Time Has Come Today" after they kicked Marky out, while they were making *Subterranean Jungle*: Billy filled in for Jerry sometimes, toward the end of the Heartbreakers, and he was also in Walter Lure's band, the Waldos.

So, anyway, two days later, I was back at Daily Planet for round two. Johnny and Dee Dee were tuning up, and I was adjusting the height on my snare stand, when Monte walked in, with Joey behind him. Joey was wearing a long, black winter parka—as with the others, not the leather jacket I expected. I'd forgotten how tall he was, too. Even with the way he stood, kind of hunched over, he was still about three inches taller than me. People talk about there being all this tension in the band back then, but I didn't see any of that. Maybe they were trying to keep it nice around me, so I wouldn't get scared off.

Monte introduced Joey and me. I was sitting behind the drums, all ready to play, and Joey shuffled over to where I was and leaned over at me. I could just barely make out his eyes behind those little rose-colored glasses he always wore.

"Hey man, good to meet you," he said, smiling a little. "Monte said you were in the Shirts. That's cool. I know Annie and Ronnie. They're great." By Ronnie, he meant Ronnie Ardito, the Shirts' lead guitar player. Ronnie, who died in 2008, was a sweet guy. Besides playing in the Shirts, he ran sound at CBGB's. He'd invite me there to jam and record all night when the club was closed, and we'd do blow and steal beers from the cooler. Those were some fun nights.

Right away, I got a really good feeling from Joey. He was definitely this sort of strange, quiet, awkward dude. But he was really friendly, and it felt like he was really happy to see me—even though we'd literally just met. Hey, whatever, he seemed like he liked me. I took that as another good sign.

With Joey, we played the same three songs as the last time: "Blitzkrieg," "Sheena," and "Sedated." They all sounded great, and we ran through them all again. And they sounded great that time, too—again, just like the records. Especially now, with Joey singing.

Joey turned around and looked my way. He was definitely digging it. "Hey, you're good, man," he said. "That was really good."

Dee Dee said the same. But Johnny kept quiet, and he didn't have any kind of expression on his face—he didn't want to show his hand around me or the other guys. He did give me a nod, though. And he perked up when he heard me mention to Joey that I sang, too.

"Really?" Johnny asked. "You can sing and play the drums *at the same time?*"

"Yeah," I said. "Been doin' it since I was, I dunno, fourteen, fifteen."

That got a pretty strong "hmm" out of Johnny. It seemed like he was even more impressed now.

Monte came in and told them to wrap it up and get ready for the next audition. Once again, I left feeling really confident. I lit up a joint and walked back up toward Grand Central.

20

Looking Like a Gang

Monte called again the morning after the second audition. "Hey, so, the band thinks you're the guy, man," he said. "You're ready to go, though, right? You don't have anything else goin' on or anything, do ya?"

A tingly wave went up my back. I got goose bumps. Holding the phone in my hand, I felt like I was going to blast off like a rocket, right through the ceiling of Annie's apartment.

"No, no," I told him, trying hard to stay cool. "Nope, nothin' else goin' on." I was ready. *Totally* ready.

"Okay, great," he said. "How much do you want?"

That was kind of . . . hmm. I didn't expect that. Going into the auditions, I never had a number in my head or anything like that. I just figured, hey, the Ramones were a big band, and whatever they'd be paying would be way more than I'd been making in Remod or Velveteen or any other band I'd been in. I was expecting *them* to make *me* an offer, and I'd bargain my way up from there. But, instead, they put the pressure on me, and I didn't want to fuck things up and scare them off up by asking for too much. I told Monte I had to think about it, and I'd call him back that day.

I asked for $400 a week, and we ended up settling on $375. Not a lot, but still decent money in 1983, for a guy who'd never really made anything in bands before and wasn't paying rent (thanks, Annie). The band agreed to that amount right away, making me think I should have asked for more. But, oh well, I was young and naïve, and I'd never been in a national act before.

I wasn't *totally* naïve, though. They wanted me to sign a contract right away, and I knew enough to say I wanted a lawyer to look at it first. That was fine, Monte said, but while that stuff was getting figured out, they were starting rehearsals at noon that Monday, and they'd see me then.

I had Annie Golden's lawyer, George Fearon, negotiate the contract: a three-album deal with a decent percentage on the first album that got better with each one after that. So at least I'd be making money from the records, if I couldn't make that much from the gigs. Obviously, the Ramones liked my playing enough to hire me. They were drawing up contracts, scheduling rehearsals. My five-year plan had worked. And now everything was happening really fast. Man, I was totally floating on air. I was a Ramone! Or was I?

If you've ever seen that Metallica documentary, *Some Kind of Monster*, there's that part where their bass player quits, and then they audition all these guys, looking for a replacement. Then, after they pick the new guy, they have a little hang to let him know he's the one, and they're looking forward to playing with him and all that. Well, it was nothing like that with the Ramones. Not at all.

To me, this is still one of those weird things. When I joined the Ramones, nobody ever actually said, "Okay, you're in the band." Forget about any kind of formal welcome, like in the Metallica movie. There was no party where everybody gets together to celebrate getting a new guy in the family by going out somewhere for dinner or drinks or anything. There was never that vibe of, "Hey, man, good to have you here, we're gonna have fun." With the Ramones, the vibe was just, "Okay, this is what we're doin'. Now get to work." And that was it.

I'm not saying I expected a party or any of that stuff—I didn't know *what* to expect. I'd never dealt with a band as big as the Ramones before. I didn't know what was normal. And I didn't know Joey, Johnny, or Dee Dee yet, personally. All I had to compare it to was what happened with the bands I'd been in before—and, with pretty much all of them, when I first joined, we at least went out for beers and tried to get to know each other a little bit.

Yeah, I'm talking about it now, but I really didn't think that much about it at the time, when I got in the Ramones—I was still just a kid, pretty much, and I was happy as hell just to be in the band, y'know? But today, I see how that whole vibe kind of set the scene for a lot of stuff that came later, between me and the other guys. That was still a long ways off, though.

Anyway, whether they literally said it or not, I was now the drummer for the Ramones. And I was fuckin' psyched, and so were Flash and all my other friends when I told them. Of course, I had to look the part, so the Ramones' management bought me a new black leather motorcycle jacket, and I ditched my Echo and the Bunnymen–style overcoat.

It's interesting that, even though I had light brown hair and Tommy and Marky had had dark hair, no one got on my case about it and made me dye mine. If I'd been blond or had red hair, I'm sure it would have been different. Looking back, I appreciate that they didn't try to turn me into a Tommy or Marky clone. John—inside the band and the road crew, nobody ever called him "Johnny," always just "John"—probably felt like he couldn't say anything, because he had brown hair himself. Maybe he thought we balanced each other out? I don't know. During the second audition, though, totally out of the blue, he did ask me, "Hey, you're not losin' your hair, are ya?" I thought that was really weird, because my hair definitely wasn't thinning. I told him no, not at all. It seemed really random, even though, yeah, I get how they didn't want a bald guy in the band. Later, I learned that Marky had been losing his hair and wore a wig. So I guess maybe John was hung up about that stuff at the time. Funny.

To kids in bands now, all of this might sound like minor stuff. These days, no one cares about bands having a united image anymore. Now, it's like, in the same band, you can have one guy with a beard, one guy with long hair, one guy with a shaved head and glasses or going bald or whatever. And, yeah, individuality is cool. I get that. But back then it wasn't like that. Having a unified image was important. Especially for the Ramones, more than any other band at the time. You had to all look like you were on the same team. Like you were in a gang. That was the Ramones' whole thing, image-wise: looking like a gang. They pretty much invented the whole idea of that, and I really respected it. I still do today.

So, now I had to learn the rest of the Ramones' songs. And, like I said, I'd never owned *any* Ramones records before I was in the band. Of course, I didn't tell anybody that. I just made up some bullshit about my record collection getting stolen, and said I needed to replace my copies of the Ramones albums so I could refresh my memory of the songs a bit. They sent me up to Sire Records, our label, to get copies of everything.

Sire, which back then was on West Seventy-Fourth Street between

Broadway and Columbus Avenue, was started in 1966 by Seymour Stein and this producer and songwriter, Richard Gottehrer. Both of them used to work as interns at King Records in Cincinnati, which was the label that James Brown had all his big early hits on. Gottehrer was also in the Strangeloves, the '60s band that did the original version of "I Want Candy," which Bow Wow Wow had done a big hit cover of right before I auditioned for the Ramones. Bow Wow Wow weren't on Sire, but they were one of the hot new English bands I'd been following. WNYU had started playing imports of their stuff a couple of years before, and I dug the crazy African drumming they had on their songs—plus their singer, Anabella Lwin, was pretty cute. So, when I heard that one of the guys who wrote "I Want Candy" ran Sire, I thought that was really cool.

I also remember going into the record vault at Sire with the secretary there, and watching her unlock the doors on these big metal cabinets where they kept extra copies of every album by everyone who was ever on the label. At that time, besides the Ramones, they had Talking Heads, the Pretenders, Madness, Depeche Mode, the Cure, Echo and the Bunnymen, even Madonna. (The Dead Boys and Richard Hell and the Voidoids had been on the label, too, but they were broken up by then.) It was a pretty amazing roster. It really started hitting me, right then, how big-time all this was, when she handed me this big stack of all the albums: *Ramones, Leave Home, Rocket to Russia, Road to Ruin,* everything . . .

I walked out of the office to get the elevator, and I just remember thinking, on the way back down to the street, holy shit, man, this is *it*. This is really happening. From now on, it's going to be *my* picture on the Ramones' record covers. *My* name. It was insane, y'know?

Of course, thinking about stuff like that was getting way ahead of things. Before it came time for the band to make any records with me, they had to tour to promote the one they'd just made with Marky, before they kicked him out. I holed up again down in the Shirts' basement for the whole weekend, playing along to all of the records and concentrating the most on the songs Monte told me they wanted in the set that tour. Besides the obvious ones I'd already played with them—"Blitzkrieg," "Sheena," and "Sedated"—there was "Rockaway Beach," "Teenage Lobotomy," "Rock 'n' Roll High School," "Beat on the Brat," "Cretin Hop," "Pinhead," "Do You Remember Rock 'n' Roll Radio?," "53rd & 3rd" . . . all the classics.

I said before how I wouldn't really have called myself a Ramones fan before I auditioned for them. And that's the truth. Yeah, I loved seeing them that one time at the Showplace in 1976. But, after that, I'd gone off on a different trip and paid more attention to all the English post-punk stuff. That all changed, though, when I actually got in the band; once I got *inside* the songs. That's when I became a fan—and suddenly wondered where the fuck I'd been for the last seven years. This stuff was amazing.

All of a sudden I really got it—how perfect and streamlined the songs were. How compact. And how pure and catchy the melodies and riffs were. There was no room for any needless bullshit. Again, it was like what I loved about seeing Nigel Olsson play—his whole thing of just focusing straight ahead and powering everything along. That wasn't just there in the way the Ramones' songs were supposed to be played. It was also there in the way they were *written*. It was like whoever was writing the songs—Joey wrote some, but usually it was Dee Dee; sometimes Johnny with Dee Dee—when they were doing it, coming up with riffs and putting them together, they were doing *that* in the same way Nigel Olsson played the drums. Keeping everything tight and powerful. So I saw how the *act* of songwriting itself was, like, an extension of the way the songs were designed to be played. That was something I'd never really thought about before, even though it was right there in front of me. I was suddenly, like they say, seeing the forest for the trees. And it made me appreciate the music on a whole other level.

Then there was Joey's voice, which was also so perfect. The vibrato he had. Man, the first time I heard "Here Today, Gone Tomorrow," when I was listening to *Rocket to Russia* and cramming for that first tour . . . that totally made the hairs on the back of my neck stand up. And John's guitar playing. The way he played everything with that downstroke he did. Playing that way all the time isn't easy to do at all. Yeah, it *looks* and *sounds* easy. But it takes total physical strength to play like he did, song after song, show after show. And you can't fuck up or cheat by playing up and down, because Ramones songs don't sound right if you do. Most guitarists can't play the way John played, or at least not for more than one or two songs in a row. There has to be that totally consistent attack that he had—that unbroken sound, with all the overtones that only come from hitting the strings the way he hit them. I totally got chills in that basement when all of this started to hit me, about how incredible this music was.

And now I was going to be a part of it.

21

These Dirty Kids

There wasn't a whole lot of time to rehearse before the tour, which was starting up in February—about two weeks after I'd passed the audition. When you're a New York band, if it's cold out and you're going to go play someplace nice and sunny—like South America or Florida, or somewhere down South—that can be kind of nice. But my first tour with the Ramones—and pretty much all the ones I'd do with them after that—started in the northeast. Not a fun place to be driving around in a van in the dead of winter. But of course, at that point, I wasn't going to let something like the weather bother me: I was in the Ramones, and I couldn't wait to get on the road and live it up like a real rock star at last. And, hey, at least we weren't going all the way up to Newfoundland, where it's *really* cold in the winter, like I did with Madison. I wouldn't be eating bologna off the end of a string again. Ever. There were going to be real restaurants with real food. Real clubs with real crowds. Real drugs. Real girls. Lots of 'em. Man, I was jumpin' out of my skin.

We did exactly two rehearsals before that first tour, just to run the set a couple of times. That was it. I was pretty much going to have to hit the ground running and find my place while we were on the road. But that's how it is with bands, really. Yeah, of course you've got to rehearse a lot to get the basic stuff down. But you only really start to develop together as a band once you're on the road, playing night after night, on one totally different stage after another. That's the only way you get to where you can read the minds of the people you're playing with, and catch all their little signs and signals, and learn to match what they play and give it the right feel. I knew all that already, from the times I'd gone out with Madison and Open Road. Sure, I was a little nervous, because now I'd be playing way bigger places than I had with those bands. But it was a good kind of nervous.

An interesting thing about Daily Planet was that it was right near Gleason's Gym, where all the really famous boxers used to train—Jake LaMotta, Roberto Duran, Muhammad Ali. There was a bar up the block where Little Matt and I used to hang out after rehearsals, and some of the boxers used to come in there after they worked out. We met Gerry Cooney there a couple of times, which was pretty great. Years later, Daily Planet closed, and the Ramones moved their rehearsal space to a place in Chelsea called SIR. But when we were still at Daily Planet, I kind of felt like I had this sort of brotherhood with the boxers. We were all down there together, training and doing our thing, y'know? Hey, there it is again: that connection between Steve Hamas and me, the two Passaic Pounders.

Subterranean Jungle was the Ramones' new album—the one they recorded with Marky, right before they got rid of him, and the one we'd be touring to promote. The photo on the cover is of the band on a subway car, the "B" train, which connects Manhattan to Brooklyn. It's funny: I used to ride that train all the time back then, when I was living at Annie's. In the picture, John, Dee Dee, and Joey are just inside the open train door, but Marky is all the way at the end of the car, totally separated from the other guys, and looking pretty lonely. Also, the "M" in the big pink "RAMONES" graffiti on the side of the car has arrows pointing away from it, as if the graffiti artist is saying the "M"—for "Marky"—should come out. So I guess maybe those things were supposed to be little hints to the fans that Marky was gone. I don't know. No one in the band ever mentioned anything to me about any of that, and I never asked. To me, though, the cover said that Marky was getting off the train. And I was getting on.

The first thing we did together as a band, besides the minimal rehearsals, was fly out to L.A. to shoot the video for "Psycho Therapy," a song that Dee Dee and John wrote that's maybe the best one on the album. Man, flying out to L.A. to make a video—big time. For me, at least. Not so much for the other guys. Besides having played L.A. tons of times already, they'd been out there to film *Rock 'n' Roll High School*, and to record *End of the Century* with Phil Spector, and both of those things had been ordeals for the band. So to them going there was just another part of the job. As a city, though, John and Dee Dee must have liked the place, because they both ended up there after the Ramones broke up. But, on this trip, it seemed like the only thing they were looking forward to was eating at Los Tacos on Santa Monica Boulevard, which they did every time they were in town. We went when we were there, and I had to admit, it was great. Back then, you couldn't get real Mexican food like that in New York.

The video was shot in a loft somewhere on Hollywood Boulevard. We did it in a day. We played mental patients in a psych ward, as if the Ramones had gone crazy from playing rock 'n' roll. Which is almost how it was in real life, when I think about it. There were all these extras playing other crazy people, and we were in the middle of them, wearing hospital gowns and acting like we were playing, even though we didn't have instruments. They had me sit on a stool and gave me an old pot and a wooden spoon to pretend to beat it with. There was this really hot chick named Mercedes who danced around us while we were supposed to look like we were playing. I tried to chat her up when we were taking breaks, but nothing happened. At least it made the endless takes and sweating under the boom lights a little more fun. John wasn't having any fun, though.

"Aw, come on, *again?*" I can still picture him moaning while he stood there in his hospital gown and the director, Frank Delia, had to reshoot a scene.

Man, did John *hate* doing that video. He complained the whole time about having to stand around between takes, or when they had to stop shooting to mess around with the lighting or whatever. John always hated doing photos or videos or any of that stuff. Some of it was just because he hated standing around or waiting for *anything*, but mostly it was because he knew that the people who worked on that stuff got paid by the hour. They were hired by the record company, and whatever they got paid came out of the production budget for the record—which had to be paid back out of record sales before the band got paid. So, the way John saw it, *any* expenses that had to do with the band were taking money out of his pocket.

Since I didn't play on *Subterranean Jungle* and I wasn't going to make anything from it anyway—plus I still couldn't believe I was even in the band—I didn't think much at the time of how John was carrying on about that stuff. But, as time went on, I'd start to really find out how cheap he was—the extremes he went to with his cheapness. And that would cause some headaches.

Anyway, the "Psycho Therapy" video actually turned out to be pretty funny, I thought, even though, when we were making it, none of us really understood exactly what was going on. We just did what Delia told us to do for about ten hours, and that was it. He also did videos for "Weird Al" Yankovich and Jefferson Starship. Why he ended up doing a Ramones video, I don't know. Someone obviously thought he could do something that would get played on MTV, but in the end they barely played it at all. Maybe that was because there's a gory part in it, where this monster that looks like the one in *Alien* blows up out of this guy's chest. Or maybe they thought we were making fun of people with mental problems. (Hey, it's the Ramones, what do you expect?) Who knows. It did get picked by *Rolling Stone* as one of its "Top 100 Videos of All Time," though, so that's pretty great. A few months later, we shot a video at a church on the Lower East Side for the second single off *Subterranean Jungle*, a cover of the Chambers Brothers' "Time Has Come Today."

After two days of L.A. insanity, pretend and real, it was time to fly back to New York to start the tour—and a whole other kind of insanity. My first show with the Ramones was on February 13, 1983, at Mohawk Valley Community College in Utica, which is in Upstate New York. By then, in the US the band were playing colleges as often as they could, because a lot of those gigs paid better than clubs; colleges usually have a "student activities" grant that comes out of the funding they get every year, and the money from that tends to be pretty good.

That was something I learned about right away that I didn't really know before. Something else I learned about right away was all the stuff that happened backstage just before a Ramones show. Remember a couple of chapters back, I mentioned how there was something the band would do before playing, to keep from cramping up? Well this is it.

Playing in the Ramones was like being an athlete. Even though John never partied—at least not that I ever saw—and the rest of us did, we all *had* to warm up before we went on. That was mandatory. Yeah, you get to move around and play a little during soundcheck. But if that's all you do, when it comes time to do the show, you're still basically going from sitting all bunched up in the van all day, straight into having to play insanely fast. And play pretty much nonstop, for a full hour, because, live, the Ramones would just go from one song right into the next for the whole show. And you can't just go from zero to a hundred miles per hour like that. If you do, your muscles are just going to totally lock up on you.

So, while Joey would be off in the corner doing his little vocal warm-ups or sniffing his nasal sprays, John, Dee Dee, and I would be in the middle of the dressing room, going through our nightly warm-up routine. We traveled with a small practice amp that John and Dee Dee would plug into, I'd grab a pair of drumsticks, and the three of us would sit in a circle. With me playing the beat on my thighs, we'd spend about twenty minutes running through, like, five or six songs, just to get the blood flowing and get our arms, hands, and legs used to moving fast. This works pretty well, and I still do it now before every gig.

There was this other thing that was part of the pre-show stuff that John and Dee Dee always did, though—something I thought was weird, and probably most Ramones fans will, too.

"Aw, jeez, we gotta go play for these *dirty kids* again," John would say, sounding like he was really tired and annoyed about having to play the show. "We gotta do this *again*? Aw, Jesus Christ, not again. These dirty kids again . . . ."

And Dee Dee would say back to him, "Yeah, man, these fuckin' dirty kids. Oh, man, what the fuck. Again, we gotta do this? Shit . . . ."

It sounds crazy, but that was how they psyched themselves up to play. By getting it into their heads that the people coming to see them were all a bunch of dirty losers who they didn't want to be there playing for. They didn't *really* think that, of course. They loved their fans. But I guess working themselves into the frame of mind where they were unhappy about playing, and wanted to take that out on the audience, helped get them in the mood to play harder and more aggressively. Like I said, it was weird.

So, after experiencing all that for the first time, it came time to play. And that was weird, too.

We always used a recording of the theme from *The Good, the Bad, and the Ugly* as our intro music the first couple of years, until we switched to that cut from the album *The Spirit of '76* by the Eastman Symphonic Wind Ensemble. The four of us walked on, and the whole house just started cheering like crazy. It sort of felt like it all was happening in slow motion. I went into auto mode, doing what I was there to do. I stepped up onto the drum riser, and, not being able to see anything through the thick cloud of smoke, I waited. The lights went up, Dee Dee counted us off, and we went into it.

We opened with "Durango 95," a new instrumental John wrote that the band hadn't recorded yet. (We did it later on *Too Tough to Die*, and it stayed in the set as the regular opener after the '83 tour.) I wasn't worried about that tune as much as I was about some of the big Ramones hits, which, with me being the new guy, the audience would be listening to more closely. Remember: I'd had to learn, like, thirty-five songs, with only two rehearsals.

Anyway, a few songs in, everything was going great. We'd blasted through "Teenage Lobotomy," "Psycho Therapy," "Blitzkrieg Bop," "Do You Remember Rock 'n' Roll Radio?," "Outsider" off the new album, and a few others, and they all felt really good. When I looked out at the crowd, everyone was bouncing up and down and going crazy, totally loving it. I was digging it, too. I wasn't so nervous anymore.

And then, about halfway through the set, John stopped the band.

It turned out I was off. I forget what song we were doing, but I knew right away it was my fault, and I felt like shit about it. I can't remember if it was because I was playing too slow or too fast or what. Any other band would have just played through until everybody found their place, and then maybe dealt with the mistake *after* the show, to make sure it didn't happen again at the next one.

Not the Ramones, though. It had to be right. From the beginning. If it wasn't, the other guys would get so thrown off that they'd have a really hard time figuring out where they were. Especially John, and he ran the band. He gave me a look and said something to me about how I was playing it wrong. Dee Dee turned from me to the mic and told the audience, "Sorry, we have a new drummer tonight." And then he just counted it off again, and we started the song over.

The rest of the set went fine, and I don't remember having any other problems. But it was crazy, to me, how they stopped the song like that.

So, that was my first show with the Ramones. Definitely an unusual night. And there were many more to come.

22

Milk and Cookies

After almost every gig, on the way to the hotel, we *had* to stop at 7-Eleven, so John could get his little carton of milk and his little package of cookies.

Usually it was Fig Newtons or Oreos—y'know, those little packs they sell with, like, six or however many it is cookies in them. Skipping the milk and cookies wasn't an option with John, just like not playing the songs right wasn't an option. If he didn't get his milk and cookies, I started to see on that first tour, he could be really grouchy, and he'd rag about everything when we were in the van. Actually, he could be grouchy and rag about everything anyway—mainly he ragged on Monte, who always drove, and who he always sat next to in the van—but it was worse if he didn't get them. He loved Yoo-hoo, too. Drank a lot of that. Liked his dairy and sugar, that guy.

The thing was, after a while, the kids in pretty much every American town the Ramones played in had caught on to how our van—or bus, if we had one for that particular tour—would be at the nearest 7-Eleven after the show. So they'd all be there waiting for us, and then maybe they'd follow us after John ran in and out of the store to get his milk and cookies. There'd be this convoy of cars full of kids behind us, on the way to the hotel. It was nuts.

When we finally got to the hotel, John always disappeared for the night. He'd head straight to his room, which was always on an entirely different floor from the rest of us. Sometimes, the rest of us would hang out and talk to the fans for a little bit, or grab the beer the club gave us for our rider and go hang out in one of our rooms. Just stay up, drinking and talking. Or maybe we'd go to a bar or a club, if there was one close enough. Not John, though. We never saw him until the next day, and he never wanted to see anyone else.

I was a really quiet guy then. I just kind of took it all in and tried to get used to how to act around everyone. John was definitely not the social butterfly of the band; that was Joey. But even though John knew I liked to party and get fucked up after the gigs, he liked that I kept my mouth shut. Which I did. For a while, at least.

Getting fucked up *before* a gig, though, was a big no-no. I remember on the first tour, the promoter took us out to a Benihana restaurant for dinner before the show. I ordered a sake, and didn't think anything of it. I figured, hey, it's a Japanese restaurant, that's what you do, right? Drink sake. But when John heard me ask the waiter for one, he shot me a mean look. He had a smirk on his face, and he was shaking his head.

"What?" I asked.

"You gonna be able to play?" he snapped at me. "We got a show to do. You do know that, right?"

I told him I'd be fine. I was just having *one* little sake with my dinner, and that was it. Which it was. And the show went great. By then, it'd been years since I'd played with anyone while I was drunk; I hadn't done that shit since Madison. Plus, of course, I didn't want to blow it with the Ramones. I didn't say anything back to him, but at the time I kind of resented John getting on my case about it. The whole thing with Mark's drinking was still fresh in his mind, obviously. He was probably worried that maybe the band had replaced one alcoholic with another, which of course I knew wasn't true. I get where he was coming from now, though. These days, I can't put up with bullshit like that if it happens with anyone in my band. You can't play your best if you're drunk. And, besides that, you fuck it up for the rest of the band, because they have to try and cover for you. So, fuck that. But, at the same time, being honest here, I—along with Joey—did mess up like that before one show. I'll get into that later, though.

Other than that little blowup, though, and John just being a standoffish guy in general, he and I did manage to bond a little on that first tour. His other big thing, besides milk and cookies and collecting movie posters (which Joey also did), was baseball. God, did he love baseball. Especially the Yankees—that was his team. When we were in the van, he always had the ballgame on the radio; there was no listening to music stations. Well, maybe the oldies station, once in a while. But that was rare. Usually, it was the game. Or, if we were somewhere with a TV and there was a game on, or ESPN, he'd be watching that.

Even though I was never that into sports, I did like to see a ballgame once in a while. So a couple of times, when the stadium was close by and there was enough time before the gig, or if we had a day off, John and I went to catch a game. And, if the club was big enough, we'd play stickball out on the floor while the gear was being set up, just to kill time. I stunk at it, though. I'd always swing and miss. It didn't take more than a few of our little stickball games to figure out how much John loved to win. I think he loved winning more than anything. That was his personality: being number one.

Once in a while one or two people in wheelchairs would come to the shows, and the club would block out a spot for them on one side of the stage, so they wouldn't be stuck behind the people who were standing, and could actually see the show. But the thing about that was, I guess, when they were onstage, John and Dee Dee really fed off the energy of the people who were jumping up and down and going nuts, and the people in the wheelchairs—through no fault of their own, of course—kind of distracted them from that. So whenever Monte came backstage and said, "Hey, guys, we have a wheelchair tonight," Dee Dee would always say, "Well, don't put them in front of me," and John would always say, "Well, don't put them in front of me, either." Joey never said anything about it when there were people in wheelchairs out front—that didn't seem to bother him.

The '83 tour ran from February all the way into August and looped from the East Coast, down through Georgia into Texas, over to California, and up the West Coast; from there, it cut over through the Midwest and up into Canada for a week, before starting up again in the South and running back up to the northeast, to finish with one night apiece in Queens and Brooklyn. By this time, the band had been touring for eight years, and they really knew what they were doing when it came to booking the right places to play in the different markets. Every room we headlined on that tour was *jammed*. In the smaller towns, it might not necessarily be the biggest club around, but it would be sold out. And that's how it was for all the tours. So, right away, I got used to playing to packed rooms *only* with the Ramones, which was definitely a nice change from most of the bands I'd been in before.

Another thing I noticed immediately was the amount of T-shirts and other merchandise the band sold on tour. There'd be long lines at the merch table every night, and it seemed like almost every kid who came to the show walked out of there with at least one T-shirt. I'd never been in band that sold merch before, so that got my attention.

Besides playing to packed rooms, the other nice little perk I got to enjoy pretty much right away was the women. I guess maybe by now you've figured out that I wasn't really too faithful to Annie. I'm not proud of that, but that's how it was. I got the feeling she was seeing other people when I wasn't around, which was fine. Even though we lived together and all that, we were never really all that serious as a couple. We were more friends than anything else. I'm also pretty sure she knew what was going on with me. I mean, I'm a couple of years younger, and still kind of wild, and then all of a sudden I'm in this famous band that's on the road all the time? Come on. She *had* to know. Women always know, right?

Anyway, a lot of times after the shows, there'd be girls waiting for us at the hotels. Sometimes they'd even find out which rooms we had, and there'd be a line of them there. Some nights I'd be in my room with one girl, and there'd be another one waiting right outside the door for her turn. It didn't matter that I was the new guy, and that I wasn't that well known yet—I was in the Ramones, and for some girls that was all it took. It was definitely fun.

What was also fun on the first tour was headlining at the Hollywood Palladium, with the Dickies opening, one night, and the next day playing this huge show with Tom Petty and the Heartbreakers, the Stray Cats, and Bow Wow Wow at Jack Murphy Stadium in San Diego. What *wasn't* fun, though, was waking up after San Diego to find out all our equipment and other stuff had been stolen. Right out of the parking lot of the Holiday Inn that used to be where the Hollywood and Highland Center is today. They drove off with the whole truck! Luckily, Matt had taken John's guitar into his room that night, to restring it, but all the amps and everything else—including the beautiful 1964 oyster-black pearl Ludwig kit I'd had since I was a kid—were gone. Even our leather jackets—the ones we wore onstage— were missing. And, of course, we were playing that night, and it was a week before we had a day off—which was a driving day anyway. So we spent all afternoon running all over L.A. to different Guitar Center stores, looking for replacement gear, plus we had to find new jackets.

The cops found the truck, which was a rented U-Haul, later on, and they got some of the gear back, too, I think. But not my beautiful Ludwigs. My first kit. To this day, I still get heartbroken and pissed off about that whenever I watch myself playing them in the "Time Has Come Today" video. Assholes. I hope they ended up in jail.

Oh well, the drums were gone, but now I had new ones, and the tour went on. And the shows got better and better. One of my favorites was on July 16, at Pier 84 in New York, with the Divinyls opening up. I usually don't like outdoor shows—sometimes the sound is weird, and the audience can be too far away and hard to connect with—but that was a good one. It was part of this summer concert series they used to do on the pier back then, which was sponsored by Miller Beer. The weather was perfect that day, and the crowd was really into it.

In August, we played Philadelphia and Cape Cod with the B-52's. I was a B-52's fan, so I remember really looking forward to those shows. I loved pogoing to their stuff back when Flash and I were out looking for girls at the clubs—"Rock Lobster," "Planet Claire," all those songs from their first two albums. Just a couple of years later, they had that big hit album, *Cosmic Thing*, which sold way more copies than any of the Ramones' albums ever did. The two bands shared dressing rooms, and we really got along well.

I'd gone to those baseball games with John, and I was getting to know Dee Dee and, especially, Joey, better. I even went sightseeing with Monte a couple of times. But, early on, I felt the most comfortable around Little Matt and the other roadies. They did the most partying, and I hung out with them more. I guess I felt okay around them because, even though I'd signed the contract and everything, nobody from the band would tell me if I was a *real* Ramone. I felt like maybe I was just a hired gun, which was what most of the roadies were. For the first three or four months, I was signing autographs as Richie Beau, because the band *still* wouldn't totally commit and make me a real member. I don't know what the problem was. Those first few months must have been some kind of test.

Anyway, I guess I passed the "extended audition," because finally, after all that time had gone by, they realized how goofy it was for me to be Richie Beau, and they said I could call myself "Richie Ramone." That was a big deal for me. But when that happened, I was still mainly hanging with the roadies. I got to be really good friends with Little Matt, who, it turned out, had another job besides being John's guitar tech: playing second guitar. Yeah, the Ramones' songs are known for being really bare bones, with just John playing. But on some of the recordings, like "Time Has Come Today," there are all these little lead parts and harmony lines that session guys like Walter Lure from the Heartbreakers did in the studio. Live, though, John was just one guy, and he couldn't play two parts at once. And a lot of the parts he just couldn't play, period. But even he knew that some of the songs wouldn't sound right without those riffs, and he still wanted them in there.

So, on just those songs, Matt, who actually learned to play from Tommy Ramone, would sit there on a chair with his guitar—hidden behind John's Marshall stacks, so the audience couldn't see him—and play the extra parts. He wore headphones with the monitor mix piped into them, and his guitar was plugged into a little amp that was miked up to the front-of-house mix. Most people in the audience never even knew he was there. There may be some diehard fans out there who know about that. It's one of the Ramones' open secrets, I guess. But there were other secrets, too. And some of them weren't so open.

23

Drive the Night Away

Backstage at every show, there was a wardrobe case. One of those heavy-duty rolling Anvil road cases that opens up like a closet, with "RAMONES" stenciled on the sides. And the *only* things that were in that case were four leather jackets. The ones we wore onstage.

The jacket. That was another thing I had to get used to when I got in the band. Just as you'd expect, playing the drums with a leather jacket on is not exactly easy or comfortable. Especially when you're doing shows in July or August—which we did a lot of, because that's when all the concert festivals are happening, and those shows paid well. But what made it *really* tough were the stage lights. These days, most bands use all LED lighting, which hardly gives off any heat. At that time, though, the lighting rig we toured with—which was run by Arturo Vega, the artist who designed the "screaming eagle" Ramones logo you see on T-shirts all over the place today—used all these PARCAN lights. The PARCANs we had were, like, 200 watts each, and they just got *insanely* hot. So, when we were playing, I'd be sitting there on the drum riser, way above everyone else, with these burning-hot lights just a couple of inches from my head. It didn't matter if the club was air-conditioned or that we had electric fans onstage. It was still ridiculous, how hot it was.

But, y'know, the jackets were the Ramones' uniform. That was the image, and that's what the fans expected to see. So, of course, just like Joey, Johnny, and Dee Dee, I had to play with mine on. Thankfully, though, I didn't have to do it for the whole show. There was a plan we followed every night. The other guys would keep their jackets on for longer, but I got to take mine off after the fourth song. We'd take a break then, just for a couple of seconds, for me to take it off. Man, I couldn't wait to get to the end of that song. It was "Blitzkrieg Bop" on the first tour. The thing was, though, if I didn't get my jacket off in time—I think I had, like, five or six seconds, while Joey asked the crowd how they were doing or whatever—the band was still going to start the next song. And, no matter what, I still had to go along with them. I couldn't hold up the show. And the next break wouldn't be for another *eight* songs.

Usually, I could get the jacket off in time on my own, but sometimes I'd have to have one or two roadies help me with it, because I'd be all sweaty and it would be stuck to me. There were a few times, though, when it didn't come off quick enough, and—*bam!*—right away I had to jump back in and play those eight extra songs with the coat on before I could finally get rid of it. That was rough. Those were the times I was really happy the Ramones had short songs. But that's also the kind of stuff that makes you stronger as a performer: if you can get through things like that on the road, you can get through most of the other pain-in-the-ass crap that comes your way.

Speaking of pain-in-the-ass crap, there was another weird Ramones rule I had to get used to early on. The rule was this: if we were playing anywhere within a five-hour drive of New York, we drove back home after the gig. Always. Always. Always. That was another one of John's things. Mostly it was because he wanted to save money. We were already paying for the road crew's hotel rooms, so they could go ahead to the next town and get the gear set up for the next show, but he refused to pay for rooms for Monte and the band if we could be back in New York in five hours or less. And I guess I got that, sort of; rooms for the five of us could easily add up to $500 or more. But, mainly, this rule of John's seemed to be because he hated being away from New York, and he wanted to sleep in his own bed at night unless it was literally undoable. And that I *didn't* get. I mean, I stayed quiet, and I went along with it—what was I going to do?—but I always thought it was totally insane.

We'd have a gig in, say, somewhere in Vermont. We'd leave around 10 or 11 a.m., drive up there—what is it, five, six hours?—eat dinner, do the gig, and then get right back in the van. Then Monte would do a couple of lines of coke and drive all the way back to New York, with John sitting up front and hassling him the whole way, and Joey, Dee Dee, and me crashed out in the back. It didn't matter if the gig the next night was in someplace close to Vermont, like maybe Albany or Boston. It could be the middle of winter, with snow coming down, ice on the road, and no streetlights outside; didn't matter to John. Instead of getting a decent night's sleep at a Holiday Inn close to wherever we'd *just played* in Vermont, or maybe heading on to wherever we were playing next and getting a hotel there for the night, we'd drive back down Route 7—this crazy, two-lane highway through the mountains that always has a lot of car accidents—and get to New York right when the sun was coming up. And then, just a couple of hours later, we'd all get back out of bed and go do it all again. Even if we were playing in Providence the night after Boston—those two towns are about an hour apart—we were *still* going to drive way the hell back to New York from

Boston, and *then* get up and go do Providence, and then go back to New York that night.

There were so many nights when I was sure we were going to get in some horrible crash somewhere, just because everybody was so tired. Everybody had assigned seats, and mine was all the way in the back; I called it the "death seat," because I was really afraid of us getting rear-ended. I'm still amazed we never had an accident. Yeah, we were saving some money on the hotel rooms. But how much were we spending on gas and wear and tear on the van?

Like I said, I thought it was a crazy way of doing things. But it was a way of doing things that had been around since way before I was in the band. I was the new guy. I was supposed to play the drums and that was it. What did I know?

I talk about this stuff now—the hot stage lights and the crazy driving and all that—as being hard. And, yeah, it was. But at that point, when I was first experiencing it, it really didn't bother me as much as maybe I make it sound. I was in a real band that was doing real stuff. With roadies, and even my own drum tech. The music was awesome, and I was getting laid and partying a lot. Plus, now I always had some money in my pocket. If I wanted a cheeseburger and a beer, I could walk into any restaurant and order them, or whatever it was I wanted. If there was a break on the tour and I had a day off to visit my folks back in Jersey, I could take Lenny and Eddie Slivka and some of my other old friends out for hot dogs and beers at Rutt's Hut in Clifton. So, overall, I was feeling great, and it was still a whole new adventure.

Part of that adventure was getting to know Joey. If you've ever seen that documentary *End of the Century* or read any books about the Ramones, you already know how he had OCD (obsessive compulsive disorder) really bad, and you can see how that made life really difficult for him and the band. If we were going out of town for a gig, Monte would have to tell him we were leaving at least an hour before we were really supposed to leave, just to make sure he was ready on time. We'd all meet outside Joey's place, which was on Ninth Street between Second and Third Avenues on the Lower East Side, and we'd all wait in the van while he went up to Joey's apartment and helped him get dressed and everything.

Usually, Joey was still asleep, so Monte would also have to wake him up. It wasn't like Joey literally couldn't dress himself. I think it was more that it just took him forever to do it, because the OCD made it hard for him to pick out stuff to wear and do the regular stuff that you do when you're waking up and trying to get out the door and start your day—the stuff most people do without even really thinking about it. On the way out, he'd want to touch and re-touch every little thing in the building and out on the street. Monte would do his best to make him stick to the program and get him to the van on time.

It was a definitely a weird scene. I'd never been around anyone with really bad OCD before. So that was something else that was totally new for me. But, after a while, I didn't really think that much about it. It was just how Joey was, y'know? He even thought it was funny himself, sometimes. He and I would be out somewhere, and he'd get all confused trying to cross the street, and then he'd look at me and we'd both just start laughing about the whole thing.

Yeah, the Ramones had this tough-guy image, with the leather jackets and everything. But Joey was a fragile guy. He needed to be taken care of. He was like a little kid in a lot of ways. A six-foot-six kid who people recognized everywhere he went. I'm sure he wished he was more normal, like everybody else, and didn't have to go through life with OCD. They know a lot more about that stuff now than they did back then, so maybe if he were still around now, he would've had it easier. But, at the time, it was what it was, y'know? Backstage, before the show, Monte would have to help him put on his little fingerless leather gloves, help him get his sneakers on. He'd ask Monte every couple of minutes if it was time for us to go on: "Hey, Monte, is it time yet? Is it time yet, Monte?"

Joey also had this other weird condition where the nerves in one of his feet didn't have any feeling in them. So he'd walk around barefoot at home and his foot would get cut up, because he'd stepped on something sharp and hadn't even realized it, and then he'd get a really bad infection. That stuff was so bad that he had to go in the hospital a couple of times because of it. And he always wore white socks—usually two pairs. I guess maybe the second pair was to help protect his feet. Sometimes, one of the socks from the first pair would get all bloody from some cut he had, so then Monte would have to help him change his socks, too.

Dee Dee never really said much—to me, anyway—about the stuff going on with Joey, but I could tell it bugged John. I saw how he didn't like anything that slowed the schedule down or had everyone worrying about Joey. He'd make fun of Joey behind his back. "Hey, Richie," he'd say to me, when we were at a truck stop somewhere, and Joey was stepping in and out of the doorway, or going back in to make sure he touched the water fountain or some doorknob an even number of times. "Look at Joey. Look at how he's walkin'. Why don'cha ask him why he's walkin' like that? C'mon, Richie. Go ahead 'n' ask him. See what he says." I never did, though. I was still getting to know everyone, and I didn't want to get in the middle of anything.

I'll say this. Everyone always talks about the bad feelings between Joey and John that started when Joey's girlfriend, Linda, left him to be with John. About how they wouldn't talk to each other, or even look at each other—even when they were stuck together in the van on tour, sitting just a couple of feet apart. But, to be honest, other than the thing I just told you about, with John making fun of Joey behind his back a couple of times, I never really saw any animosity between the two of them the whole time I was in the band. That's the truth. Sure, I could tell they weren't *best friends*. And, no, they didn't hang out together or anything like that. But they were professional, and they'd at least talk to each other. Usually about stuff that had to do with the band. I'm not saying it didn't get to that point later on, but it really wasn't like that when I was around. Things got worse between them after I was out of the band, I guess.

Back then, besides dealing with Joey's OCD and his foot infections, another thing John didn't like was when Joey and I started getting to be friends. Even though the whole rivalry between them didn't really blow up until later, I got the feeling from John that he saw me becoming friends with Joey as me not being "on his side." Which, if that was the case, was just some bullshit thing in his head. Joey was just a really great guy, and, for me, really easy to get to know and be friends with. In fact, Joey would become one of the best friends I ever had.

24

The Primer

I taught Joey Ramone how to play poker.

Once we got to the part of a tour when the shows were outside the five-hour radius from New York, we'd stay at Holiday Inns and have a rented tour bus. One of those big buses with a bathroom, a little kitchen with a microwave, a couple of tables, some couches, and some bunks. None of us ever actually slept in those bunks. All we'd ever use them for was storage—mostly we kept our clothes in there, and posters and other memorabilia, and stuff we picked up on the road. If we were tired, we'd just crash out on the couches instead.

All the way in the back of the bus was a little lounge area, and that's where Joey and I always hung out. John would be up front by the TV, probably watching a ballgame, and Dee Dee would usually be somewhere in the middle. The lounge part had sliding doors, so you could close it off from the rest of the bus, so Joey and I would shut ourselves off back there and pass out or listen to tapes on the stereo. I remember us blasting "For Those About to Rock" by AC/DC and "Panama" by Van Halen a lot on those first tours.

So, one day, we were in the kitchen of the bus, and I found a deck of cards in one of the drawers.

"Hey, man, let's play poker," I said. "You play, right?"

Joey seemed kind of embarrassed.

"Uh," he said. "I don't really know how, man. I never played it."

I told him it was easy—I'd teach him. So I did. And he kind of got addicted to it.

Joey and Dee Dee and I would spend hours and hours in the kitchen, playing cards. The thing was, even though all of a sudden Joey was really into poker, he wasn't any good. He was a really easy tell—terrible at bluffing. He'd get that little smirk and raise me on whatever bet I put down, and I'd always know when he had a lousy hand. We were playing for cash, and all his money on the road was from per diems, so his per diems were pretty much just going right to me, because he always lost. He kept thinking he'd start winning at some point, but it was hopeless. Monte kept track of the band money and handed out the per diems, so Joey was always going to Monte, asking for an advance so he could pay us what he owed us.

After a while, Monte took me aside. "Listen, man," he said. "You *gotta* stop playin' poker with Joey, okay? He's into us for three weeks of per diems!"

So that was the end of our little poker club. I did kind of feel sorry for Joey when he kept losing. But, hey, it killed time on the bus, and he seemed like he was enjoying it, so . . .

Besides poker, and, especially, booze, Joey liked cocaine a lot. I never really did. For me, the first hit would be fun, but then it just made me really depressed. Barbiturates were still my thing—*they* made me happy. And pot. Joey *never* smoked pot, but Dee Dee sure did. Constantly. John, not as much. Maybe a puff once in a while, after the show. Anyway, Joey was the one I was hanging out with the most on that first tour, and I wanted us to be friends. So, after the gig, a lot of times I'd end up sitting around the table in one of our rooms, doing coke with him and drinking the beers from the club, and we'd stay up to, like, four or five in the morning. That's when I got into taking Excedrin PM for a while, just to be able to go to sleep for a couple of hours before we had to get up for eleven o'clock check-out and get back on the bus.

Then there was the "Primer." The Primer was the secret term the two of us had for grabbing a beer and drinking it down really fast right before we went onstage. If you drink a whole beer really fast—y'know, just chug it—it gives you that little lift that kicks in really quick. It only lasts a couple of minutes, and it's not enough to actually get you drunk, just kind of pumped up and buzzed for the first two or three songs. Like I said before, I'd try not to get full-on smashed or anything like that before playing with the Ramones. And for Joey it was the same. John would have had a fit if we did that. But the Primer thing was different. Just that one fast beer, five minutes before we went out and started the set. We'd be backstage with Monte, and the intro music would start playing. The smoke machine would start up, the lights would go down. People out front would start screaming. And then Joey would lean over to Monte and ask him, "Hey, Monte, how much time we got?" Monte would check his watch and say eight minutes or six minutes or whatever it was, and then Joey would lean down toward me. He'd look at me over the tops of his glasses.

"Hey, Richie," he'd say, with this little bad-boy smirk on his face. "Primah? Yeah? Primah, Richie? Whaddya think?"

So, when it got to the five-minutes-to-showtime mark, we'd both grab a beer from the fridge and slam it straight down. The Primer was something that was just between me and Joey; John and Dee Dee weren't in on it. They had their own spots they stood in when we were just about to go on—who knows what they were doing at that point to get themselves ready. Probably still bitching about having to play for the dirty kids again. Whatever they were doing, though, I'm pretty sure they never knew about Joey and me, with our little pre-show ritual. So, hey, maybe now *you* know something even the other Ramones didn't know. How about that?

I guess most people do know, though, about how Dee Dee had a big problem with heroin. As far as I know, that was something that only went on before and after I was in the band. The whole time I was in the band, I never saw any of that stuff. Besides staying clean, Dee Dee was also trying to stay off booze, which of course isn't the easiest thing to do when you're in a rock 'n' roll band that tours. He needed some help with that, so he was on Antabuse. Antabuse is a prescription medication that, if you drink any alcohol when you're on it, makes you feel like you have a massive hangover, and makes you want to puke. I guess the idea was that, if he wasn't drunk, there was also less of a chance that he'd go looking for other stuff.

Like I mentioned earlier, though, Dee Dee still smoked pot all the time. And, since he wasn't doing heroin, he really took his pot smoking to the next level. Same thing with hash, too. He loved that, when he could get it. He had connections *everywhere* on the road—in every town we played in. I remember this one dealer he had in San Francisco. We called her the Tube Lady, because the pot she sold us always came in these little cigar tubes.

On the days when Dee Dee couldn't get something to smoke on the road, he had a really hard time. Especially after a long flight to Europe or England or somewhere like that, he always needed his hash as soon as we got to the hotel. When we went over to England to do some shows in July of 1986, the promoter was supposed to have some hash waiting for him there. I was sitting with some of the roadies on the plane, and we were drunk the whole flight, which probably tortured him. But I guess being on the Antabuse and knowing he had the hash to look forward to helped him keep it together. After we landed in London, though, the promoter told us that something had happened, and he couldn't get Dee Dee's hash. When we finally did get to the hotel, he freaked out and drank every bottle of booze in the minibar—and then started puking his guts out, because of the Antabuse. I think he spent the whole night with his head in the toilet.

I got to be smoking buddies with Dee Dee, even though I mostly hung with Joey. Since John was the responsible guy and Dee Dee was totally the opposite, Dee Dee made John crazy most of the time. Dee Dee lived in his own world. He lived the way he wanted to, did what he wanted to do—or as much as he could get away with, anyway. And it could be pretty amazing sometimes, how much he would get away with.

There was one time when we were flying from New York to go do some shows on the West Coast. I knew Dee Dee would be getting some pot for the road, so I gave him some cash and asked him to get me four ounces. It's hard to believe now, but back then, before 9/11 and all the terrorism stuff, the airline security people didn't really look that closely at what you had in your luggage. You still had to be careful, but we used to bring weed with us all the time when we were flying somewhere. Anyway, we were all there at the airport, waiting in line at the counter to check in. I was standing in front of Dee Dee, so I turned around and whispered to him to see if he'd remembered my pot.

"Oh, right," he said, totally stoned at, like, ten in the morning. "Yeah, man! I got it right here!"

And then he just unzipped his shoulder bag, dug around inside it, and pulled out this huge sandwich bag just *filled* with pot. A quarter pound! Right in the middle of the airport!

"Here ya go, man," he said, handing it to me. "Good stuff!"

I couldn't believe it. I looked at Dee Dee and almost had a heart attack.

I grabbed the pot from him really fast, stuck it straight in my bag, and looked around really quickly, to see if anyone noticed the whole thing. Amazingly, no one did. Or, if they did, they didn't want to get involved, so they pretended not to. I broke out in a cold sweat. I was sure some undercover cop was going to tap me on the shoulder and tell me to come with him. Luckily for us, back then there weren't as many undercover security people, watching everybody, as there are in airports today.

"Are you fuckin' crazy, man?!" I asked Dee Dee, trying to keep it to a loud whisper.

"What, man?" was all he said. It didn't even register with him that we could've both gotten busted right there in the airport. Dee Dee was a total legend at *hiding* drugs. Man, he hid them in places you'd never even think of. So I couldn't believe it when he just whipped out this big bag of pot for the whole world to see and didn't think anything about it. Just totally nuts. But that was Dee Dee.

When I hung with Little Matt or John Markovich, our front-of-house soundman, after the shows, we were always trying to get away from Dee Dee. All of us would drink and do drugs, and that's what Dee Dee wanted to do, too, but, like I said, he was supposed to be staying away from that stuff. Plus he was just hard to be around all the time, because he was always just so *on*, y'know? He would just talk and talk and talk and never shut up. I loved the guy, but, man, he was a lot to handle sometimes. On that first tour, he was always knocking on my door at, like, eight in the morning, wanting me to smoke pot with him. And, since I was new then, and I wanted to be friends with everybody, I'd drag myself out of bed and let him in, and we'd smoke. But a few weeks into the tour, Matt and the road guys and I started pretending we weren't in when he came around looking to party.

I remember a funny thing that happened relating to that, in New Orleans, when we played there in 1985. I made plans to meet up with Matt and the other guys in Matt's room after the gig and go downtown to check out the bars, and of course we kept that a secret from Dee Dee. We were all in Matt's room, just about to leave, and who's outside in the hall but Dee Dee, banging on the door and calling Matt's name.

The rest of us ran out on the balcony, and Matt shut the curtains behind us. "Hang on a minute," he groaned, trying to sound really tired when he went to the door.

"Hey, let's go find some blow, maaan!" said Dee Dee. He sounded pretty excited about the idea.

"Nah," Matt told him, throwing in a yawn. "I'm pretty beat, man. I'm gonna crash."

I was listening in from the balcony with the other guys, cracking up. We were like a bunch of schoolboys, trying to keep from laughing too loud.

"Okay, man, okay," said Dee Dee. You could tell he was bummed out. "Hey—do know where Richie and the other guys are?"

"No, man," said Matt. "Maybe try their rooms."

Dee Dee told him thanks and took off. No surprise, later that night we ran into him when we were out barhopping in the French Quarter. Dee Dee didn't care, though. We were all so fucked up by then that everybody just laughed about it.

Jumping back to 1983, though, that whole first tour went really well. I'd proven myself to the band, and everybody liked me. I was now officially Richie Ramone. But about six months after I'd played my first show with them, something horrible happened—and it looked like the band might be over.

25

Add It to the List

On August 14, 1983, I was at Annie's place, and I got a call from Joey. I guess it was around noon.

"Hey, man, we just found out John's in the hospital," he said.

What?

"Yeah, he got beat up. He has, like, a concussion or somethin'. They got him up in Saint Vincent's."

The night before, we'd played at L'Amour, this big metal club out in Queens. After the show, like always, Monte dropped us all off near Joey's place on Ninth Street, and I took the train home from there. For a couple of years, John had been living on Tenth Street, between Third and Fourth Avenues, right around the corner from Joey, with this girl Cynthia, who everyone called Roxy. By then, though, he'd actually left Roxy and moved into a place on Twenty-Second Street with Joey's ex, Linda. I think Joey knew John and Linda were seeing each other, but they didn't want to let him know they were actually living together; John was afraid it would break up the band if Joey found out. So John and Linda were keeping it a secret. What John would do is, after every gig he'd ride back with the band to the usual drop-off spot near Joey's place and get out there, to make it look like he still lived on Tenth Street. Then he'd just sneak around the block and catch a cab up to Twenty-Second. I only found out about this later. Talk about crazy.

As far as I can tell, what happened after the L'Amour gig was this. John got dropped off at the regular spot, and he was walking by his old place on Tenth Street on the way to hail a cab at the corner when he bumped into Roxy. She was hanging out on the stoop with this kid, Seth Macklin, who was the singer in some punk band I never heard called Sub-Zero Construction. Roxy drank a lot. I guess even though they weren't together anymore, John was still worried about her when he ran into her that night because she was really drunk, and Macklin seemed kind of creepy and fucked up. John didn't want to just walk off and leave her there with the guy, so he tried to get her to just go inside. And then, out of nowhere, Macklin just coldcocked him and started kicking his head against the sidewalk after he went down.

So now, John was in Saint Vincent's Hospital with a skull fracture, and there was bleeding on his brain. They had him on anti-seizure meds, and he had to have brain surgery. He almost died. I went to see him a couple of days later, and he didn't look too good. They'd shaved his head and it was all bandaged up. I didn't stay long, but he thanked me for coming anyway. In his book, John didn't mention that I visited him, in the part where he talks about that whole incident. He says Linda, his mom, and Tommy Ramone were the only ones who went. But I definitely went, too. He was pretty out of it on meds at the time, though—plus he had a fractured skull—so I'm not too surprised he didn't remember.

Anyway, of course it was all really scary, and I was worried about John. Everybody was. Joey was really pissed off and hurt about John getting together with Linda, but I'm sure he was still worried about John, at least a little bit. And even though Joey was just as important to the band, I knew that, without John, that would be it for the Ramones. He was the one who kept the music in line and stayed sober while everyone else got fucked up and flew off in different directions. (I think the part of his personality that made him so disciplined was also the part that made him such a right-wing conservative guy—not that he and I really ever talked about that stuff.) But even though everyone was worried about John dying or ending up like one of the vegetables Dee Dee wrote lyrics about, I still couldn't help thinking, oh, shit, this really might be it, man. This might be the end of the Ramones. And I hadn't even been in the band a year.

But John recovered really fast. He was only in the hospital for ten days, and, barely three months later, he was playing again. By the middle of December, we were back doing gigs—not a full-on tour yet, but shows in New York and close by, in New Jersey, Long Island, Upstate New York, Rhode Island, Connecticut—places like that. If you see photos from around that time, you can tell they were taken at those gigs because John has short hair, since it was still growing back from when they shaved it off in the hospital. I'm still amazed by how he bounced back so fast like that. It was unbelievable. But, like I said before, winning was John's favorite thing. So, even though he'd been beaten up, he wasn't going to give the other guy the satisfaction of seeing him lose. Never. No matter what.

We spent the first half of 1984 at home, playing a few times a month around the northeast, doing the usual drive-to-the-gig/do-the-gig/drive-straight-back-home thing. Instead of paying us after the shows or mailing us our checks, John would have Monte meet the roadies and me once a week at the rehearsal space to pay us our salaries—even if there was no rehearsal that day. So all of us would have to take the subway in from Brooklyn just to get paid, and then turn around and get back on the train. That was one of those instances where John just got off on being a dick, knowing he was putting us out, and we couldn't do anything about it, because *we* didn't make the rules.

I did have time to do other stuff here and there while we stayed close to New York, though. Around that time, Fred Schneider from the B-52's was making his first solo album, *Fred Schneider and the Shake Society.* I got to know Fred a little when we did those shows with the B-52's in the summer of '83, and he also knew Ronnie Ardito from the Shirts from the early New York punk days. Fred was looking for new songs to record, so he asked Ronnie to write something for the album, and Ronnie brought me in as a collaborator. We came up with a fun song called "Orbit"—very B-52's-sounding—and played on the recording. Bernie Worrell from Parliament and Funkadelic is on it, too, playing synth bass.

I hadn't really been a songwriter before—I'd only ever been in bands where other people wrote the songs. But after the Fred Schneider thing, I was starting to feel like maybe I should try to do some more of it. And it turned out other people were thinking that, too.

Paul's Lounge was this little bar right around the corner from Joey's building. When we weren't on the road, he'd be in there every night. It was almost like that place was his living room. Take it from me: besides his own apartment, there was *no place* in New York that Joey Ramone spent more time in than Paul's. Even CBGB's. Paul's was his hang. During the week, it was usually a pretty quiet place, but it was never so dead that it felt depressing or anything like that. And they had great pinball machines in there. Joey loved pinball, and he and I would spend hours in there, getting smashed and playing it.

So, anyway, one night Joey and I were at Paul's, sitting at the bar between games. He was saying how it was going to be time soon for the Ramones to make a new album.

"Hey, man, you should write some songs for the band," he said.

Whoa. Me? Write songs for the Ramones? The idea freaked me out. Yeah, I'd done the Fred Schneider song with Ronnie. But Dee Dee and Joey were the main songwriters for the Ramones—all the fans knew that. They invented a whole songwriting style, and the thought of me trying to come up with stuff that fit in with what they did was a little scary. I'd barely written *anything.* What if I wrote something that sucked? It might not just make me look bad—it might make the whole band look bad. It was a lot of pressure. Pressure I wasn't sure I wanted. I told Joey all that.

"Nah, man," he said. "You can do it. I know you can do it. You know what makes a good song good. Besides, we need more songs for an album. Come on, man. You *gotta* write some stuff, okay?"

The more I thought about it, the the more it hit me how cool it was that Joey was asking me to do this. It made me feel good that he had that much confidence in me as a songwriter when I hadn't really written anything on my own. I told him I'd give it a shot. At home, I had a cheap little Casio keyboard I was messing around with, just for something to do when the band wasn't busy. So I started making up riffs and melodies on the Casio, and coming up with lyrics that I could picture Joey singing.

My friend Phil Caivano—who was in this New York band that used to open for the Ramones called Shrapnel, and was in Monster Magnet later on—would transpose my Casio riffs for guitar. With Phil playing

He probably got a better drum sound than the one on Subterranean Jungle.

guitar, I started making these home demo tapes, with me singing and programming the rhythm track on the Casio. Once I had a few tunes recorded, it was time to bring them to the band; Joey told me that whenever they were getting ready to make a new album, they'd have a meeting with their manager and listen to everyone's demos, to decide what would get recorded. Phil seemed to think I had some cool songs, but I had no idea what the other guys were going to think.

The Ramones' manager was Gary Kurfirst, this tall bald guy from Forest Hills, the part of Queens where the band had started and the other guys had grown up. He took over from Danny Fields, the Ramones' first manager, a couple years before I joined; he also managed Talking Heads, the B-52's, Blondie, and, a little later, Jane's Addiction, Garbage, and some other bands. He started out as a promoter back in the '60s, booking shows by the Shangri-Las and the Ronettes, and putting on this big festival in Flushing Meadow Park with Jimi Hendrix, Janis Joplin, the Doors, and the Who; after that, he worked with Chris Blackwell from Island Records and helped break Bob Marley and some other reggae acts in the US. Gary, who died in 2009, worked hard, and to me he really seemed like he knew what he was doing. Plus, I got the feeling he really did love the Ramones and felt the band deserved to be bigger.

So now I was in this meeting at Gary's office with him, Joey, John, and Dee Dee, to pick out songs for the new album. The other guys played tapes of their songs. Joey had a few (two of his were co-writes with outside guys), but most of the songs were by Dee Dee alone, or Dee Dee with John, who hadn't written anything in years. Anyway, all their songs were great. I was blown away by how great they were, actually. And then it was my turn. I handed my tape to Gary, and he popped it into the stereo.

Humankind, it's not fair, why should we all live in fear
Humankind, it's a test, to see who's the very best
Humankind, don't know why, no one cares who lives or dies
Humankind, don't look at me, look at yourself, what do you see

"Humankind" was a fast rocker I wrote about how messed up the world was in 1984. Back then, there were all these Wall Street assholes just out to get rich and screw everyone else, and on the news there was always terrorism happening everywhere. And, of course, all that's still going on today—the cycle always repeats itself. The lyrics weren't super-deep or anything, but they had an edge and an attitude that fit the music. That's what *I* thought, anyway.

Joey looked up. "Hey, this is pretty good," he said. "Yeah, I dig this."

There was something about the music, though, that was different from the regular Ramones formula. The opening riff used a minor chord—a C sharp—and Ramones songs always stuck to major chords. Right off the bat, that made John uncomfortable.

"Ah, I dunno, man," he said. "There's a minor chord in there . . . ."

"Yeah, I know," I said. "But it's cool, y'know? Minor chords add tension, right?"

John looked at the floor and grunted.

"It's true, it's a little different for you guys," said Gary. "But in a good way. I think it works—it still fits. Maybe as a deep cut."

"Yeah, I like it," said Dee Dee. "I think it's cool, John."

There was a long silence.

"Okay," John grumbled. "Add it to the list."

26

Keep Doin' What You're Doin'

We spent the first six months of 1984 doing the usual hit-and-run shows, mostly in the northeast. What shows do I remember from that year? Well, there was one with Cheap Trick and David Johansen in Cortland, New York. And then one in Rochester with Billy Idol, right when he was having his big MTV hits—"White Wedding," "Rebel Yell," all that stuff. Those were some pretty big shows. And then, later in the year, we toured the South and the West Coast, where we did shows in L.A., San Diego, and Phoenix, with Black Flag opening for us. Those three shows were a really important thing at the time, because they brought together the two generations of punk: the older '70s people and the hardcore kids. The one in L.A. was at the Hollywood Palladium, and there was this huge riot after the show, with hundreds of cops with billy clubs beating up kids in front of the place. We were still inside the venue, and we didn't hear about it until later.

Black Flag were one of the main pioneering bands of hardcore—the younger wave of punk that came up in the early 1980s, when most of the original '70s punk bands had either broken up or gone commercial. And, in the early '80s, the Ramones did try to go more pop in the studio, on albums like *End of the Century*, *Pleasant Dreams*, and *Subterranean Jungle*. So, when that was happening, the hardcore kids held on to the fast, raw, hard sound of the Ramones' earlier albums and made that same sound even faster, rawer, harder, and more violent. Dee Dee was always interested in whatever new stuff was going on, and he was a big hardcore fan. Joey dug some of it, too, but he was more of a pop head.

I think John saw the hardcore bands as stealing away the Ramones sound—and now he wanted to steal it back. Y'know: give the kids what they wanted, which was faster music, but from the guys who invented the stuff in the first place. Let the originators show 'em how it's done. And, with me on drums, the Ramones were the fastest they'd ever been, so I was perfect for that, and I loved it. If you watch the *End of the Century* documentary, there's a scene where Joe Strummer remembers John telling him how our set had gotten two minutes faster in the space of just a few months. All the same songs, in the same order—just with the speedometer cranked up all the way.

So, with John and Dee Dee, at least, the hardcore thing was really on their minds when they were writing stuff—on their own and sometimes together—for the new album. And, when it came time to make the album, they had more songs than Joey; from what I knew about the other records, it was Joey and Dee Dee, who wrote most of the songs on those, separately, and John didn't write that much. So that was one thing I knew was going to make this record different for the band. I was always blown away by how Dee Dee could just *bang* out songs. Especially lyrics: Dee Dee always had these little notebooks with him, and I'd see him writing in them a lot.

Since the new album was about getting back to the Ramones' roots,

Tommy Ramone and Ed Stasium, who co-produced *Road to Ruin*, were brought back to co-produce it. (Ed had also been the engineer on *Leave Home, Rocket to Russia*, and *It's Alive*.) I loved the demos of the songs, and I knew this album was going to be a really big deal, especially for the fans, because it was like a total dream-team reunion. Yeah, for me as the new guy, there was the whole legacy to live up to, and I guess if I'd stopped to think about that, it might've made me a little nervous. But with Tommy and Ed there, I knew I was going to be in good hands when I was making my first album with the Ramones. It couldn't have been a better situation, really.

We played Washington, D.C., on July 1, and then took the rest of the month off to make the record. I'd never made a whole album before, but the other guys talked like it wouldn't really take the whole month to do it—it *couldn't*. The studio time, producer's and engineer's fees, and all the other costs had to be paid back from the record sales, so by then the band had learned how time was money when you were in the studio. All those big bands from the '70s, like Boston or Deep Purple or whoever, would spend months and months in the studio making an album. They'd take a whole week just to get the drums dialed in. Not the Ramones. I could see how part of the reason for that was because it would have driven everyone crazy—no one had the patience for it. Especially John, who Phil Spector had forced to do, like, sixty takes of just the opening chord of "Do You Remember Rock 'n' Roll Radio?" when they were making the *End of the Century* album. He said that scarred him for life. But mainly it was about keeping the cost down; the budget wasn't huge, and the band still hadn't made any hit albums, so John told me how the only way to make money off the records—or, at least, not lose any—was to spend as little money as possible making them. And, of course, John being John, he was always reminding everyone of that. The clock was running.

The routine for every album I made with the band was that we'd rehearse for a whole week before we went into the studio, to make sure we really had the songs down. (Joey wasn't at these rehearsals, though; I think he was in the hospital with one of his foot infections.) I knew I had to give my best performance right out of the gate, because I'd only have time for one take of every song.

Besides bringing in Tommy and Ed to do the record, we were booked in to a studio that also fit in perfectly with the whole "classic Ramones" vibe the band was going for: Media Sound, the same studio where *Rocket to Russia* and *Road to Ruin* were recorded. It was a really huge place on West Fifty-Seventh Street. Originally, it was built as the Manhattan Baptist Church, so the main room had really high ceilings, and the acoustics were amazing. After a week of rehearsals and studying the demos at home, I definitely felt like I was ready for the session. And it went *great*. I asked Tommy at one point how he thought I was sounding. He was the producer, but I also felt like I really wanted to get his approval, because he was the guy who originally came up with the Ramones' drumming style. All he said to me was, "Man, just keep doin' what you're doin'." And that was all I needed to hear.

I knocked out all my basic tracks for the album, plus some extra songs, in one day. There were still vocal and guitar overdubs for the band to do (Walter Lure ended up doing a lot of guitar overdubs, like he did on *Subterranean Jungle*), and after that there was the mixing, which was done at Sigma Sound Studios in Philadelphia, where David Bowie's *Young Americans* and all the big Philly soul hits were cut in the '70s. But I wouldn't need to be around for any of that, so I could just party and sleep late while the other guys did what they needed to do. I remember feeling really good about everything when I got done with the tracking. The album was going to be called *Too Tough to Die*, which was the name of one of Dee Dee's songs, about a guy with a halo around his head who tries to be good, likes chocolate, and goes to the gym a lot—typically funny, weird Dee Dee stuff.

We did the shoot for the cover photo really early one foggy morning in a tunnel in Central Park. George DuBose, who had also taken the picture for the *Subterranean Jungle* cover, was the photographer. George did good work, and he worked really fast, which is why John liked to use him. During one shot, something went wrong with one of George's strobe flashes, and it didn't go off. The picture came out really shadowy—you couldn't see our faces, and we were just bluish silhouettes against the fog at the end of the tunnel. We looked like "droogs," the gang members in the movie *A Clockwork Orange*, which tied in well with an instrumental John had written for the album, "Durango 95": the Durango 95 was the name of the sports car the droogs drove when they were going around terrorizing people in the movie. Anyway, that was the photo that ended up being on the cover, and it still looks awesome. It says, "Here's the Ramones, coming out of the fog of the last few years, back again to show the world how this punk rock stuff is done."

And the songs totally live up to the cover. The first one, "Mama's Boy," which was written by John, Dee Dee, and Tommy, maybe wasn't the song I would've expected the band to pick as the opener. Instead of the usual fast, four-on-the-floor Ramones beat, it's more mid-tempo, and I play this circular pattern between the snare and the rack toms. But it totally works as the opening song, because it has enough of the regular Ramones ingredients in there—especially the pissed-off, paranoid lyrics about jerks with jellybean brains being all the same, and about not wanting to be stuck in a shitty job that you hate. The main guitar riff has a surf-rock feel that's just unusual enough, musically, to make people go, "Hmm, this is kind of different, but it still sounds like the Ramones, and it's cool." And it has this dark, menacing feel that sets the scene really well for the rest of the album; the next tune, "I'm Not Afraid of Life," is even darker and more menacing.

After those two songs, the album really starts picking up steam with the fast songs. Next is "Too Tough to Die," then "Durango 95" and "Wart Hog," which has these crazy lyrics Dee Dee wrote when he was in rehab, about heroin and "drugs and bitches and junkies and fags." Joey didn't like the lyrics—I guess he thought they were mean—so Dee Dee sang it. Joey actually wanted to leave "Wart Hog" off the album altogether, but John pushed to get it on. And I was really glad he did, because I sang the chorus, and it became one of the Ramones' most popular live tunes. (Besides Joey, I guess someone at Sire was also afraid the lyrics would be offensive, so they blacked them out on the lyric sheet.)

I started singing more with the band after that. Joey, John, and Dee Dee all liked what I brought with my songwriting and singing, but I think they were mostly happy about it because it meant there was less work for them. I wrote another song around that time called "Smash You" (there's a demo of me singing it), which was my first shot at really trying to come up with something that had the classic, upbeat "pop" Ramones style—all major chords, along the lines of "Sheena Is a Punk Rocker" or "Blitzkrieg Bop." It didn't make it onto the album, but it did end up on a British EP—thanks to Martin Mills, who ran Beggars Banquet, the label that put out our records in England—and it became another fan favorite. Since my songs from that session sounded good, it became a regular thing that John would let me have one song on the album, and Martin would make sure I also got one on a B-side, or as an EP track.

I loved the production of the album by Ed and Tommy (who's credited on it as "T. Erdelyi," his real last name). My drums are really clear and have a great, natural sound, and the guitars are nice and raw. It pretty much sounds like the band did playing live in the room—which, for a major-label album back then, was kind of a radical thing. I could picture the hardcore kids really loving "Endless Vacation," which Dee Dee sings in this super-super-snotty, little-kid voice, and there are songs like "Daytime Dilemma" (which Joey wrote with Daniel Rey from Shrapnel) that really did sound like they'd fit in with the stuff on *Rocket to Russia* or *Road to Ruin*. The most commercial-sounding track is "Howling at the Moon," a song Dee Dee wrote about pot smugglers that was produced by Dave Stewart from the Eurythmics (he was also managed by Gary Kurfirst, so I guess that's how that came together) and has Tom Petty's keyboard player, Benmont Tench, on it. That one made the Top 100 in England when it was released there as a single, and we made a video for it where we're all playing inside this wooden crate, like we're being smuggled into the country. The video's funny, but it wasn't that funny for us making it, being crammed inside a hot crate all day, shooting the thing.

Of course, picking *Too Tough to Die* as the album title came from how John almost died when he got beat up. But it was also supposed to be a comment about how the Ramones were still around and still going strong after, at that point, ten years. The band still had never had a US hit, and they were being written off because they'd made some so-so records in the last few years. And there'd also been all this insane stuff going on inside the band that had people thinking things weren't going to last much longer. But now—*bam!*—here we were, in 1984, with a killer record that was going to prove the doubters and the haters all wrong. And that's what ended up happening.

When the album came out that July, the press went crazy for it, saying it was the best Ramones album in years. Kurt Loder, who was one of the big MTV VJs at the time, reviewed it for *Rolling Stone* and called it "a return to fighting trim by the kings of stripped-down rock 'n' roll." Even the kids in the hardcore scene were raving about *Too Tough to Die*. Suddenly, it was like there was this whole new generation of fans who were just finding out about the band. The Ramones were back in a big way, and the whole band was really happy about that.

"Richie saved the band, as far as I'm concerned," Joey told the *Providence Local*. "He's the greatest thing to happen to the Ramones. He put the spirit back in the band."

27

Clap Test

When the Ramones weren't on the road, you never saw John or Dee Dee hanging out. Like I said, John wasn't a socializer, and Dee Dee lived out in Queens with his wife, Vera, who was trying to keep him there and keep him straight. But Joey went out every night, and most of the time I went with him.

By the time we made *Too Tough to Die*, Joey and I were really close. Mostly, it was just me and him hanging out, but a lot of the times we went out, it'd be us, Joey's brother Mickey, and the lead guitarist from the Plasmatics, Richie Stotts —"Stotts," we all called him. All four of us were really tall, so I'm sure we were quite a sight—especially Stotts, who was almost seven feet and had a crazy Mohawk. Even at six-three, I was still the shortest of the bunch—Mickey's an inch or two taller than me—so I never had to look down when I was talking to any of them, which I have to do when I'm talking to most people.

We'd usually all meet up at Joey's place and then go from there. We'd go see other bands play at CBGB's or the Ritz, or the Pyramid on Avenue A, or the Lismar Lounge on First Avenue, or some other

Lower East Side club. Then we'd hang all night and drink at the Scrap Bar over on McDougal Street in the West Village, or, almost always, Paul's Lounge. People recognized Joey wherever we went, and he always seemed happy to talk to them and sign autographs for them if they asked. I never, ever saw him turn anybody down when it came to that stuff. Not even once. You could always see how good it made him feel, that people loved him and what he did so much.

Joey's whole world was the Ramones and the rock scene. But, after a couple years of us playing and partying, as a friend, I thought it might be good for him if he tried doing some non–rock 'n' roll stuff. Y'know— "normal" things that were fun and had nothing to do with the band. I got him to go bowling a couple of times—that was fun. By that time, my dad had retired and sold his landscaping business and opened Secluded Acres, a horse-boarding stable in West Milford, New Jersey. West Milford's a little town a half-hour north of where my folks lived in Wayne, and about an hour from where I grew up in Passaic. Probably the thing most people know West Milford for is Jungle Habitat, this wildlife theme park that was there in the '70s. After it closed down in 1976, someone jumped over the fence to see what was left and found an elephant carcass and all these other dead animals in there. The park owners had just taken off and abandoned them. Thinking about that today makes me sad and pissed off. I guess I also see now how my dad's love of horses helped fuel my love of animals; if you go to my website, www.richieramone.com, you'll see links there to some of the animal rights organizations I support.

Anyway, one weekend I organized a little party for us at Secluded Acres. Monte got the van and drove me, Joey, Joey's girlfriend Angela, and a couple of other people out there for the day. We all hung out and drank and rode the horses with my parents. Horseback riding was definitely a new thing for Joey, being this total New York guy. I remember my mom helping him get on a pony. Man, Joey Ramone on a pony. I really wish I had a picture of that, but no one there had a camera. It wasn't like it is today, with everyone having one on their cell phones.

There's another image of Joey in my memory, though, that's maybe even better than the one of him on that pony. After a show on the tour for *Too Tough to Die* in 1985, Joey and I went back to his room to party with this girl he met at the show. We all hung out for about an hour, drinking the beers from the club. I could tell Joey and the girl wanted to be alone, so I said I was tired and left. A few minutes later, on the way back to my room from the lobby, I heard something going on in Joey's room as I was walking by. I'm kind of ashamed I did it, and I've never told anyone about this, but the door was cracked open a tiny bit, and I couldn't resist sneaking a peek inside. I guess it goes back to my peeping-paperboy days—some things never change. Anyway, the two of them were on the bed, going at it. I'll never forget seeing Joey's bony ass, going up and down, up and down, up and down, really fast. It reminded me of, like, a jackrabbit or something.

As far as me banging groupies on the road then, I guess I wasn't as wild as some guys are. But I was still kind of a pig. Mainly, at that point, I was into oral sex. Once in a while I'd meet a girl I thought was special and wanted to have full-on sex with, but usually I'd just go for the BJ. It was quicker, and there was less of a worry about catching something. If I was with someone I *did* want to fuck, though, I'd ask her where her boyfriend was. If she said she didn't have one, I figured she'd probably been with a lot of guys, so I'd back off. If she said, "Oh, he's at home tonight," then I'd be attracted to her, because there was less of a chance of her having any diseases. If she happened to be a nurse, that was even better. Then I knew she'd be clean. I liked nurses. I was so paranoid about getting something on the road, whenever I did have sex with a girl, I'd always find a hospital the next morning, before I had to be on the bus, and get checked out. But even though I was a good boy like that, it all caught up with me when the bill for a clap test I got in Germany got sent to Annie's place in Brooklyn, and she opened it. That wasn't a fun day.

Back to the fun, though. On tour, the band and the crew loved pranks. Monte got hit with lots of those. We'd do things like balance a bucket of water on top of the dressing room door, and then yell for him to come in. Or stick a sign that said "kick me" on his back. Stupid shit like that—total school-kid stuff. But one of the funniest things we'd do—we thought so, anyway—was to sneak a piss in an open beer and then give it to someone we met backstage. Sometimes the club would have pitchers of beer there for us, but we *never* drank those. We'd drink the sealed bottles, yeah, but never the pitchers. We'd all take turns peeing in them. Dee Dee would always pee too much; we'd have to tell him to stop, so the people we were pranking wouldn't taste anything and figure it out. The idea was just to leave a little bit of a head on the beer—a little piss foam, right there on top. But Dee Dee was like that—you always had to tell him to slow down, with everything. We'd go out to eat breakfast, and he'd take the little bottle of maple syrup and keep pouring it on his pancakes until his plate was overflowing and it was all over the table. He did everything to excess, that guy. Anyway, we'd offer these pitchers of beer we'd pissed in to the poor victims we met in the dressing room—promoters, journalists, people from the other bands, anyone from the house crew who'd been uncool to us. Yeah, it was childish. And mean, too, I guess. But, y'know, it can get boring on the road. And to us, hey, it was entertaining. The only other thing I'll say about that is that, to this day, I never drink anything backstage that's already open. Ever.

In February 1985, after we'd done a few months in the States, we flew to London to do four nights at the Lyceum Theatre. The Ramones hadn't played in England, or anywhere in Europe, since 1981, so all four shows sold out immediately. It was the first time I'd been to England, so for me that part was amazing enough, besides just the whole experience of playing there. Everyone was going crazy the whole time, talking about the shows, and we even played on TV. Most people reading this probably know how the Ramones pretty much kicked off the whole British punk scene when they played there in 1976, and made the guys in the Sex Pistols, the Clash, and everyone else want to start bands. To people in England and Europe, they were heroes.

Joey and Dee Dee loved playing overseas, but John definitely didn't. He hated the food and the hotels—there weren't too many Holiday Inns in Europe back then—and all that stuff, and of course he hated being so far away from New York. I think that was a big part of why the band put off going back there for so long. But I guess maybe with John being so excited himself about *Too Tough to Die*, and everyone in the press talking about it being a "return to form," he figured it was time to go back.

That June, after five more months of East Coast and Midwest shows in the US, we went back over to do two weeks in the UK and Europe. *Wow*, I thought. Me, this suburban Jersey kid, getting to see all these places I'd never been. It was crazy. I couldn't wait to get over there. And the first show of the tour was pretty amazing: this big festival called the Longest Day, which was in Milton Keynes, England, not far from

London. We were opening for U2 and R.E.M., two of the biggest bands in the world at that time. The show was in the Milton Keynes Bowl (now called the National Bowl), this insanely huge amphitheater that holds sixty-five thousand people—and it was totally sold out. I couldn't believe I was about to play in front of that many people. It definitely wasn't something I *ever* would have thought I'd be doing, back when I was playing with Madison and living on frozen Newfoundland steak in Canada.

Backstage at Milton Keynes, they served us *T-bone* steak, made by these amazing gourmet chefs the promoters brought in. And the backstage bar had whatever fancy beer and booze you could think of, which was tough to stay away from, before the gig. The dressing-room trailers and little hangout areas were all really nice, too. Everything was totally *big time*. It was funny: U2 really worshipped the Ramones—like with the Pistols and the Clash, the Ramones were what inspired them to start a band in the first place—and they all wanted to meet us. Especially Bono. He was dying to meet Joey, and when he went to shake his hand, I could tell he was really nervous about it. I remembered thinking about that little scene when U2 came out with their song "The Miracle (of Joey Ramone)" after Joey died.

When we were getting ready to go on, after Billy Bragg had played, I was in a slow-motion haze. It felt a lot like that very first show I played with the band, two years before. I remember sitting down behind the drums, looking out, and there just being people for as far as I could see. It was totally nuts. I mean, after the first hundred rows of people, it just doesn't even look real anymore. It's like a big, moving painting or something. The roaring was so loud I could barely hear myself breathe while I was adjusting my stool and checking my kit.

I looked out again. There were these giant lighting and camera towers sticking up here and there out of the crowd, and people up front were waving flags and homemade "RAMONES" banners. They went wild right from the first song, which of course was "Durango 95." We only did three other songs off *Too Tough to Die*—the title track, "Danger Zone," and "Wart Hog." The rest of the set was pretty much all the hits, and it went great. I don't think R.E.M. or U2 were too happy about having to follow us, even though more people were there to see them. But, for me, it was a friendly rivalry. After we were done, Larry Mullen Jr., U2's drummer, made a point of finding me backstage and telling me "great show," which was really nice of him.

After Milton Keynes, we took the ferry over to Ireland to do two nights in U2's hometown of Dublin; from there it was Belfast, and then Scotland, followed by Denmark, Germany, and Belgium. All the places we played were packed, and, just like in the US, the fans were buying tons and tons of T-shirts and other Ramones stuff at the shows. I remember thinking, wow, man, that's got to be a lot of money from the merchandise. But I really didn't think much more about it than that. I was having way too much of a blast, visiting all these amazing countries, playing to huge crowds, and getting fucked up every night on awesome European beer and whatever else was around.

We did some festival in Germany, and right before we went on, Dee Dee and I were talking with Lemmy Kilmister—the legendary leader, singer, and bass player of Motörhead, in case you somehow don't know who he was. Lemmy loved the Ramones from day one; he even wrote a song as a tribute to the band called "R.A.M.O.N.E.S." So, the three of us were backstage, and he was cutting up some white powder on a tray. "Fancy a bit, then?" he asked, and Dee Dee and I both snorted a line off Lemmy's personal switchblade. As we were going on, I remember thinking, holy shit, I just did coke with Lemmy!

Somewhere around the third song of the set, I looked over and saw Dee Dee puking next to his amp. It turned out what we thought was coke was really speed. I didn't know then that Lemmy was, like, the biggest speed freak in rock 'n' roll—that was his thing. I don't know if coke would have hit him the same way or not, but the speed definitely wasn't working with Dee Dee's Antabuse. It didn't mess with me too badly, but the set was definitely a little faster, that show.

There was another show in Germany where Joey and I had spent the whole day drinking, and we were drunk when we went on. Of course, John had a fit about that. We never did it again, though. But there was something else that's memorable that happened on that tour while I was enjoying some of that great European beer—and it was almost a total disaster.

On July 6, we played in Tourhout, Belgium. After the show, Little Matt and I were hanging out with these kids who lived in some kind of commune. We were drinking Carlsberg Elephant beer, which has a really high alcohol content. Very strong. One of the kids who lived at this place had a moped, and, after I'd had a few Elephants, I talked him into letting me take it for a ride. I got on the thing and started riding it into this field next to the commune. I was pretty buzzed, but I figured, hey, it's this big, open field, there's no way I'll run into anything. I was wrong.

I was riding along, having fun—and then, all of a sudden—*pow!*—I was off the bike and up in the air. I hit a gopher hole or something and flipped the thing. Trying to stop my fall, I stuck out both my arms in front of me and came down with all my weight on my right hand. Crack.

Now that hand was broken. Elephant beer or not, I was in *incredible* pain. The girls at the party felt bad for me, and they all lined up to kiss the boo-boo, which was a cute scene. But my hand still hurt like fuck. The next morning, I could barely close it. The pain was indescribable. And, that afternoon, we were doing another giant festival, this one in Werchter, Belgium, with U2 and R.E.M. again, plus Depeche Mode, Joe Cocker, and a bunch of other bands. At 1 p.m., I had to play in front of 250,000 people—almost four times as many as Milton Keynes.

Luckily, the promoter found me a doctor. He taped my hand up to where I could just about hold a drumstick and shot me up with some kind of painkiller, and we went on as scheduled. Without the meds, it would have been totally unbearable, but the pain was still insane anyway. Any drummers out there: try playing sixteenth notes for a whole show with a broken hand sometime. Talk about murder. Goddamn, I can still feel it now.

I don't know if Matt was still a little fucked up, or maybe he was just trying to be funny and take my mind off the pain, but for most of the set he stood off to the side where I could see him, laughing and pointing at me. Yeah, real funny, Matt. The only thing that *almost* distracted me a couple times was watching the crowd. Everybody was drinking out of these half-gallon plastic bottles, and they were literally throwing them everywhere the whole set.

Thankfully, it was the last show of the tour, and, when it was over, we went straight to the airport and got on a plane back to New York. By the time we landed at JFK, I think I must have drunk every one of the little plastic bottles of booze they had on the plane. Going through customs, I was pretty happy the band had the next month off.

I didn't know it then, but another one of my crazy drinking incidents would lead to something that was actually good. Really good. For me *and* the Ramones.

28

Somebody Put Something

One of the cool bars in the Village I used to hang out at with Flash, before I was in the Ramones, was called One U (short for the address, 1 University Place). We used to love to go to that place because there were always cute NYU girls there. Mickey Ruskin, who ran Max's Kansas City, opened it, and you'd always see all these big-name rock 'n' roll people there—David Byrne, Lou Reed, Johnny Thunders, David Johansen, people like that. It wasn't really a super-expensive place or anything, but neither of us ever had enough money to buy drinks for ourselves *and* for the girls we were trying to pick up there. After a while, though, we noticed that the little deli right next door sold St. Pauli Girl in bottles, just like One U did. So we'd just buy it cheaper at the deli, and smuggle the open bottles into the bar in the pockets of our Bunnymen coats. We were sneaky guys. But that's not the drinking story I was talking about at the end of the last chapter, the one that turned into something great. This is . . .

There was another money-saving thing Flash and I would do when we were out at the bars and clubs: steal people's drinks. We'd hang around some table full of buzzed NYU kids or bridge-and-tunnel idiots, wait until they got up to dance, and then just sneak over to their table and walk off with their drinks. Sometimes, if it wasn't that crowded and we were afraid of getting caught, we'd just drink half the glass or take a couple quick sips and leave it there. Whatever it was I ended up drinking that way, though, I didn't care. I thought the whole thing was totally hilarious. And all I wanted to do was get fucked up and not have to pay for it. But there was this one time, in the summer of 1981, when our little scam really came back to bite me.

We were at the Ritz for "Mod Monday," doing our usual drink-stealing thing, and getting more and more wasted as the night went on. About an hour after we got there, I was dancing with this cute girl who looked like Siouxsie Sioux. The DJ was playing "To Hell with Poverty" by Gang of Four, the strobe lights were flashing, and I was feeling good. It was looking like the night was going to end well. And then, out of nowhere, things started getting weird. Really weird.

All of a sudden, I felt really hot and dizzy. The whole dance floor got all wavy, and all the people around me looked like they were melting—except the girl I was dancing with, who went from looking like Siouxsie to looking like some monster off *Star Trek*, with holes where her eyes were supposed to be. I started freaking out and crying. Somehow, Flash got me out of the club and back to his mom's place, where I spent the next couple of hours hanging onto the toilet, puking like crazy, and hoping like hell the bathroom would stop moving. All I could figure was that one of the drinks that I stole that night must've been spiked with LSD. Whoever put it in there meant it for someone else, and they got me instead. So, once again: never drink anything that's already open if you don't know where it came from.

By now, I guess you're probably thinking, "Okay, but how did this whole crazy drinking story with the acid and the freak-out and the puking turn into something great?" Well, in early 1985, I was goofing around on the Casio at Annie's place, trying to come up with songs for what was going to be my second album with the Ramones. I hit on this really cool descending riff: A to F to G, letting each of the notes ring out a little. Then that led me to a chorus that used the same notes in the same order, but doubled them up in the classic Ramones way and added an E major at the end of it. The rhythm was mid-tempo, and that brought out the dark feel of the chord progression. I recorded it and listened back to it over and over again the next day. It was totally stuck in my head. I didn't have a title or words for it yet, but it definitely felt like something good.

Later in the week, Little Matt and I were hanging out at the bar near the Shirts' place, and something we were talking about—I think my beer tasted weird, and I made a joke to the bartender about him dosing me—reminded me of that whole insane night at the Ritz, and I told Matt the story. I was still thinking about it when I got back to Annie's that night, so I started writing down some words that came to mind:

It feels like somebody put something
Somebody put something in my drink
Somebody put something
Somebody put something
Blurred vision and dirty thoughts
Feel out of place, very distraught
Feel something coming on

For the rest of the lyrics, I made the scene a bar instead of a nightclub, which I thought worked better, because it helped keep it simple. I also used some details I thought would remind Joey of hanging out at Paul's Lounge. He always sat in the same spot at the bar ("*Stopping for my usual seat*") and, when he wasn't sitting there, he'd always be checking out the jukebox ("*Yeah, kick the jukebox, slam the floor*"—I never actually saw Joey kick a jukebox or slam the floor, but sometimes, when he was really wasted and playing pinball, he'd get a little out of hand and tilt the machine a bit too hard). Phil Caivano came over, and we made a demo of the song. I sang it in a low, mean voice, and gave it an obvious title: "Somebody Put Something in My Drink."

A few months later, when the band got together at Gary Kurfirst's office again to pick out songs for the next album, I played it for them. Like some of the older, darker Ramones songs—say, "I Just Wanna Have Something to Do" off *Road to Ruin*, or even "Mama's Boy"—it wasn't a super-fast song. But it still had the usual things people would expect a Ramones song to have, like the choppy guitar riffs and the catchy chorus. And, with the tension of the sustained chords, it also had a twist that made it a little different.

Going in, I was afraid that Joey, John, and Dee Dee might think it was a little *too* dark for the band. I really had no idea how any of them were going to react to it at first. I was nervous. I kept thinking back to John's crack about "Humankind" having a minor chord in it and all that. But, right away, John and everybody else saw how the song could work. Especially Joey—he really loved it. And he dug the way I sang it on the demo so much that, when we finally recorded it, he even sang it a little like I did, in that really low, growly voice. That was kind of a new style of singing for him, and he ended up using the voice he uses on "Somebody Put Something in My Drink" more and more after we recorded it.

Joey also started singing that way just because he was getting older.

HUSKER DOWN: Pre-show laughs in Lincoln, Nebraska, on what is now officially referred to as the Cold as Fuck Tour, winter 2014. *Photo by Jeff Jones*

DOG DAY: Me and my girl, Gretta, hanging out in Los Angeles, California, 2014. (Hey, everyone, please be nice to animals.)
Photo by Steve Appleford

ALWAYS BE PUTTING: Practicing the short game in Tandil, Argentina, 2014. *Photo by Daniel Watanabe*

BLACK SKY AT NIGHT: Hi-Fi Rock Festival, Long Beach, California, 2015. (I remember very little.) *Photo by Daniel Noble*

FUCK YOU LOOKIN' AT?: Mid-show intensity at Chicago's famed Mayne Stage, 2014.
Photo © Dave Hedstrom

UP TO SKATE: At the Hollywood premiere of *We Are Blood*, with hip-hop great, Lil' Wayne, 2015.
Photo by Brett Smith

STRAIGHT CHILLIN': A moment of relaxation in Venice, Italy, 2015. *Photo by Alex Ruffini*

MOMENTS AWAY: Moments 'til showtime at the UniClub in Buenos Aires, Argentina, 2017.
Photo by Daniel Watanabe

PUNK AS FUCK: Club Amparo, Carlos Casares, Argentina, 2018. Protect ya neck. *Photo by Ivan Weingart (ph:saturno)*

BSAS, CHE!: There is no place like Buenos Aires. More UniClub madness, this time in 2018.

Photos by Ailiñ Gómez Caraballo

His voice was more worn by then, and of course it was never going to be exactly the same as it was when he was younger. But that deep growl he used later on started with "Somebody Put Something in My Drink." So, in a way, I think my vocal on that demo influenced the way Joey ended up singing in his later years. I'm sure there are bootlegs around that have the demos I made. Listen to those and then listen to the way Joey sings before and after the song was recorded, and see what you think.

"Somebody Put Something in My Drink" became one of the Ramones' biggest songs. It made no. 69 on the singles chart in the UK, and it's been covered by bands all over the world. (Joey said in an interview he did with the *Los Angeles Times* in 1986 that I wrote it about getting dosed in a bar in San Francisco, but I don't know where he got that from; I told *East Coast Rocker* I was in a mental institution for two weeks after getting dosed and wrote it there—a total lie.)

The song also became the opening track on our next album, *Animal Boy*. The producer this time was Jean Beauvoir, who'd played bass in the Plasmatics, and with Little Steven after that. Sire kind of pushed him on us, but Joey and Dee Dee were sort of friends with him anyway. Back then, the Plasmatics were the most outrageous thing around: this crazy "shock rock" band who came out of the punk scene in New York and did insane stuff onstage, like smashing TVs and blowing up cars. Their singer, Wendy O. Williams, would do shows with only shaving cream covering her tits or electrical tape over her nipples, and their lead guitar player, Richie Stotts, who I mentioned earlier, had his crazy Mohawk and wore a dress onstage. They were a wild band. Anyway, Beauvoir produced a British single we put out a few months before we did the album called "Bonzo Goes to Bitburg." That sold really well as an import in America, plus the critics loved it, and it was a hit on college radio.

Ronald Reagan was president then, and he'd visited this graveyard in Germany where S.S. soldiers were buried. People were mad about that because it was like he was formally recognizing these Nazi soldiers or something. Joey was Jewish, so of course he thought it was fucked up for Reagan to do that. Dee Dee grew up in Germany, which was still kind of like the motherland to him, and I guess the whole thing bugged him, too. So the two of them and Jean wrote "Bonzo" about seeing that story on the news. I'm guessing they probably also thought it would be good to have an anti-Nazi song, too, because in the past some people hadn't gotten that Dee Dee's lyrics to "Today Your Love, Tomorrow the World," off the first Ramones album, which talk about Nazis and shock troopers, were really just making fun of that stuff; maybe "Blitzkrieg Bop" confused those people, too, if they only knew the title.

I didn't think anything of this at the time, though—it was just another song to me. But John was a conservative, and he loved Reagan, so he had a problem with the title, when he found out what it was by seeing it on the record cover. (In case you're too young to know, Bonzo was Reagan's nickname because he'd been in this movie about a monkey in the 1950s called *Bedtime for Bonzo*.) People talk like there was this whole huge thing where John flipped out about it, and in his book he also kind of makes it seem like that's what happened. But I really don't remember it being that big a deal. He and Joey and Dee Dee just agreed to change the title to "My Brain Is Hanging Upside Down," which is one of the lines in the song, when it came out on the album. Then everybody just moved on, and we didn't talk about it anymore. And that was that.

We started recording *Animal Boy* in early December 1985, at a studio in New York called Intergalactic. Just like with *Too Tough to Die*, we did it really fast. I played my parts and I was in and out in a day. Again,

Dee Dee wrote most of the songs, either by himself or with John or Jean Beauvoir. One of the ones Dee Dee wrote with Jean is "Something to Believe In," which we did a really funny video for. The video was kind of making fun of the phony side of all the celebrity charity things that were big then—"We Are the World" and all that. It shows us playing this benefit show called "Ramones Aid," and there are all these guest appearances by famous people and people from bands, like Penn and Teller, Spinal Tap, Weird Al Yankovic, Afrika Bambaataa, Sparks, X, the Circle Jerks, and the B-52's. I think it's probably my favorite video we did during the whole time I was in the band.

Animal Boy came out in May of 1986. It didn't end up doing as well as *Too Tough to Die*. A couple of songs, like "Eat That Rat" and "Apeman Hop," kept up the hardcore style Dee Dee and John were into then, and "Crummy Stuff" and "Love Kills" (a Dee Dee song about Sid Vicious and Nancy Spungen) have the old Ramones sound, but it's a little slicker. Jean Beauvoir tried to make us sound more commercial and put too many synthesizers on some of the songs, which a lot of the old fans didn't like.

Joey only had two songs on the album, "Hair of the Dog" and "Mental Hell." During the sessions we also recorded a song I wrote and sang lead vocals on called "(You) Can't Say Anything Nice." It sounded really great, but it got left off the album. Originally, it only came out in Europe on the B-side of the "Something to Believe In" 12-inch. I wonder if John ever figured out it was about him (the line "You know your biggest problem / is the way you comb your hair" came from the way he always leaned forward and combed his hair, from back to front, before we'd go onstage).

We got George DuBose to shoot the cover photo again. He wanted to shoot us in the monkey house at the Bronx Zoo, but none of us wanted to stand around in a cage for an hour, smelling monkey shit and trying not to step in it. So he built a fake cage in his loft, got Legs McNeil from *Punk* magazine to dress up in a gorilla suit and stand behind us, and hired Zippy the Chimp, who was the Monkey Cam on *Late Night with David Letterman*, for one of us to hold in the picture. Originally, Joey was supposed to hold Zippy, but Zippy was afraid of him and kept hopping off. When John, who didn't even want to touch Zippy, tried holding him, I'm pretty sure Zippy pissed on him a little bit. Dee Dee, forget about it—he wouldn't even get near the little guy. So in the end, it wound up being me and Zippy, together forever on the album cover.

29

Joey • Johnny • Dee Dee • Richie

Christmas Eve, 1985.

I was at Joey's mom Charlotte's house in Queens with him, Mickey, and Dave U. Hall, who was the bass player in Mickey's band, the Rattlers, and had been in Remod with me for a little bit. Originally, I was planning to go out to my folks' place, like I always did every Christmas Eve. But the whole New York area was getting hit with this big blizzard, and the buses weren't running out to Jersey. Joey felt sorry for me, not being able to visit my family on Christmas Eve, so he invited me to his mom's for dinner.

Of course, being Jewish, Joey's family didn't actually celebrate Christmas. But he and Mickey and their mom were still into the whole holiday vibe—the part about bringing family and friends together. And the holiday cheer, or maybe I should say holiday beer, started flowing pretty much as soon as I got to the house. We all had drinks while we watched the snow coming down outside. It was nice.

So we were all sitting there in the living room, a couple of hours after dinner. I think it was about nine when Joey suddenly said, totally out of nowhere, "Hey! Ya know what we should do? I got this new song I've been workin' on that I really wanna record." He was all excited. "We should find some studio and record it!"

"*Now?!*" I said. "Joey, man, it's Christmas Eve. Nobody's gonna be open, man."

"No, man," he said. "There's this one place, right near here. They're open, I know the guy. He'll totally do it. Just this one song, c'mon."

By then, we were all feeling pretty good, so it was, like, hey, why not. We went over to the studio, which was somewhere close by, in Queens—I forget where. But when we got there, it turned out the engineer was closing up, and he didn't want to take a chance on getting stuck there during the storm. Joey was bummed out. He was hung up on recording this new song. I guess maybe he thought there was still enough time for him to get it on the new album, even though we'd already cut all the songs for it with Jean Beauvoir. But it turned out Joey was in luck: the engineer told us about this other studio over in Flushing, so we gave that guy a call, and he said to come on over.

The song was called "Elevator Operator." It was pretty good, very poppy. I liked it. The bass intro was kind of like "Stand by Me" by Ben E. King, and the rest of it was a lot like "Then He Kissed Me" by the Ronettes, one of Joey's favorite groups. Joey showed us the parts on guitar, and then Mickey, Dave, and I recorded the music. But by the time everything was ready for Joey to do the vocals, he felt like he was too drunk to sing.

"You do it Richie," he said.

"Me? It's *your* song, man."

It felt good that he asked me. Besides, of course, being Joey's brother, Mickey was the lead singer for the Rattlers, so he could have asked him to do it. But he didn't.

"I dunno," I said.

"No, no, man, you do it," Joey said. "C'mon. It's just a demo for the other guys to hear. You sounded great on those demos of your songs. C'mon, man. Just do it. It'll be good."

So I sang it. The lyrics were about this girl Joey had a crush on who worked at the Peppermint Lounge. And, yeah, she actually did run the elevator there. I kind of remember her. There was one weird line in the song, "I was coming from a garden party." I always wondered where that line came from, because I could never picture Joey at a garden party (in New York?). He probably got the idea from that Ricky Nelson song, "Garden Party." Or maybe it had something to do with this art gallery in Astoria that Charlotte ran called the Art Garden (the Ramones used to rehearse in the basement there when they were just starting out). I don't know—I never asked him. Anyway, the demo stage was as far as "Elevator Operator" got. The Ramones never did the song. John didn't like it. Now, it's just another bootleg rarity. But recording it with Joey and the other guys during that crazy Christmas Eve blizzard is still a great holiday memory for me. The following week, the Ramones played the World, this big club on Second Street and Avenue C, for New Year's Eve. That was a fun night, too.

A couple of weeks after the sessions for *Animal Boy*, I went to meet Joey at Paul's Lounge. There was this amazing-looking girl with him, playing the jukebox. She was, like, *wowwww*. I was very, as I like to say, enthusiastic. I grabbed Joey by the shoulder and pulled him over to the bar.

"*Who* is *that*?" I said, talking over the music but also trying to keep my voice down. I knew she wasn't his type. Joey liked smaller girls. Not long-legged, model types like this one.

"Aw, man, you'll *never* get that," he said to me, rolling his eyes under his glasses and drinking his beer. I used to laugh at how fast he drank beers when we were out. One after another. The way some people chain-smoke cigarettes. "She's *waaay* outta your league, man. Forget about it."

But I wouldn't forget about it. "Yeah, we'll see," I told him.

Seven months later, that girl and I were in Las Vegas. Getting married. But let me back up a bit, to before that happened.

I won't mention her by name, but she was from New York. She was a music journalist, which is how Joey knew her.

The night we met ended up being our first date. Sort of. Monte picked the three of us up in the van, and we all went out to Brooklyn to see this metal band, King Flux, who she was writing about at the time. At twenty-eight, I'd just learned this new word: *fellatio*. I thought it was a hilarious word. I was such a kid then. When we were getting in the van, I said to her, "Hey, you gonna give me some *fellatio*?" She told me to fuck off. I liked that.

King Flux's lead guitar player was Richie Stotts, and their drummer was . . . Marky Ramone. That night would be the first and, so far, only time Marky and I would meet. If you can call it meeting. After the show, everybody was backstage, and Marky was cutting through on the way somewhere. He walked by me, our eyes met, he nodded, and he said one word: "Hey." That was all. I nodded and said "hey" back. I got the feeling he wasn't exactly happy to see me, which wasn't really a surprise. He'd been kicked out of the Ramones, and I was the guy who'd replaced him. What was he going to do? Wish me luck? Of course not. I got that. That was as far as the conversation went.

Anyway, soon after that, I got an apartment of my own on the Lower East Side, on Eleventh Street and Avenue A. Right near Joey's place. It was great, because I was close to all the action; now, when Monte dropped the band off after gigs, I could just walk home. I didn't have to take the train all the way back out to Prospect Park anymore. That always sucked, after driving back all night from Boston or D.C. or wherever. Anyway, my new girl would stay over at my new place, and sometimes I'd stay with her out at her folks' place. But she refused to move in with me unless we were married, so that would come later.

Animal Boy had been released on the last date of the English tour, May 19, and now the band was booked to tour the US for the rest of the year. Like always, we started on the East Coast with five-hour-New-York-radius shows, spread out to one-week runs in the Midwest and on the West Coast, and then finished up back east. We did dates in Virginia and D.C. with the Smithereens, who were really big on MTV right then, and Social Distortion opened for us at the Hollywood Palladium.

Metallica even came to see us play on one of their off days, at the Jockey Club, this old casino in Newport, Kentucky, that had been remade into a punk club. James Hetfield, their singer, came up to me and told me how much they all loved "Somebody Put Something in My Drink." "Man, I wish *we* could write a song like that," he said. I sure wish they'd done a cover of it, like they did with a couple of the Misfits' songs. That would have been very nice for my bank account. Oh well. I remember talking to their bass player, Cliff Burton, a really nice guy—two months later, he was killed when Metallica's tour bus crashed in Sweden. I remember we'd just gotten back from the West Coast when I heard about that, and I was totally in shock. Really sad.

Now that I had a serious girlfriend, I was being a good boy. Sort of. After the shows, I was still partying with Joey, Matt, and the crew. The shows in the US on that tour were really good, and, like always, totally packed. But I knew the places we would have been playing in Europe were bigger, so I didn't get why we weren't doing more shows over there. We did fly over in August, to do a couple of quick shows in Belgium and Holland, and those were huge gigs. The Belgian show was with Public Image Ltd., which was a cool one for me since—maybe you remember from chapter 15—they were one of the English bands Flash and I had been really into back in the day.

I was proud of seeing my name on the T-shirts the band sold at shows—the official Ramones "screaming eagle" logo, with "Joey • Johnny • Dee Dee • *Richie*" in a circle around it. That was a big deal. It said my name was etched in stone as a Ramone, and it felt awesome.

What didn't feel so awesome was something else to do with those shirts, and it came up on that tour. It was the morning after the last show in Europe, and we were all in the van, heading to the airport to go home. Arturo Vega was sitting next to me. Besides running the lights and designing all the graphics, Arturo also handled the merch business for the band when we were on the road.

"Last night was really good," he said. "We sold a lot. Especially the new shirts."

I watched him reach into the inside pocket of his jacket. He pulled out three envelopes that were each about an inch or two thick and handed them to John, Joey, and Dee Dee. The driver stopped the van and, without saying a word, they all got out and ran into a bank to exchange the currency before we flew back to the States. I just sat there in the back. All by myself. This was, like, the sixth time I'd watched Arturo hand out those envelopes stuffed with cash to everybody else. And, while I was sitting there, something started to hit me. Hard.

I'd written the lead song off the new album, and people in the press were pointing that out. To the outside world, I was a Ramone. My name was on the shirts that Arturo had just been talking about. People were buying those shirts. But it didn't seem like it had occurred to anybody in the band that maybe offering me a couple bucks from the huge profit the shirts were making would be a nice gesture. An equal share wouldn't have made sense, I knew that. Only an idiot would have thought I should get anywhere near what Joey, John, and Dee Dee got and totally deserved; they started the band, and they were total legends. But *my* name was also on the shirts, which to me meant I was part of the Ramones brand.

I was getting my weekly salary, and, when we made the albums, I got a percentage off those. My bills were getting paid. I was comfortable enough, money-wise. What started to bug me that morning about the T-shirt thing wasn't really about money. It was about wanting some kind of token acknowledgment between us that said I was valuable to the band. That they were happy to have me and wanted to keep me around. That I was past the point of just being some hired gun. But when the three of them were done in the bank and got back in the van, I didn't say anything. I just kept it to myself. And hoped something would change down the line.

Those three European dates and the two weeks we did in England were the only overseas shows we did that year. Mainly that was because Joey was in and out of the hospital a lot again for his foot stuff, and of course John still hated traveling and the expense of touring over there. Instead of playing Paris and renting a van and all the gear to do that, he would have rather just played Providence, Rhode Island, gotten five grand for the band, and been able to sleep in his own bed that night. But there was also this big push from Gary Kurfirst to get the band to finally make it in the US. I got the sense that it could happen, because it was during the time that the whole "alternative rock" scene—which the Ramones had pretty much started—was getting to be a big thing, and MTV and commercial radio were paying attention to all that. In a lot of markets, alternative bands like R.E.M., Modern English, XTC, the Smiths, Love and Rockets, and New Order were going from just being college-radio stuff to getting played on the commercial stations; even Hüsker Dü, one of the underground/D.I.Y. hardcore bands who'd covered Ramones songs when they were learning to play, got signed to Warner Bros., which would have been unthinkable a couple years before. So it was looking like maybe the mainstream was finally ready for the Ramones, and we could ride that whole wave along with these other bands.

I also felt like I was getting more and more invested in the band, since I was writing more songs, and people were calling "Somebody Put Something in My Drink" an instant classic. Even though *Too Tough to Die* and *Animal Boy* didn't sell a lot in America—they both barely made the *Billboard* 200—they mostly got good reviews. Way better reviews than the ones for the last couple of albums the band had made before I joined.

It seemed like bigger things were right around the corner.

30

Whaddya Mean, "Skip That Part?!!"

The next big thing that happened was at the beginning of 1987. On January 30, we flew down to South America to do three shows: two in São Paulo, Brazil; and one in Buenos Aires, Argentina. It was the first time the Ramones would be playing down there. A couple of people I'd mentioned it to had told me the band was popular in South America, but I still didn't have any idea what to expect. I figured "popular" meant it would be like it was when we played the clubs in England or Europe. Man, was I ever wrong.

It was way beyond that. It was fuckin' amazing. The most incredible thing ever. The only thing I could compare it to is how it looks like in those old TV reports about the Beatles when they first came to America, in 1964. Seriously. The kids down there had been waiting forever to see us. And, now that we were there, they all came out and followed us everywhere we went—like, literally, *hundreds* of them. And they were all totally going out of their minds. It was actually almost scary at times. We had guards stationed outside our hotel room doors, and we had to have these big security guys around us when we were walking to and from the van, because the kids would surround us and start touching and grabbing us, trying to get pieces of our clothes and our hair or whatever.

When we were in the van, they'd chase us until we got to a traffic light and had to stop. Then they'd all run over, grab the sides of the van, and start rocking it up and down. Driving up to the club or the hotel was like parting this huge sea of people. I was always afraid someone was going to get run over. Luckily, that never happened, which is kind of a miracle, when I think about now. At the hotels, the fans would find out what rooms we were in and then stand outside on the street and keep yelling our names, until we finally came out on the balcony and waved to them. It was insane.

The places we played each held about five thousand people, and they were sold out way in advance. The newspapers said there were some problems with skinheads starting fights outside the Palace Theater, the place we played in São Paulo. But the shows themselves were great. So was the one in Buenos Aires, at the Estadio Obras Sanitarias, this giant basketball arena. The audiences just went crazy every night. They all knew the words to every song, and they all sang along—loudly, I could tell, even though I couldn't hear them over the band—the whole time. I remember looking out at the front row when we were doing "Somebody Put Something in My Drink" and seeing all these kids' mouths moving along to the words I wrote. Most of them probably didn't even speak English. But they knew those words. That was a pretty incredible moment. To me, South America still has the best audiences. I *love* playing down there, and I always have a lot of fun every time my band tours there.

After all that, coming back to the States and playing much smaller places just a couple weeks later, in Pittsburgh and Allentown—even though they were great, sold-out shows—definitely felt a little different. We also played at William Paterson University in Wayne, New Jersey, which was cool for me, because it was right near my folks' place. My whole family came to the show—my mom and dad, Lenny, my sisters, my cousins, everybody. After that, in March, we went back down south again for a couple weeks, hitting Texas, Florida, Georgia, and Louisiana.

One cool thing I remember about playing in the South that tour was running into Bananarama in New Orleans. If you're too young to know (or too old to remember) Bananarama, they were a British girl group who were the hottest thing on MTV back in the mid-'80s. Three really cute singers—Sara Dallin, Keren Woodward, and Siobhan Fahey—who played with a backup band, like the '60s girl groups used to do. They first got together when they were in fashion school in London when punk was happening over there, and they all loved the Ramones from way back. So, when we bumped into them, they really wanted to hang out. We all went to this riverboat bar/restaurant for drinks. I can't remember the name of the boat—I wonder if it's even still there, after Hurricane Katrina. They'd had a couple of hits before then, but when we ran into them it was right after they'd had a no. 1 hit in the US with their cover of "Venus" by the Shocking Blue. So they were everywhere then, on front of the all the magazines. They were all really nice, and we had fun hanging out. I got pretty flirty with a couple of them, too. But by then I was engaged, and I was staying true to my fiancé, so I didn't try anything. Man, that was definitely a tempting situation, though.

We got married in the spring of 1987. I remember looking in Monte's tour itinerary book with him to figure out what days the band had off, so the two of us could go to Vegas, get married, and have a quick honeymoon there. Once we were married, my place on Eleventh Street didn't last long. She knew this real-estate investor guy who hooked us up with an awesome apartment in the Beaux Arts Building on Forty-Fourth Street, right near the UN—at market value, really cheap—and we finally moved in together. So now I had this beautiful new wife, and, after being out in Brooklyn for years, I was living in this amazing, super-classy place right in Midtown Manhattan. Things were good.

In April, the band started working on the next album. The last two hadn't sold as well as Sire thought they would, so this time John was pushing even harder to spend as little time and money as possible in the studio. He got Daniel Rey (the guy from Shrapnel who'd worked on *Too Tough to Die*) to be the co-producer, because he'd heard some demo of a local band that Daniel did in his basement and liked it—plus he knew Daniel was still kind of a starstruck kid who wouldn't want a lot of money. Sire gave us an advance of $150,000 to do the album, and we blocked out a week at Intergalactic—the same crappy studio in Midtown where we did *Animal Boy*—for something like $4,000. Out of the money that was left over after that, there was Daniel's fee, which was really low, and then it got split up from there according to the percentages on our contracts. Since it was my third album with the band, my higher percentage kicked in, and I got the biggest check I've ever gotten for playing on a record. Not bad for a day and a half in the studio, I remember thinking.

As with the other albums, we rehearsed (without Joey; he wanted to rest his voice) the week before, to get the arrangements worked out, and, when we went in, I definitely felt like I was ready. Again, I knew John would only want to do one take per song. It was just, "Bang it out right the first time and then move on to the next one," and I was fine with that: besides keeping the cost down, it keeps the feel of the music more fresh, more alive. After you've done, like, thirty takes of something, it gets to be a drag. It starts to suck for everybody. And I think people will pick up on that feeling, if they hear it on a record. So that's still the way I do it today, whether I'm playing on one of my own records or someone else's.

I wrote two songs for the album, and both of them made the final list this time: "I'm Not Jesus," the hardcore song about going to church when I was kid that I talked about earlier, and "I Know Better Now," another song that had to do with being a kid. This one was about looking back at when you're a teenager, rebelling against your parents' rules, and then thinking about how much you've learned about life since then:

> *When I was your age*
> *I heard it all*
> *Like livin' under*
> *Your martial law*
>
> *I would think it was*
> *For my own good*
> *I would think it was true*
>
> *Nobody*
> *Can tell me*
> *I know*
> *I know better now*

Like Ramones songs always are, "I Know Better Now" is a pretty simple song. Most people would probably think recording it would have been totally easy. Just bang it out and move on, like I said. But when I was teaching that song to the band in rehearsal, that wasn't how things went. It actually turned into a pretty major, fucked-up thing— between John and me.

The intro to "I Know Better Now" isn't just a straight "one-two-three-four!" count-in that goes right into a four-four rhythm, like on other fast Ramones songs. The guitar, bass, and drums do start together, but for the first eight measures, before it goes into the main riff, the drums do this sort of staggered pattern between the snare and the tom-toms. It isn't anything super-complicated. It's kind of a surf thing. Maybe like something you'd hear on a Ventures record, but a little heavier. The Ventures and surf music had influenced the Ramones, so I guess that was probably somewhere in my head when I was writing it. Anyway, for some reason, when we were rehearsing it, John just couldn't get that opening part. He was having a really hard time locking in. I guess what I was playing was throwing him off, and I could see he was really getting frustrated. After he'd screwed it up it a couple of times, he put his hand up for us to stop.

"Fuck this," he said. "This isn't a drum record. Let's just skip that part."

What?

I couldn't believe it. It was a great song, and Joey, Dee Dee, and I weren't having any problems with it. But now, all of a sudden, just because John was having a hard time, we were just going to change the song? No way. I was *pissed*, y'know? I'd been the quiet guy the whole time I was in the band. Never talked back to John. He ran the show. Fine. And I knew we were trying to stick to the one-take-only plan, and not mess with anything that might slow us down in the studio. I got that, too. But *I* wrote the song, and, to me, that intro was a really important part of it. I couldn't hold back about that. I blew up.

"Whaddya mean, 'Skip that part?!'" I yelled, standing straight up off my stool. "That's the way the song is *written*, John! That's how the fuckin' song *goes*. The intro is the coolest part. That's what makes it different, y'know? C'mon, man. What the fuck? Jesus fuckin' Christ, man."

The room got totally quiet. *Nobody* was expecting that. Even me, I've got to say.

A couple of seconds went by.

"All right, all right, fine, let's try it one more time," said John, afraid to look me in the eye. "Fine. C'mon, let's just fuckin' *go*, then. We've wasted enough time already."

So we did it again. And this time, we nailed it. I listen to the studio version of that song now, and I hear how pissed off I was in the way I hit the drums so hard. I was probably wishing they were John's head. And you know what? It sounds great.

Word about that whole rehearsal incident got around to everyone who worked with the band. All the guys in the crew and all the wives and girlfriends were all saying, "Wow, did you hear how Richie stood up to John?" Nobody ever really stood up to him. Even Joey and Dee Dee. So that was definitely a big deal, and it changed the dynamic inside the band.

I was never around for any of the overdubs, but I think Daniel went in and replayed some of John's parts on that song, which he did on a lot of the other songs. John never had a problem with that, though, because even though he didn't want to spend the time doing them himself, he still wanted everything to be precise. If something he played was a little off, it was usually quicker—and cheaper—for one of the studio guys to just punch in and do it. It was the same with Dee Dee's parts. Dee Dee was a "live" guy, not a technical guy, and he played sloppy sometimes.

Live, that doesn't matter. But in the studio, when you're recording, it needs to be *tight*. So I'm sure Daniel redid a lot of Dee Dee's stuff. For the basic tracks, though—the foundation of everything—it was always me, John, and Dee Dee in the room, playing together. Always. And I never went back in and redid anything I played. Never, ever. With the drum parts, what you hear on all the records I'm on is *exactly* what I played. And, 99 percent of the time, it's the first take.

Even after my drum tracks were all done and I'd gone through all that insanity in the studio with John, though, I still wasn't done with the insanity of making that album—the one we ended up calling, for all kinds of reasons, *Halfway to Sanity*.

31

Trouble Bubbling

The week after we recorded *Halfway to Sanity*, my wife and I were visiting her folks and staying out at their place. The phone rang at four o'clock in the morning. It was Joey, looking for me. By now, I knew early morning phone calls were never good. I was hoping my new in-laws weren't having heart attacks in the other room.

I was afraid Joey was going to tell me somebody died or got beat up again. It turned out it was something serious, but not *that* serious.

"Listen, man," he said. He sounded really stressed out. "You *gotta* come help me mix this album. It's not soundin' good at all. I dunno what I'm doin' wrong, but it sounds like shit, man. Y'know . . . John doesn't wanna spend any more time on it. And he won't lemme give it to someone else to mix. Man, I'm, like, really freaking out here. You think you can come down later?"

I said "yeah" and took down the address. I wasn't going to ask him why he didn't ask Dee Dee to help him. Joey and I were friends, and it actually meant a lot to me that he wanted my help with something as important to the band as mixing the record. Besides, I knew Dee

Dee didn't have the patience to do mixes. That was never his thing. He and John both hated hanging out in the studio, unless they really had to be there. They just wanted to get their parts down, be done, and let the producer do whatever he needed to do from there to make things sound good.

So, that week, I started meeting up with Joey at Unique Recording, where he was working on the mixes with Daniel and the engineer, Joe Blaney. It was a total change of scenery there from doing the tracking the week before at that cheap place, Intergalactic. Unique took up the top three floors of the old Cecil B. DeMille Building in Times Square. It was this really slick, high-tech place where people like Madonna, the Stones, Aerosmith, and Mariah Carey recorded. They always had all the newest gear there—samplers and all that stuff—when it was brand new; the companies who made the gear would actually give it to Unique to try out before anyone else got it. Because of that, a lot of the MIDI and sampling techniques you hear today in rap and hip-hop music were pretty much invented there.

We got a good rate on one of the mixing suites because we were willing to do the graveyard slot. So we got the place for something like eighty-five bucks an hour, instead of the two hundred an hour they charged during peak times. We'd go in around eight and work until around four, five, six in the morning. At the time Joey brought me in, there were about five or six songs left to do, so we worked on those. We blocked out, like, four or five nights at Unique, and we'd usually do two songs a night. Even though Daniel was there, he pretty much just sat in the back of the room and let me tell Joe Blaney what to do, and then Joey would say what he thought of that. Usually, he liked my ideas.

If you've ever been in a studio during a mixing session, you know how insane it can get—changing the levels of different instruments or vocal tracks, trying different effects on different things here and there. When you change one little thing on a song, it can throw all kinds of other stuff off and change everything else—even though that wasn't at all what you were trying to do in the first place! You have to listen to little parts of songs, and even whole songs, over and over and over again when you're running the mixes, and it's easy to start zoning out and losing track of what's going on. It can really make you crazy, after a while. Of course, John wasn't happy about the idea of Joey and me doing too much of that. When he heard about it, he got really pissed off, telling us we weren't listening to Daniel about what he was doing with the production, and how we were getting in the way of him doing his job and all this other stuff, which caused even more stress.

On the third night we were there, John showed up at the studio, unannounced.

"Hey, we need to hurry up and finish," he said, like he was our dad or something. "This is all a waste of money. Nobody's gonna buy the record, anyway."

But Joey and I still kept working hard, because we really cared about the music. With every album we worked on, Joey would always say to me, "This is gonna be the one, Richie. This is gonna be the one!" Joey really wanted us to get on the radio and have hits. Maybe John had cared about that in the past, but by this point I think he'd given up on that whole idea. To John, the records were just a reason to go on tour and sell more T-shirts, which was the only thing the band made money from. Well, everyone in the band besides me, anyway. But when I asked John for a mixing credit on the album—I told him I didn't want to be paid for it, I just wanted the credit—he said no.

By the time we got done with the mixing, and all the other craziness had quieted down, I really felt like I had—like one of the songs Dee Dee wrote for the album says—lost my mind. But *Halfway to Sanity* still came out pretty good, I think. And a lot of people tell me it's one of their favorite Ramones albums. I love Joey's "Bye Bye Baby," one of the best '60s-girl-group-style ballads the band ever recorded. He did some great crooning on that one, which he always really loved doing. Especially then, since on a lot of the fast, hardcore-type songs we were doing, all he could really do was yell his brains out. "Bye Bye Baby" sounds a lot like something the Ronettes would have done; actually, their lead singer, Ronnie Spector, sang a great version of it with Joey later, on *She Talks to Rainbows*, a record of hers that he produced in the '90s.

"A Real Cool Time," which was one of the two singles off the album, is a song Joey wrote about some girl at the Cat Club he had a crush on. That was another club he and I used to hang out at a lot. It was on Thirteenth Street. Joey used to do DJ nights there sometimes. Cool place.

The other single was "I Wanna Live." Dee Dee wrote that one with Daniel Rey. I always thought it was just a good, catchy tune. But now, when I read Dee Dee's lyrics about executing killers, and loading his pistol made out of "fine German steel," I wonder who at Sire thought a song with words like that was going to get played on the radio and decided to put it out as a single. It was hard enough to get airplay for a song like that back then, but it would be totally impossible today, with all the mass shootings and everything going on everywhere. Forget it.

Debbie Harry from Blondie did the backup vocals on "Go Lil' Camaro Go," a surf song Dee Dee wrote. She was one of Joey's good friends, so it was no big deal for him to ask her to do the song, but for me it was a total honor that she sang on it. It still blows me away, being on a record with her; I'd loved Blondie since I first heard them back in the late '70s.

Besides the two songs I wrote for it, *Halfway to Sanity* has some other good rockers. I really like "Death of Me," a Joey song that has this really good, tough, mid-tempo riff. Like with "I Wanna Live" and most of the other songs we recorded for the album, I really didn't pay that much attention to lyrics of "Death of Me" at the time. But looking at them on the inside of the CD booklet now, it seems like Joey was facing his demons on that one, talking to himself about his crazy lifestyle and how he was doing too many drugs. Or maybe it's about him seeing Dee Dee doing the same. Or maybe it's about both of them. I don't know.

George DuBose shot the cover photo again. We did it in front of a restaurant somewhere down in Chinatown. Again, John didn't want to spend a lot of time on that, either. After ten minutes, he told George that was enough. So that was the end of the shoot.

From late April to late June, we went back to playing the usual close-to-New-York shows, mostly on the weekends: Albany, Western Massachusetts, Providence, Poughkeepsie, Philly, D.C., those kinds of places. On June 27, we did a big outdoor "Queens homecoming" show with the Wailers (without Bob Marley, who was dead by then) and Meat Loaf at Flushing Meadows-Corona Park, where the 1964 World's Fair was. Definitely a weird bill. What's also interesting to me now about that gig is that, in 2016, the Queens Museum—which is literally right there next to where we played in the park—had a big exhibit of Ramones memorabilia called "Hey! Ho! Let's Go: Ramones and the Birth of Punk." It got written up in the *New York Times* and all the other big papers, and people came from all over the world to see it. Plus Monte went on to work with the New York Hall of Science, which is right there, too.

After the gigs, whenever it was just me, Joey, and Dee Dee hanging out and partying, I'd bring up to them how much it bugged me that I was doing so much for the band—that I *loved* doing all that, and *loved* being in the band—but felt like I wasn't being allowed to really be a *part* of the band. There were times when I couldn't figure out if they wanted me to be Richard Reinhardt or Richie Ramone.

I played great. I'd written songs. I'd done a great job on the albums, even mixed some of the new one. I was never late to the rehearsals or to the studio or the gigs. Other than those *two* times in Germany, first with Joey and then with Lemmy from Motörhead (how I could say no to drugs from Lemmy?), I never got fucked up before any of the shows. We'd toured all over together, and I'd done almost *five hundred* shows with them—without ever missing a single one.

Obviously, I pointed out to Joey and Dee, they wanted to keep me. If they hadn't wanted to keep me, they would have gotten rid of me a long time ago. But they didn't. I was still there. So didn't that mean I really *was* a Ramone? And after four and a half years as a Ramone, didn't I deserve more of a stake in the band—which meant at least a little bit of the money from the tour merch?

Every time we had those talks, though, Dee Dee and Joey would always say, yeah, that made sense to them; they agreed with me, they totally understood how I felt, and blah, blah, blah—but they'd have to talk to John about it. I got that. He definitely would have listened to them before he would've listened to me about anything.

"Yeah, man," they'd say. "We'll back you up, man. We'll talk to John."

But then they never would. I don't know if it was just because everyone was fucked up when we were talking, or they were just "yessing" me because they were too afraid to bring it up with John themselves or what. But it would always just get forgotten about, and nothing would happen.

We went up to Canada to do some gigs in July. After one of the shows there, I overheard some of the roadies talking, and I found out I was making the *same* salary they were. I almost fell over when I heard that.

What the fuck?

That was it. No one else was going to stand up for me. *I* had to do it. I had to talk to John myself.

32

Time Has Come Today

People always want to know if I ever got into arguments with John about politics, because our views were so different. Nope, never. John hardly ever said anything about anything to me. Besides once in a while at rehearsals or song-pitch meetings, and the times when I went to those baseball games with him when I first joined, the whole time I was in the band, we never talked *at all*. Like I said, in the van he was always sitting up front, away from the rest of us, listening to his ballgames and not talking to anyone—except to get on Monte's case about his driving, and say he was making us late or getting us lost. We pretty much never did soundchecks, so I'd see him in the dressing room for our little warm-up set with Dee Dee, and then onstage. After that, I'd just see the back of his head in the van on the ride to the hotel or back to New York. That was it.

And when we were in New York, unless there was band stuff to do, we never saw each other. The whole time I was in the band, we didn't even have each other's phone numbers. Joey and Dee Dee and I all had each other's numbers, but not me and John. If he wanted to ask me something or tell me about something to do with the band, he'd just have Monte give me a call. That was how he wanted things. Yeah, he liked my playing and my songs, but it wasn't like he cared about us being friends or anything. To him, our relationship was just a business thing. Like I was an employee.

And, on top of that stuff, there was still this whole bad feeling between him and me leftover from when we were making *Halfway to Sanity*. I knew he was still pissed off about me getting in his face in front of everybody at that one rehearsal, and about how Joey let me take control of things when we were mixing the album. He was probably starting to see me as a threat. I didn't want to be a threat, though. I just wanted to be treated fairly. Since there was a bad vibe between us, it definitely didn't feel like the best timing for me to be asking for more money. But I was married now, and I felt like I had to think about my future and my financial security and all that. Plus, I had my pride, y'know? Sure, John was pissed at me. Fine. I was pissed at him, too. I was still nervous as hell, but I *had* to talk to him about the situation with the merch money. I couldn't just keep on living with the feeling that I was putting so much into the band and still being treated like crap.

So, finally, backstage after one of the Canadian shows, I went up to John. He was sitting by himself in a corner of the dressing room.

"Listen, man," I said. "I gotta talk to you about somethin'."

I went into the whole thing. I guess I got pretty worked up. Like I said, I was really pissed off by that point. I'd been carrying this stuff around inside for a long, long time. I told him how, yeah, I totally got that I didn't deserve as much as what he or Joey or Dee Dee got from the merch. I must've said that, like, three or four times.

"Look," I said. "I really respect you guys. But I'm feeling like you guys aren't respecting me, y'know?" I told him, "Man, I *know* all you guys are making *tons* of money off the shirts and the other stuff we sell on the road. Don't think I don't see those envelopes every night, and that I can't guess how much is in there." I told him, "Listen, man, I'm not looking for a raise in my salary. I'm not looking for a higher percentage on the records. Or a bigger piece of the publishing, or any of that. Just a measly couple of bucks from the T-shirt money at the end of the night. That's all. Just so I can have a little something in my pocket between paychecks. *Four years* I've been in this band. Don't I deserve a little something for that by now?"

I pretty much poured my guts out. And, when I was done, I was really feeling like I'd made my case pretty well. But John didn't say anything. He just sat there on his folding chair, listening and looking straight at me. No expression. When I'd said everything I had to say, he finally spoke.

"Uh-huh," he said, really flatly. Like this whole serious talk by me— the guy who never talked—was just ten or fifteen minutes of dumb, boring bullshit he'd had to sit through. "So, how much you askin' for?"

I'd thought about that. I came up with an amount that was so low I figured he'd give me an easy yes, just to shut me up about the whole thing.

"Ten percent," I told him. "Ten cents outta every dollar. That's all. Just from the T-shirt money. That ain't a lot. Right?"

There was a long pause.

"Well," he said, "you're asking for way too much. *Way* too much."

Huh? My heart stopped. *What?*

"Sorry, man. But no."

And that was it. He got up and walked out of the dressing room.

I just stood there.

What? Seriously? Ten cents on the dollar was "way too much"? Man, that was nothing. *Nothing!* Like any of those guys would have even *noticed* a tiny amount like that not being in their big, fat envelopes. For every hundred bucks they got, I would have got ten bucks. *Ten fucking bucks.* I mean, everybody knew how cheap John was, but come on. He didn't even take two seconds to even think about making me a counteroffer. Y'know, I was figuring I'd get a "Well, lemme think about it," or "I'll talk it over with the guys and we'll see." But, nope, not even that. That was it. Conversation over. Goodnight. See ya.

We all got in the van while the roadies were still packing up the gear. Nobody talked. Like always. We stopped at the 7-Eleven so John could get his milk and cookies on the way to the hotel. Like always. When we got there, I called my wife from my room to tell her what happened. She knew I'd been waiting and waiting to have this talk with John, so she was pissed off, too. I didn't need her to remind me how true it was, but she did anyway: after all this time, anyone from outside the band who knew what was going on would have seen how I was worth a lot more to them than what they were paying me. And they would have also seen how I was being treated like shit.

I took a shower, cracked open a beer from the club, and lay down on the bed. I watched TV with the sound off. And wondered what the hell I was going to do.

Back in New York, I had some time to think about that. It was late July, and the next leg of the tour wasn't going to start until mid-August. My wife and I talked and talked and argued a lot about what I should do. But mostly I was inside my own head. It was just me. I seriously think I wore out the tiles on the hallway floor at our place in the Beaux Arts Building, from all the back-and-forth pacing I did those four weeks. I'd already been round and round and round with Joey and Dee Dee about everything, and it was easy to see they weren't going to help me out. And, obviously, John wasn't going to give an inch. About anything. It seemed like he thought it was funny, keeping me in my place. And, besides, he was too busy planning for his retirement, stuffing the cash he was making in some kind of secret safe he had hidden in the floor of his closet. That's what I heard, at least. John really didn't care who was playing the drums at that point in his career. It was just about money.

I felt like there really wasn't anyone else I could talk to about any of this. From the way everything looked, I could see that nothing was ever going to change. The other guys knew I was unhappy, but they didn't seem to care. The fans accepted me as a Ramone, but I had to face up to the fact that I was never going to be accepted as one by the other Ramones. I felt like I'd run into one of the brick walls they used to stand in front of for the album cover photos.

So that was it. I decided the next show, on August 12, 1987—the day after my birthday—was going to be my last.

It was at a club in East Hampton, Long Island, called the Jag. The set was pretty good, from what I remember. We started with "Durango 95," of course, and we did a couple of other songs off *Animal Boy*, and "Somebody Put Something in My Drink" and a few more from *Too Tough to Die*. It was definitely a weird feeling, being up there, playing the songs, and knowing that was going to be it. And, also, being the only one onstage who knew.

I remember looking out in the crowd at one point, and there was a guy holding up a homemade banner that had one word on it, in two-foot letters: "RICHIE." That had never happened before. I'd played hundreds and hundreds of shows with the band, and I'd seen all kinds of crazy audience banners with Joey, Johnny, and Dee Dee's names on them. But this was the first time I'd actually seen one with *mine* on it.

Finally, I thought. But why *tonight*, of all the nights? In a way, that was tough to see—bittersweet. I'm sure the other guys saw it, too. I remember thinking, gee, maybe *now* they'll get how the fans actually do see me as a Ramone. But that feeling didn't last long. I knew, even with that, things wouldn't be any different. By now, Joey, John, and Dee Dee were just the guys they were. They weren't going to change. My mind was made up, and I was going through with it. I'd had my five-year plan, and, by now, I'd been in the Ramones for, basically, five years. It was time for a new plan. Not that I really had one—besides not wanting to get pushed around anymore.

We finished with "Pinhead," and we all walked offstage and went back to the dressing room.

I reached into my bag for some dry clothes, and my hands were shaking. I was nervous. Okay, I thought, there's no turning back now. I've got to do this.

Since it was summer, the back door of the room was open, to let in some fresh air. There was a white stretch limo parked in the back lot, right outside the door.

"Hey," said Monte. "That's weird, there's a limousine out there. Maybe it's somebody famous."

I grabbed a towel and went over to the open doorway. Then I turned around, so I was facing everyone.

"That's my ride," I said. "I quit, guys. I'm leaving. Thanks for everything. Bye."

All of a sudden, everyone stopped talking. It was dead quiet. Everybody was standing there with their mouths open, staring at me, with their eyes bugging out—Monte, John, Dee Dee; even Joey, behind his glasses.

I turned around and walked out.

I got in the back of the limo—which I'd hired to pick me up—and the driver started the engine. My wife was already inside, along with our friend Jacqueline, two quaaludes, and a bottle of Cristal. Jacqueline handed me the 'ludes, and I chased them down with a glass of the champagne. When we started pulling away from the club, I stood up through the open sunroof.

And waved goodbye.

33

Aftermath

The next morning, I woke up to all these people from the management company in the hallway outside my apartment, banging on the door. "Richie! We gotta talk, man," they were yelling. "Come on, Richie. Open the door!" But I wouldn't open it. I didn't want to see these people. I didn't want to talk to *anybody*.

I finally did talk to them, though. I stood there in my boxer shorts, with the door shut, and argued back and forth with these guys for *hours*. I think my neighbors were afraid to leave their apartments. They must've been, like, "What the fuck is happening out there?" I'm surprised nobody called the cops. I mean, this thing felt like it went on all afternoon. It was like there was some kind of hostage negotiation or something going on. It was nuts. Finally, they got that they weren't going to talk me out of my decision, and they left.

The band really wanted to get me back in, immediately, because we'd had shows booked at the Ritz in New York that night and the next night. The Ritz shows were big shows, and they really didn't want to cancel those. So they offered me more money to do those two gigs—five-hundred bucks a night, way more than I'd been making for a whole week during the last four-and-half years—and hinted around that we'd talk more after that. But my wife had heard from someone, probably Joey, that John just wanted to get me back in the band to do the two Ritz shows and was planning to fire me right after that. Years later, he *said* that wasn't true. But I don't know—I wouldn't have put it past him. It would have totally been like him to do that. Y'know, like, "I'll show *you* who's boss!"

Anyway, I didn't take the bait. If there was any bait to take. Now that John's gone, I guess I'll never know for sure.

Later, John made it seem like he was shocked when I quit, because he thought we were "still in negotiations." But he'd flat-out said no when I tried to talk to him about money. He didn't say, "We can't do that much, but we can do such-and-such an amount," or, "Lemme think about it," or, "Let's talk later." So what else was I supposed to think, y'know? Maybe he really did think he was being a tough negotiator, and he was waiting for me to come back and ask for less. But there was no way I would have known that from the way he talked.

Looking back on it now, the whole thing could have been avoided if we'd just had the lawyers work it out. I really should have handled it that way from the beginning. Like I said, it looked to me like everyone in the band liked what I did and wanted to keep going with me. So I'm sure some kind of deal could have been figured out. Who knows what the Ramones would have gone on to do, musically, if I hadn't left? I was still just getting started as a songwriter, so I'm sure I would have kept bringing more and more songs in. Now, whenever I think about that whole scene with the limo, I laugh at myself and think, man, what a prick I was. But, y'know, I was really young, I felt like

I was being mistreated, and I kind of had an attitude then. I didn't think things through, the way I would today. Oh well.

The band ended up canceling the Ritz shows (both of them got rescheduled) and getting Clem Burke to take my place. Clem's an incredible drummer, but he wasn't right for the Ramones, and he only lasted for two gigs, in Providence and Trenton. They kicked him out and rehired Marky, who had gotten sober by then. It's interesting how, when I joined, the Ramones were touring with me on the album they recorded with Marky just before he was out of the band—and now they were touring with him on the album they recorded with me just before I was out. He should have had a dozen roses delivered to my doorstep for giving him his life back.

When I left, I didn't give a shit what John thought, but after things had settled down a little, I did feel kind of bad for hurting Joey. Yeah, he and Dee Dee didn't stand up to John for me, like they said they would, and I'd been pissed about that. But Joey and I were really good friends, so it bugged me to think he was feeling like I betrayed him, which is what he said in interviews for a while, after I was gone. He went from saying I saved the band to saying I screwed them. I guess I couldn't have blamed him for feeling that way at the time. But, again, I was doing what I thought I needed to do: stand up for myself.

Dee Dee didn't really care too much about it, though. He got how I was frustrated with the way things in the band were. "Man, I wish *I* could quit," he'd always tell me, "but Vera won't let me."

Dee Dee started getting into rap around the time I left. Whenever he wasn't on the road, he'd take the train in from Queens really early and get to my place about 8:30 in the morning. We'd call up Weed

Deliver, this pot dealer who'd bring the stuff straight to your door, and then we'd usually hang out until about one in the afternoon, getting stoned and recording his crazy rap songs with my keyboard and my little home studio. Dee Dee always had endless ideas for music.

A couple of years later, parts of some of the songs we came up with ended up on *Standing in the Spotlight*, the solo rap album he made under the name Dee Dee King. Toward the end of his time in the Ramones—he finally did quit in 1989—he even started dressing like a rapper. Instead of the Ramones uniform of the leather jacket and jeans, he started walking around in these fancy velour sweat suits and Kangol hats, with gold chains around his neck. I heard Dee Dee's new look really drove John nuts, and, of course, John wouldn't let him wear any of that stuff onstage. Mostly, though, everyone I knew just thought it was hilarious. And, yeah, it was. Definitely kind of weird, too. But, hey, that was Dee Dee. Just him being himself and wanting to be different.

One afternoon, the two of us were at my place, getting high, while I worked out beats on the drum machine. One of the melodies we came up with reminded me of "The Twist" by Chubby Checker, a song I loved when I was a kid. Right then, an idea hit me.

"Hey, y'know what would we should do," I said to Dee Dee. "We should do a *rap* version of 'The Twist'! Think about it! Man, that would be *huge*! Right?" This was when Run-DMC were the biggest thing on MTV, with their version of Aerosmith's '70s hit "Walk This Way." A big part of why that record did so well was because it appealed to rap fans *and* rock fans. But, with a rap version of "The Twist," there would be a similar kind of crossover thing, *plus* a nostalgia angle that would also get the older generation. And it was also an easier song to dance to; when I was a kid, whenever the Exceptions or any of my brother's other bands played "The Twist," it would always get the older people *and* the kids dancing. So I figured it couldn't miss.

Dee Dee loved the idea, too. We came up with a version that combined the 1960 version of "The Twist" with the follow-up from 1961, "Let's Twist Again," and Lenny played sax on it. We figured we should get Chubby Checker himself to sing it, but with some rap group that was really hot then. Who, though?

Dee Dee had the answer right away: "The Fat Boys!"

The Fat Boys were a rap trio from Brooklyn with gold- and platinum-selling albums. They were kind of a goofy/novelty group, so I could see why Dee Dee thought they'd be a good fit for the song. Plus, y'know, Fat Boys, Chubby—geddit?

We heard Chubby was playing in Atlantic City, so we went down to pitch him on the idea, and he loved it. Chubby and I clicked. "I see something in you," he told me. "I wanna work with you." And, for a little while after that, I *did* work with him, as his music director, writing arrangements and leading his band through their charts at some shows in Canada, and mixing tracks with him at Victory Studios, near his place outside Philadelphia.

After Dee Dee and I went to the Fat Boys' label, Tin Pan Apple, though, their producers, the Latin Rascals, ended up going straight to Chubby, produced the song with him, and totally cut us out of the deal. Or maybe Chubby did—I never found out. Anyway, "The Twist" featuring Chubby Checker ended up being the *lead single* off the Fat Boys' 1988 album *Coming Back Hard Again*, which went gold. It got released all around the world, they made a video for it that got played a lot on MTV, and it became a Top 20 single—but Dee Dee and I never got anything for it. Even though it was us who came up with the idea.

That definitely opened my eyes up even more to how shitty the music business can be. It brought me back to what happened with Velveteen; how so many people from the business side are totally greedy, and they'll just use you and your ideas to make money for themselves. That kind of stuff's been going on forever. I'm sure it always will, too. You've really got to be careful who you trust if you're going to be a musician. Take it from me—that's one of the really big things I've learned from doing this for so long.

By the time the Fat Boys and Chubby were having their hit with our idea, I was long gone from the East Coast. Since I'd left the Ramones, the scene in New York was getting harder and harder for me to be around. I didn't want to go out to any of the clubs I used to hang out at, because I didn't want to run into Joey or any of the people who worked with the band. And, everywhere else I went, I was always running into fans or music-scene people who wanted to ask me all these questions about why I quit and what I thought about them having Marky back in the band and everything else. I knew if I stayed there, I'd be dealing with all that forever. It was time for another change.

So, in November of 1987, three days before Thanksgiving and three months after I'd left the Ramones, my wife and I loaded everything we owned into the back of a twenty-foot U-Haul truck and moved to L.A. We went out there like cowboys, without a lot of money, and with no idea what either of us was going to do for work. We also didn't really have any idea as far as the lay of the land went. I rented an apartment from an ad, sight unseen, in Simi Valley, and right away when we got there we realized it was way too far away from everything, so I found us another place in North Hollywood, a cool neighborhood in the San Fernando Valley. It was the beginning of a whole new adventure—one that would have way more twists than Chubby Checker ever did.

34

We Never Spoke Again

Since L.A. is such a big place for music, I figured it would be easy to get in a happening band as soon as I got there. I thought, man, all I have to do is just get to L.A. and spread the word that, hey, I was in the Ramones and I'm looking to play, and that would be it. It wasn't that easy, I found out.

This was right at the time when hair metal and glam metal were the big thing coming out of L.A.—Guns N' Roses, Poison, L.A. Guns, all those bands. I grew my hair long again and started playing with different bands, trying to find a way in. The first thing I did was a project with Dave Wayne, who'd been the singer for Metal Church. He had an amazing voice, but we never got beyond making demos in my apartment. (Sadly, Dave died in a car crash in 2005.)

I spent some time playing with a band called Male Order Brides, who I was introduced to by Brett Smith, one of the first people I met in Hollywood. Brett was the drummer in a cool band back then called Gang War (no relation to the Johnny Thunders/Wayne Kramer band of the same name), and he was always pushing me to get back into music;

he was a big supporter then, and he's still a good friend today. I also met Charlie and Will Sexton, two brothers from Texas who played awesome blues-rock guitar. A couple of years before we met, Charlie had been an MTV teen idol with his hit "Beat's So Lonely," and he went on to play with Bob Dylan. The Sextons flew me down to Austin, to jam with their band Will and the Kill, but nothing else happened with that.

It was definitely a shock, going from being used to someone else always moving my drums and setting everything up for me—I barely had to lift a drumstick when I was in the Ramones—to suddenly having to do everything for myself again. I mean, just having to carry my snare and my stick bag to go play the Coconut Teaszer, or some other little place on the Sunset Strip like that, was depressing. It was like I was back in Tapestry, cramming my kit in the back of a car again, only now I was old enough to drive.

I was getting to know people here and there, though, like Taime Downe, the singer from Faster Pussycat. I used to play Nintendo hockey with him a lot. Good guy. But the L.A. scene, and hanging with West Coast musicians, was way different from how it was with bands on the East Coast. A lot of the West Coast guys seemed more pretentious than I was used to. I could never really get to the point where I felt like I was fitting in.

Paying the bills by playing music wasn't happening, either. I needed to do something for work. When I talked about my childhood earlier, I said how I was never into sports, but that not's totally true. I did like golf. I still do. There's something about that game that's both challenging and relaxing. Some people in the rock scene make jokes about golf and say it's something for retired executives or whatever, but Iggy Pop and Alice Cooper are both golfers. And so am I, though I've never played with either of those guys. So there you go.

Anyway, I got a gig caddying at the Lakeside Golf Club in Burbank, which was pretty cool. In a lot of ways, it was the perfect job for a rock 'n' roll bum like I was back then. You could work the days you wanted to work, you got to be outside, and you'd spend a couple of hours carrying some guy's clubs around and get paid pretty well for it. Plus, sometimes, after a round, the guy you caddied for would take you in the clubhouse and buy you lunch or drinks. Since Lakeside was right near where all the Hollywood studios were, I caddied for some big people: Joe Pesci, Jack Nicholson, a lot of movie moguls and people like that.

Caddying was cool, but it was still only part-time, and it wasn't what I wanted to be doing forever. So I kept playing in bands, and I even started a video-game production company with my friend John Zeiler, the same guy who rented us the flat in the Beaux Arts Building in Manhattan back in the day. The video-game thing folded in 1997, and, after ten years, my savings had started running out. My wife and I gave up on L.A. and moved back to New York.

The first job I got once we were back was as an engineer at the Cutting Room Recording Studios on Broadway, just north of Houston Street. I did that for about six months, working mainly with hip-hop artists, which was crazy, because they'd always want to bring their whole posse into the studio to party with them. I remember they all loved to drink Hennessy and milk—that was the thing then. With the engineering stuff, though, I felt like I was out of my league; it takes a lot of patience to do that job, and that's not really me.

So I kept playing. And, through my wife's connections, I got an audition with Cinderella, this glam-metal band from Philadelphia. They were one of those bands who were big on MTV for, like, five minutes, before Nirvana and grunge came along, when all those L.A. bands I was talking about before were still the thing. I heard they got signed because Jon Bon Jovi saw them at a club somewhere and liked them. They never called me back after the audition. I never heard why. I thought it went fine. At least that was my feeling. But the Cinderella guys probably wanted someone flashier than me. With bigger hair. And makeup. Whatever.

By now, it was 1998, and the money was getting really tight. I needed a *real* job—there was no way around it. And, living in New York, another caddying gig wasn't going to cut it. I'd reconnected with Flash, who was out of music and working in the hotel audiovisual business. "Hotel A/V is where all the misfit musicians go," he told me. So I answered an ad for an A/V company that worked with hotels in New Jersey. I was so broke I couldn't afford a suit to wear to the interview, so my mom bought me one, along with some black plastic shoes that looked like real leather—or close enough, anyway. I got the gig, and we moved to a bungalow on the Jersey Shore, so I'd be closer to work.

I was the director of A/V: I oversaw a staff who maintained and set up the projectors and the P.A. and other equipment used in the conference rooms and event rooms of hotels, when companies had trade shows or meetings there. It was pretty easy work, and I was good at it. From there, I kept getting better and better jobs in other places and moving around the country, working at different hotels. I was at the Adam's Mark Hotel in Charlotte, North Carolina, for a bit, but the atmosphere there was really racist, which I couldn't deal with. One day, at a meeting, the food and beverage manager complained about the servers, calling them "wetbacks." I got out of that city as fast as I could.

I worked a few years at the Westin Bonaventure in downtown L.A., and then I landed a job at a hotel in Las Vegas and moved out there. What was interesting about working in the hotel industry in Vegas was that a lot of the hotels and casinos there liked to hire Mormons for the service jobs, because they're known for being people who don't steal or drink or do drugs. I guess I wasn't a good fit, though. My management style was too "New York" for some of the people I was supervising, and I ended up getting fired after they complained about my attitude. Looking back, I think I was just unhappy. I was stuck in a straight "responsible" job, and I wasn't doing what I loved to do—play music—and that was coming out in the way I was at work. It would still be a little while before I figured that out, though.

But losing the Vegas job kind of turned out to be a good thing, because almost immediately after I was let go, I got hired as the regional manager of VER, an A/V equipment rental company in Scottsdale, Arizona. Vince Dundee, the guy who owned it, was a big rock 'n' roll fan who really loved the Ramones, so he was pretty excited to have me there. It was a 24/7 job—I had to wear a beeper, and I could get called up anytime to go and deal with some piece of gear somewhere that wasn't working—but it was still pretty cushy and easy. The company leased me a brand new SUV, and I had an expense account to take clients out for lunch or dinner—or even to play golf or go to strip clubs.

Unfortunately, my marriage ended in 2009. We were fighting a lot, and I guess the stress of moving twenty-one times in twenty years didn't help too much. After we split up, I went back to L.A., where I worked in the accounts-payable department of the same equipment rental company I'd been with in Scottsdale. That wasn't as much fun; now, instead of eating steaks and playing golf in the sun on the company's dime, I was stuck at a desk under fluorescent lights, chasing down deadbeats for money over the phone.

It was kind of a trip, working the hotel jobs. Sometimes, guests would spot me or find out who I was, which was always embarrassing.

But by the time I was directing a staff of twenty people at the Doral Golf Resort and Spa in Miami (which was later bought by Donald Trump), not that many guests were recognizing me: I had a flattop, and I weighed two-hundred-and-thirty-eight pounds. Anyone who saw me then probably figured I was just another fat Florida Republican in a suit. Or, at least, they probably didn't think I was a guy who'd once been the drummer of the best-known punk rock band of all time.

As for the fallout from quitting the Ramones, there were all these horrible things the Ramones and people who worked with the band were reportedly saying about me. Either they'd put me down or else just totally leave me out of the band's history, trying to act like I never existed. (The Internet wasn't that big of a thing yet, but once the Ramones did have an official website, for a long time it didn't even mention my name.) I got how they would have been mad at me for quitting and all that. Okay. But to flat out pretend I was never in the band, when I'd made three albums with them—with my picture on the covers—played all those shows with them, written songs, and everything else? And act like they'd never even heard of me? It pissed me off. But I didn't want to deal with it. I was still bitter then myself. So I pretty much kept my mouth shut. In fact, my first interview after leaving the band wasn't until 2003—sixteen years later—for the *End of the Century* documentary.

How hard did the band try to erase me? Well, one day when I was in Tower Records in West Hollywood, looking through the Ramones section, I came across *Loud, Fast Ramones: Their Toughest Hits*—and it had a bonus CD, called *Smash You! Live '85*, of a show I did with the band in England. Not only had a recording I played on been released without me knowing about it or being paid for it, but when I bought the album and opened it up, I saw on the CD that the song "Smash

You" was credited to "the Ramones" and not to *me*, even though we'd agreed my songs were always supposed to be credited to me as the sole writer.

I later heard John had okayed the release and said he thought I'd never find out about it. If that's true, I don't know what he was thinking—like I seriously wasn't ever going to be in a record store and see it? Anyway, I was pissed. I sued the band's estate and the Walmart, Apple, and RealNetworks digital music sites over the digital distribution of the songs I wrote. The judge ruled against me on the digital stuff because of the wording in my contract, but I did get my full writing and publishing rights back on the Ramones songs I wrote, so that was great.

All of that stuff was just business, though. The deeper stuff was, y'know, deeper.

Like, I never once spoke to Joey again after leaving the band. Never. Think about that for a second. Crazy. But when I found out he was sick, I started feeling pretty sad about the way things had gone between us. Yeah, part of the reason I quit was because I felt like he hadn't stuck up for me at times. I already told you about all that. But he was still my *friend*, y'know? I'd always hoped we'd work things out someday, because even though I'd been frustrated with Joey before I quit, I really did miss him. Some of the best times of my life were when we were hanging out, whether it was playing poker on the bus or drinking at Paul's Lounge or riding horses at my dad's stable or whatever.

When I got the news that Joey had passed, right away I was on the phone to his family, asking if it would be okay for me to come to the funeral. That was a touchy thing for a lot of reasons, of course, but one of the main ones was because they really had to keep the details secret. If the location of the service had gotten out, every Ramones fan who was anywhere near New York would have been there. That might sound really touching and nice, but it would have made what was supposed to be a serious, quiet, family thing into a total circus.

Anyway, Joey's family said it was okay for me to come, so I flew up and rented a car to get to the funeral. When I got there, it was like some unbelievable, sad dream. I guess Joey had never been the healthiest guy I knew, but, still, it just seemed like he was one of those people who was just always going to be around. Like, nothing could defeat him, y'know? I felt a little weird, being there, because of the way I'd split on the band years ago. That definitely made it uncomfortable. But I still felt like I *had* to be there, to pay my respects to Joey. Tommy was there with Monte, but the day of the funeral, Marky Ramone was on Howard Stern's radio show, complaining that no one had invited him. I guess he didn't know that in the Jewish religion, they bury their dead within forty-eight hours, and they don't send out invitations to the funeral. I heard later that Joey had been asking for me when he was in the hospital, that he wanted to say goodbye. Which of course made everything even sadder for me.

I always stayed in touch with Dee Dee. The last time I talked to him was over the phone, when I was still in Miami, in mid-May of 2002. It was a couple months after the Ramones had been inducted into the Rock and Roll Hall of Fame, and I was saying how I was bummed out that I didn't get to be part of that. "Ah, who cares?" he said, laughing at the whole thing. "How much time do we have left, anyway?" Two weeks, later he was gone.

John passed in 2004. That was another shock; I didn't even know he'd been sick. We'd had our differences and all that, but I was still sad to hear he'd died. Compared to the rest of us, he always took the best care of himself, by far. I just figured he'd eventually turn into the grouchy old man he'd always wanted to be. But when it's your time, it's your time, I guess.

When all was said and done, I still loved the Ramones' music, and I was proud of my time in the band. Mickey Leigh understood that when he reached out to me about playing the Joey Ramone Birthday Bash in 2006. I hadn't really been playing at all, so I was kind of nervous about the idea. "You should start playing again," he told me. So I gave in and played the Bash, which turned out to be a blast. The year after that, Mickey and I played the opening of the Joey Ramone Place store in Rio de Janeiro—a whole store that sold only Joey-related stuff.

I'm a driven person. But like everybody, I guess, I'm also someone who needs a push once in a while. Joey Ramone was the guy who pushed me to start writing songs in the first place, way back when. And now here comes his little brother, pushing me to be out there playing them again. Some things just make perfect sense, y'know?

Epilogue

So it's May 19, 2018, and here I am. Back again in New York to play the Joey Ramone Birthday Bash. Exactly one year after I started this book.

A lot of stuff has happened in the space of that year, and some of it's been tough. I lost my dad in February, which was definitely the hardest thing. In November 2017, my girlfriend, Clare, and I lost our home and almost everything we had stored there in one of the wildfires that destroyed so much of California. It was almost like all that crazy messing around with fire I did when I was a kid finally caught up with me. I also toured my ass off, and, in March, we had to put down Clare's dog, Roomba, who I really loved.

Webster Hall, where the Bash was last year, is gone, too. It got sold to some company that's going to make it into a "sports-entertainment" place, which definitely sounds a lot different from when it was the Ritz. So, this year, the Bash, my fifth one—I'd play it every year, if my touring schedule allowed it—is at a club called Bowery Electric, the next block up from where CBGB's was. Tonight, the Love Triangle— me, C. J. Ramone, and Mickey Leigh—are back together again, to play all of the Ramones' *Road to Ruin* album for its fortieth anniversary. And, just like last year, we get to back up some amazing guest singers, raise some money for lymphoma research, and play to a place that's packed with insanely happy Ramones fans. And, just like last time, I can feel Joey's spirit everywhere, filling the room and surrounding the whole club. I know he's happy.

Along with Dee Dee, Johnny, and Tommy (who died in 2014), we also lost Arturo Vega, in 2013. But I can feel all of them in here, too. Everybody can. Yeah, people know how, when all the Ramones were alive, there were times when some of us didn't get along. But tonight, just like the song says, we're a happy family.

I'm pretty happy myself these days, most of the time, even though I've been through the tough personal stuff I told you about above. Mostly, I'm happy because I'm really back into playing again. In 2007, I performed a symphonic piece I arranged called "Suite for Drums and Orchestra," which is based on Leonard Bernstein's *West Side Story*, with the Pasadena Pops Orchestra. That was something really different and cool. I was the featured soloist with an orchestra, which is something I don't think many other punk drummers have done. I also played four songs on the Joey Ramone album . . . *Ya Know?*, which came out in 2012 and was put together around demos Joey made before he died. In 2011, I got to make a little speech at the ceremony in L.A. when the Ramones were given a Grammy Lifetime Achievement Award—the first and only time all three Ramones drummers were under the same roof.

Since 2010, though, I've been leading my own band. When we play live, I share drum duties with one of our two guitar players, Ben Reagan, a solid guy who's been with me since I started the band. I love it when Ben plays drums, because it gives me the chance to go out front and sing while I mix it up with the crowd. We've released two albums so far, and we're on the road six months a year, touring the US, England, Europe, South America—everywhere we can go. I also run all the business stuff, which ain't easy. So now I guess I kind of get where Johnny Ramone was coming from, when he was always worrying about money and everything. Interesting, huh?

The Ramones are always going to be a part of me, and I'm always going to be a part of them. I'm a piece of their big, crazy, amazing story. And no one can take that away from me. That's just how it is.

So here I am. Still playing. Still having fun. Still a Ramone.

Still me.

Appendix 1

Ramones Performances with Richie Ramone

1983

February 13—Utica, New York

February 17—Philadelphia, Pennsylvania

February 18—Poughkeepsie, New York

February 19—Wellesley, Massachusetts

February 20—Boston, Massachusetts

February 24—Middlebury, Vermont

March 12—Southampton, New York

March 13—Danbury, Connecticut

March 14—Burlington, Vermont

March 16—Philadelphia, Pennsylvania

March 17—Philadelphia, Pennsylvania

March 18—Brooklyn, New York

March 19—Brooklyn, New York

March 23—Washington, D.C.

March 24—Washington, D.C.

March 25—New Haven, Connecticut

March 26—Hartford, Connecticut

March 30—Boston, Massachusetts

March 31—Amherst, Massachusetts

April 8—Atlanta, Georgia

April 9—New Orleans, Louisiana

April 11—Beaumont, Texas

April 13—Dallas, Texas

April 14—Houston, Texas

April 15—Austin, Texas

April 16—San Antonio, Texas

April 19—Las Cruces, New Mexico

April 20—Phoenix, Arizona

April 22—Hollywood, California

April 23—San Diego, California (Jack Murphy Stadium)

April 24—Pasadena, California

April 26—Goleta, California

April 27—Santa Cruz, California

April 28—Palo Alto, California

April 29—San Francisco, California

April 30—Sacramento, California

May 2—Eugene, Oregon

May 3—Portland, Oregon

May 4—Seattle, Washington

May 5—Seattle, Washington

May 6—Vancouver, British Columbia, Canada

May 9—Denver, Colorado

May 11—St. Louis, Missouri

May 12—Kansas City, Missouri

May 13—Wichita, Kansas

May 15—Minneapolis, Minnesota

May 16—Madison, Wisconsin

May 17—Milwaukee, Wisconsin

May 19—Chicago, Illinois

May 20—Chicago, Illinois

May 21—Cleveland, Ohio

May 22—Detroit, Michigan

May 24—Indianapolis, Indiana

May 26—Columbus, Ohio

May 27—Wheeling, Illinois

May 28—Evanston, Illinois

May 29—Chicago, Illinois

May 31—Omaha, Nebraska

June 1—Des Moines, Iowa

June 2—Rockford, Illinois

June 3—Wausau, Wisconsin

June 5—Winnipeg, Manitoba, Canada

June 7—Calgary, Alberta, Canada

June 8—Edmonton, Alberta, Canada

June 10—Toronto, Ontario, Canada

June 12—Ann Arbor, Michigan

June 13—Ottawa, Ontario, Canada

June 14—Montreal, Quebec, Canada

June 20—Virginia Beach, Virginia

June 22—Raleigh, North Carolina

June 23—Columbia, South Carolina

June 24—Hallandale, Florida

June 25—Hallandale, Florida

June 26—St. Petersburg, Florida

June 29—Washington, D.C.

June 30—Washington, D.C.

July 9—Bridgeport, Connecticut

July 11—Margate, New Jersey

July 13—Wilkes-Barre, Pennsylvania

July 14—Pittsburgh, Pennsylvania

July 16—New York, New York (the Pier)

July 22—Hicksville, Ohio

July 24—Richmond, Virginia

July 27—Buffalo, New York

July 28—Roslyn, New York

July 29—Philadelphia, Pennsylvania

July 30—Cape Cod, Massachusetts

August 5—Hampton Bays, New York

August 6—Poughkeepsie, New York

August 12—Brooklyn, New York

August 13—Queens, New York

December 20—Cedar Grove, New Jersey

December 22—Poughkeepsie, New York

December 23—Hartford, Connecticut

December 27—Levittown, New York

December 29—New York, New York (the Ritz)

December 30—Providence, Rhode Island

1984

January 5—New Haven, Connecticut

January 6—Boston, Massachusetts

January 7—Queens, New York

January 12—Philadelphia, Pennsylvania

January 14—Roslyn, New York

March 9—Portland, Maine

March 10—Providence, Rhode Island

March 16—Waterbury, Connecticut

March 17—Brooklyn, New York

March 20—Washington, D.C.

March 22—Manchester, New Hampshire

March 23—Albany, New York

March 29—Hartford, Connecticut

March 30—Brockton, Massachusetts

April 6—Salisbury, Massachusetts

April 26—Charlottesville, Virginia

April 27—Bronx, New York

April 28—Rochester, New York

April 29—Storrs, Connecticut

May 4—Ithaca, New York

May 5—Cortland, New York

May 17—Garden City, New York

May 18—New Haven, Connecticut

May 19—Mount Ivy, New York

May 31—Richmond, Virginia

June 1—Norfolk, Virginia

June 8—Ellington, Connecticut

June 9—Keene, New Hampshire

June 16—Queens, New York

June 28—Providence, Rhode Island

June 29—Taunton, Massachusetts

June 30—Syracuse, New York

July 1—Washington, D.C.

August 1—Rochester, New York

August 17—Hackettstown, New Jersey

August 28—New Haven, Connecticut

August 30—Selden, New York

August 31—Hartford, Connecticut

September 2—Lido Beach, New York

September 15—Stony Brook, New York

October 5—Spring Valley, New York

October 6—Queens, New York

October 9—Washington, D.C.

October 11—North Dartmouth, Massachusetts

October 12—Providence, Rhode Island

October 13—Manchester, New Hampshire

October 19—Bethany, West Virginia

October 20—Norfolk, Virginia

October 26—Tampa, Florida (show canceled due to rain)

October 28—Hallandale, Florida

October 29—West Palm Beach, Florida

October 30—Hallandale, Florida

October 31—Gainesville, Florida

November 2—Atlanta, Georgia

November 3—Atlanta, Georgia

November 5—Destin, Florida

November 7—New Orleans, Louisiana

November 10—Houston, Texas

November 11—Austin, Texas

November 12—Dallas, Texas

November 14—Albuquerque, New Mexico

November 15—Phoenix, Arizona

November 17—Los Angeles, California

November 18—San Diego, California

November 20—Los Angeles, California

November 21—Pomona, California

November 23—San Francisco, California

November 24—Palo Alto, California

November 27—Portland, Oregon

November 29—Vancouver, British Columbia, Canada

November 30—Seattle, Washington

December 1—Eugene, Oregon

December 3—Sacramento, California

December 4—San Jose, California

December 5—Berkeley, California

December 7—Las Vegas, Nevada

December 9—Los Angeles, California

December 12—St. Louis, Missouri

December 13—Milwaukee, Wisconsin

December 14—Chicago, Illinois

December 15—Detroit, Michigan

December 16—Detroit, Michigan

December 26—West Islip, New York

December 27—New York, New York

December 28—New York, New York

December 29—Providence, Rhode Island

1985

January 3—Boston, Massachusetts

January 4—Hartford, Connecticut

January 9—Mount Vernon, New York

January 12—Asbury Park, New Jersey

January 25—Lexington, Virginia

January 30—Washington, D.C.

January 31—Washington, D.C.

February 8—Brooklyn, New York

February 12—Bronx, New York

February 14—Lowell, Massachusetts

February 15—Worcester, Massachusetts

February 16—Manchester, New Hampshire

February 17—Philadelphia, Pennsylvania

February 18—Baltimore, Maryland

February 24—London, England

February 25—London, England

February 26—London, England

February 27—London, England

March 7—Garden City, New York

March 8—Providence, Rhode Island

March 9—Brooklyn, New York

March 14—Athens, Ohio

March 15—Detroit, Michigan

March 16—Detroit, Michigan

March 18—Columbus, Ohio

March 19—Cincinnati, Ohio

March 20—Pittsburgh, Pennsylvania

March 29—Buffalo, New York

March 30—Syracuse, New York

March 31—Hamden, Connecticut

April 4—Baltimore, Maryland

April 5—Norfolk, Virginia

April 6—Newark, Delaware

April 12—Durham, New Hampshire

April 13—Trenton, New Jersey

April 27—Worcester, Massachusetts

May 3—New Haven, Connecticut

May 4—Jamesburg, New Jersey

May 5—Trenton, New Jersey

May 7—Garden City, New York

May 9—Rochester, New York

May 10—Buffalo, New York

May 12—Hartford, Connecticut

May 20—Providence, Rhode Island

May 25—Hartford, Connecticut

May 27—Blacksburg, Virginia

May 28—Richmond, Virginia

May 30—New York, New York

May 31—New York, New York

June 7—Oyster Bay, New York

June 8—Hampton Beach, New Hampshire

June 14—Scotia, New York

June 15—Brooklyn, New York

June 22—Milton Keynes, England

June 24—Dublin, Ireland

June 25—Dublin, Ireland

June 26—Belfast, Northern Ireland

June 28—Glasgow, Scotland

June 30—Roskilde, Denmark

July 1—Münster, Germany (TV show taping)

July 2—Berlin, Germany

July 3—Hamburg, Germany

July 4—Bochum, Germany

July 6—Torhout, Belgium

July 7—Werchter, Belgium

August 9—Worcester, Massachusetts

August 10—Middletown, New York

August 11—Hampton Bays, New York

August 12—New Haven, Connecticut

August 21—Boston, Massachusetts

August 22—Branford, Connecticut

August 24—Norfolk, Virginia

August 25—Washington, D.C.

August 26—Washington, D.C.

August 27—Ocean City, Maryland

September 1—Lido Beach, New York

September 20—Hartford, Connecticut

September 21—Albany, New York

October 5—Asbury Park, New Jersey

October 11—Spring Valley, New York

October 12—Providence, Rhode Island

October 13—East Meadow, New York

October 26—College Park, Maryland

November 22—Commack, New York

November 23—Lewistown, Pennsylvania

November 27—Trenton, New Jersey

November 29—Brooklyn, New York

December 31—New York, New York

1986

April 11—Fredonia, New York

April 12—Rochester, New York

April 14—Philadelphia, Pennsylvania

April 19—Burlington, Vermont

April 20—Durham, New Hampshire

April 25—Randolph, New Jersey

April 26—New Brunswick, New Jersey

May 4—London, England

May 5—London, England

May 6—London, England

May 7—Brighton, England

May 8—Poole, England

May 9—St. Austell, England

May 11—Bristol, England

May 12—Birmingham, England

May 13—Preston, England

May 14—Edinburgh, Scotland

May 15—Newcastle, England

May 17—Leeds, England

May 18—Manchester, England

May 19—Nottingham, England

June 20—Albany, New York

June 21—Hartford, Connecticut

June 22—Hampton Beach, New Hampshire

June 24—New Haven, Connecticut

June 25—Providence, Rhode Island

June 27—Brooklyn, New York

June 28—Philadelphia, Pennsylvania

June 29—Baltimore, Maryland

June 30—Norfolk, Virginia

July 1—Washington, D.C.

July 2—Washington, D.C.

July 8—Oyster Bay, New York

July 11—Trenton, New Jersey

July 12—Asbury Park, New Jersey

July 17—Pittsburgh, Pennsylvania

July 19—Detroit, Michigan

July 20—Detroit, Michigan

July 21—Cleveland, Ohio

July 22—Columbus, Ohio

July 24—Newport, Kentucky

July 25—Chicago, Illinois

July 26—Chicago, Illinois

July 27—Minneapolis, Minnesota

August 2—Veurne, Belgium

August 3—Sneek, Netherlands

August 4—Amsterdam, Netherlands

August 5—Amsterdam, Netherlands

August 31—Lido Beach, New York

September 11—San Diego, California

September 13—Los Angeles, California

September 14—Sacramento, California

September 15—San Francisco, California

September 16—San Francisco, California

September 17—Santa Clara, California

September 19—Long Beach, California

September 21—Los Angeles, California

September 22—Riverside, California

September 23—San Diego, California

September 24—West Hollywood, California

October 10—Trenton, New Jersey

October 11—Brooklyn, New York

October 16—Northampton, Massachusetts

October 17—Hartford, Connecticut

October 18—Providence, Rhode Island

October 24—Washington, D.C.

October 25—Philadelphia, Pennsylvania

October 31—Roslyn, New York

November 1—Bridgeport, Connecticut

November 3—Boston, Massachusetts

November 6—New York, New York

November 7—New York, New York

November 15—Kent, Ohio

November 16—Buffalo, New York

November 18—Montclair, New Jersey

November 21—Sayreville, New Jersey

November 22—Medford, Massachusetts

December 4—Waltham, Massachusetts

December 5—Rochester, New York

December 6—Alfred, New York

December 19—Queens, New York

December 20—Bay Shore, New York

December 31—Roslyn, New York

1987

January 3—Trenton, New Jersey

January 4—Washington, D.C.

January 23—Providence, Rhode Island

January 24—Poughkeepsie, New York

January 31—São Paulo, Brazil

February 1—São Paulo, Brazil

February 4—Buenos Aires, Argentina

February 20—Pittsburgh, Pennsylvania

February 21—Allentown, Pennsylvania

February 26—Wayne, New Jersey

February 27—Asbury Park, New Jersey

February 28—Philadelphia, Pennsylvania

March 20—Dallas, Texas

March 21—Austin, Texas

March 22—Houston, Texas

March 23—New Orleans, Louisiana

March 25—Atlanta, Georgia

March 26—Tallahassee, Florida

March 27—Tampa, Florida

March 28—Cocoa Beach, Florida

March 29—Miami Beach, Florida

April 22—Garden City, New York

April 23—Staten Island, New York

April 25—Hartford, Connecticut

April 26—New Haven, Connecticut

April 30—Williamstown, Massachusetts

May 1—Brunswick, Maine

May 2—Albany, New York

May 3—Hadley, Massachusetts

May 8—Randolph, New Jersey

May 9—Brooklyn, New York

May 15—Providence, Rhode Island

May 16—Bay Shore, New York

May 29—Darien Lake, New York

May 30—Poughkeepsie, New York

June 18—Harrisburg, Pennsylvania

June 19—Ocean City, Maryland

June 20—Philadelphia, Pennsylvania

June 26—Oyster Bay, New York

June 27—Queens, New York

June 28—Washington, D.C.

June 29—Washington, D.C.

June 30—Washington, D.C.

July 1—Norfolk, Virginia

July 21—Toronto, Ontario, Canada

July 22—Toronto, Ontario, Canada

July 23—Toronto, Ontario, Canada

July 24—Ottawa, Ontario, Canada

August 12—East Hampton, New York

Appendix 2

Lyrics

"Humankind"

Humankind, it's not fair, why should we all live in fear
Humankind, it's a test, to see who's the very best
Humankind, don't know why, no one cares who lives or dies
Humankind, don't look at me, look at yourself, what do you see

People always tellin' lies, they can keep their alibis
People knockin' at my door, how come they want more and more
People talkin' behind your back, most of them drive a Cadillac
People starin' at your clothes, I can't take it anymore

Humankind, it's a shame, some don't even know their name
Humankind are so strange, some need to be rearranged
Humankind, don't know why, no one cares who lives or dies
Humankind, don't look at me, look at yourself, what do you see

People always tellin' lies, they can keep their alibis
People knockin' at my door, how come they want more and more
People talkin' behind your back, most of them drive a Cadillac
People starin' at your clothes, I can't take it anymore

Tell me, tell me, who's to blame, for people acting this way
Tell me, tell me, what's so wrong, if humankind just got along
Tell me, tell me, tell me please, if psychiatric help is what we need

"Smash You"

Hangin' out on the avenue
Lookin' for somethin' to do
Didn't know when we first met
That you would be such a pest

Don't go callin' on the phone
I don't need your dial tone
You've been treatin' me so bad
You're the best girl that I ever had, so

Oh, oh, oh, oh baby
Go go go go, honey
Oh, don't you know
You make me wanna smash you

Smash you

Fightin' on the avenue
I'd knock some sense into you
But I know it's not enough
You think you're so damn tough

All this talk about suicide
Too many pills, too many lies

Baby, you're no good, you see
Run, run, run, get away from me

Oh, oh, oh baby
Go go go go, honey
Oh, don't you know
You make me wanna smash you

Oh, oh, oh, oh baby
Go go go go, honey
Oh, don't you know
You make me wanna smash you
Smash you

Fightin' on the avenue
You make me wanna smash you

Fightin' on the avenue
You make me wanna smash you, go

Hangin' out on the avenue
Lookin' for somethin' to do
Didn't know when we first met
That you would be such a pest

I'm sick of all your phony friends
They make me wanna smash their heads
You've been treatin' me so bad
You're the best girl that I ever had, so

Oh, oh, oh baby
Go go go go, honey
Oh, don't you know
You make me wanna smash you

Oh, oh, oh baby
Go go go go, honey
Oh, don't you know
You make me wanna smash you
Smash you

Smash You

You make me wanna smash you
Smash you

Smash you

You make me wanna smash you
Smash you

Smash you

You make me wanna smash you
Smash you

Smash you

"Somebody Put Something in My Drink"

Somebody, somebody put something in my drink, somebody

Another night out on the street
Stop in for my usual seat
Oh, bartender, please
Tanqueray and tonic's my favorite drink
I don't like anything colored or pink
That just stinks, it's not for me

It feels like somebody put something
Somebody put something in my drink
Somebody put something
Somebody put something

Blurred vision and dirty thoughts
Feel out of place, very distraught
Feel something coming on
Yeah, kick the jukebox, slam the floor
Drink, drink, drink, drink some more
I can't think
Hey, what's in that drink

It feels like somebody put something
Somebody put something in my drink
Somebody put something
Somebody put something in my drink
Somebody put something
Somebody put something in my drink

In my drink
In my drink

Somebody put something
Somebody put something in my drink

"(You) Can't Say Anything Nice"

I'm walking away from you
Don't want to be abused
Doberman eyes
Eagle claws
And your snake body says it all

You know your biggest problem
Is the way you comb your hair
And you see that it's too late now
Everybody's putting you down

You can't say anything nice
Not willing to sacrifice
Oh you can't say anything nice
You can't say anything nice
Not willing to sacrifice
Oh you can't say anything nice nice nice nice nice nice nice

Absent minded like a zombie
I can't control myself with you
Give give give, take take take
Babe I'm through, through with you

You know your biggest problem
Is the way you comb your hair
And you see that it's too late now
Everybody thinks you're a clown

You can't say anything nice
Not willing to sacrifice
Oh you can't say anything nice
You can't say anything nice
Not willing to sacrifice
Oh you can't say anything nice nice nice nice nice nice nice nice

The pain
The pain
The pain
The pain
The pain
The pain

I'm walking away from you
I don't want to be abused
Doberman eyes
Eagle claws
Your snake body says it all

You know your biggest problem
Is the way you comb your hair
And you see that it's too late now
Everybody's putting you down

You can't say anything nice
Not willing to sacrifice
Oh you can't say anything nice
Oh you can't say anything nice
Not willing to sacrifice
Oh you can't say anything nice nice nice nice nice nice nice nice

"I'm Not Jesus"

Don't wear a crown of thorns
Got no holes in my hand
Don't accuse me of that crime
Don't hang me up to dry

It's not me
It's not me
It's not me

Don't wanna die for your sins
Got no special powers
Sacrifice and sacrilege
Hey man, I wanna live

I'm not Jesus
I can't heal you

Taste my blood
it doesn't taste like wine
Can't you see this cross isn't mine
Judas must die for what he has done
Satan's watching with his gun

It's not me
It's not me
It's not me

Father, son, and Holy Ghost
Say your prayers, it's your only hope
Twelve apostles can't help you now
I'll be back to stake my ground

I'm not Jesus
I can't heal you
I'm not Jesus
I can't heal you

Don't wear a crown of thorns
Got no holes in my hand
Don't accuse me of that crime
Don't hang me up to dry

I'm not Jesus
I can't heal you
I'm not Jesus
I can't heal you

"I Know Better Now"

Nobody
Can tell me
I know
I know better now

You're a kid
You're a brat
Clean up your room
Throw out the trash
When I was your age
I heard it all
Like livin' under
Your martial law

I would think it was
For my own good
I would think it was true

But nobody
Can tell me
I know
I know better now
And nobody
Can tell me
I know
I know better now

Gotta be in early
Gotta go to school
They don't like my friends
I don't like those rules
I'm not a criminal
I'm not on drugs
Don't wait up for me
I'm out havin' fun

I would think it was
For my own good
And I would think it was true

Nobody
Can tell me
I know
I know better now
Nobody
Can tell me
I know
I know better now

Nobody
Can tell me
I know
I know better now

And nobody
Can tell me
I know
I know better now

Appendix 3

AMBULANCE

Planet You. No label CD (US), 2012. Richie Ramone appears as Richard Beau on "Tonight" and "Believe in You," recorded circa 1979–1980.

REMOD

"Life of the Party" / "Gaygirls Dance." No label 7-inch SWM1201 (US), 1980. Richie Ramone appears as Richard Beau.

VELVETEEN

"Wild Rain"* / "Preoccupied" (vocal) / "Get Wild" (dub/vocal). Atlantic 12-inch DMD 647 / 0-86995 (US), 1983. Richie Ramone appears as Richard Beau on "Wild Rain."

After Hours. Atlantic LP 80119-1-Y (US), 1983. Richie Ramone appears as Richard Beau on "Wild Rain."

FRED SCHNEIDER AND THE SHAKE SOCIETY

Fred Schneider and the Shake Society. Warner Bros LP 1-25158 (US), 1984. Richie Ramone appears as Richard Beau on "Orbit."

Fred Schneider. Reprise CD 926592-2 (US), 1991. Richie Ramone appears as Richard Beau on "Orbit."

RAMONES
Singles/EPs

"Howling at the Moon (Sha-La-La)" / "Smash You." Beggars Banquet 7-inch BEG 128 (UK), 1984.

"Chasing the Night" / "Howling at the Moon (Sha-La-La)" / "Smash You" / "Street Fighting Man." Beggars Banquet double 7-inch BEG 128D (UK), 1985.

"Chasing the Night" / "Howling at the Moon (Sha-La-La)" / "Smash You" / "Street Fighting Man." Beggars Banquet 12-inch BEG 128D (UK), 1985.

"Bonzo Goes to Bitburg" / "Daytime Dilemma." Beggars Banquet 7-inch BEG 140 (UK), 1985.

"Bonzo Goes to Bitburg" / "Daytime Dilemma" / "Go Home Annie." Beggars Banquet 12-inch BEG 140T (UK), 1985.

"Something to Believe In" / "Somebody Put Something in My Drink." Beggars Banquet 7-inch BEG 157 (UK), 1986.

"Something to Believe In" / "Somebody Put Something in My Drink" / "(You) Can't Say Anything Nice." Beggars Banquet 12-inch BEG 157T (UK), 1986.

"Something to Believe In" / "Animal Boy." Sire 7-inch 7-28599 (US), 1986.

"Crummy Stuff" / "She Belongs to Me." Beggars Banquet 7-inch BEG 167 (UK), 1986.

"Crummy Stuff" / "She Belongs to Me" / "I Don't Want to Live This Life." Beggars Banquet 12-inch BEG 167T (UK), 1986.

"A Real Cool Time" / "Life Goes On." Beggars Banquet 7-inch BEG 198 (UK), 1987. Richie Ramone appears on A-side only.

"A Real Cool Time" / "Life Goes On" / "Indian Giver." Beggars Banquet 12-inch BEG 198T (UK), 1987. Richie Ramone appears on track 1 only.

"I Wanna Live" / "Merry Christmas (I Don't Wanna Fight Tonight)." Beggars Banquet 7-inch BEG 201 (UK), 1986. Richie Ramone appears on A-side only.

"I Wanna Live" / "Merry Christmas (I Don't Wanna Fight Tonight)." Beggars Banquet 12-inch BEG 201T (UK), 1986. Richie Ramone appears on A-side only.

Albums and Compilations

Too Tough to Die. Sire CD 92 51871 (US) / Beggars Banquet CD BEGA 59 (UK), 1984. Track listing: "Mama's Boy" / "I'm Not Afraid of Life" / "Too Tough to Die" / "Durango 95" / "Wart Hog" / "Danger Zone" / "Chasing the Night" / "Howling at the Moon

(Sha-La-La)" / "Daytime Dilemma (Dangers of Love)" / "Planet Earth
1988" / "Humankind" / "Endless Vacation" / "No Go."

Animal Boy. Sire CD 92 54331 (US) / Beggars Banquet CD BEGA 70
(UK), 1986. Track listing: "Somebody Put Something in My Drink" /
"Animal Boy" / "Love Kills" / "Apeman Hop" / "She Belongs to Me" /
"Crummy Stuff" / "My Brain Is Hanging Upside Down (Bonzo Goes
to Bitburg)" / "Mental Hell" / "Eat That Rat" / "Freak of Nature" /
"Hair of the Dog" / "Something to Believe In."

Halfway to Sanity. Sire LP 9 25641-1 / CD 9 25641-2 (US) / Beggars
Banquet LP BEGA 89 / CD 89CD (UK), 1987. Track listing: "I
Wanna Live" / "Bop 'Til You Drop" / "Garden of Serenity" / "Weasel
Face" / "Go Lil' Camaro Go" / "I Know Better Now" / "Death of
Me" / "I Lost My Mind" / "A Real Cool Time" / "I'm Not Jesus" /
"Bye Bye Baby" / "Worm Man."

Ramones Mania. Sire double CD 9 25709-2 / double LP 9 25709-1
(US/Europe), 1988. Richie Ramone appears on the following tracks:
"I Wanna Live" / "Mama's Boy" / "Bop 'Til You Drop" / "Bonzo
Goes to Bitburg" / "Wart Hog" / "Animal Boy" / "Howling at the
Moon (Sha-La-La)" / "Somebody Put Something in My Drink."

All the Stuff (And More)—Volume Two. Sire CD 9 26618-2 (US),
1991. Richie Ramone appears on "I Don't Wanna Live This Life
(Anymore)."

Anthology: Hey Ho Let's Go! Warner Bros CD 8122735572 (US), 2001.
Richie Ramone appears on the following tracks: "Howling at the

Moon (Sha-La-La)" / "Mama's Boy" / "Daytime Dilemma (Dangers of Love)" / "I'm Not Afraid of Life" / "Too Tough to Die" / "Endless Vacation" / "My Brain is Hanging Upside Down" / "Somebody Put Something in My Drink" / "Something to Believe In" / "I Wanna Live" / "Garden of Serenity" / "I Don't Wanna Live This Life (Anymore)."

Loud, Fast Ramones: Their Toughest Hits. Rhino CD R2 76101 (US) / 8122-73642-2 (Europe), 2002. Richie Ramone appears on the following tracks: "Wart Hog" / "Mama's Boy" / "Somebody Put Something in My Drink" / "Garden of Serenity."

Loud, Fast Ramones: Their Toughest Hits. Rhino double CD R2 76101 (US) / 8122-76101-2 (Europe), 2002. Includes bonus disc, *Smash You!* Live 1985, recorded live at the Lyceum, London, February 25, 1985. Richie Ramone appears on the following tracks: "Wart Hog" / "Mama's Boy" / "Somebody Put Something in My Drink" / "Garden of Serenity" (disc 1); "Do You Remember Rock 'n' Roll Radio?" / "Psycho Therapy" / "Suzy Is a Headbanger" / "Too Tough to Die" / "Smash You" / "Chinese Rock" / "Howling at the Moon (Sha-La-La)" / "I Don't Wanna Go Down to the Basement" (disc 2).

Weird Tales of the Ramones. Rhino CD boxed set 8122-74662-2 (US), 2005. Richie Ramone appears on the following tracks: "Mama's Boy" / "I'm Not Afraid of Life" / "Too Tough to Die" / "Wart Hog" / "Howling at the Moon (Sha-La-La)" / "Daytime Dilemma (Dangers of Love)" / "Endless Vacation" / "My Brain Is Hanging Upside Down (Bonzo Goes to Bitburg)" (UK 12-inch version) / "Somebody Put Something in My Drink" / "Animal Boy" / "Love Kills" / "I Don't

Wanna Live This Life Anymore" / "Something to Believe In" (single version) / "I Wanna Live" / "Bop 'Til You Drop" / "I Lost My Mind" / "Garden of Serenity."

JOEY RAMONE

. . . *Ya Know?* BMG CD 83100301-2 / double LP 83100302-1 (US) / CD 53800210 2 / double LP 53800213 1 (Europe) / Random CD RR 982 (Argentina), 2012. Richie Ramone appears on the following tracks: "Going Nowhere Fast" / "What Did I Do to Deserve You?" / "Seven Days of Gloom" / "21st Century Girl."

DAN SARTAIN

Dudesblood. One Little Indian LP TPLP1169 LP / CD TPLP1169CD (UK), 2014. Richie Ramone appears on "Love Is Suicide."

THE ROCK 'N' ROLL RATS

Rebel '67 EP. Empire Records of Canada CD 001 (Canada), 2014. Track listing: "Rebel '67" / "Dark Shadows" / "Bernadette" / "Sick of the City" / "I'm Right You're Wrong."

THE ANDERSON STINGRAYS

"Summerville Beach." RTTB digital download, 2015.

THE GOBSHITES

Various Artists. *Poxmen of the Horslypse: A Tribute to Horslips.* Shite 'n' Onions LP SNOLP003 / 7-inch SNOPL003-7 A (US), 2017. Richie Ramone appears on "The Man Who Built America" (included as a bonus split single with the Larkin Brigade).

RICHIE RAMONE

Singles/EPs

"I Fix This" / "Pretty Poison." Outro 7-inch OUTRO-002 (US), 2017.

"The Last Time." Outro 7-inch flexi-disc (given away with *New Noise* magazine) / digital download (US), 2018.

Albums

Entitled. DC-Jam CD DCJ-0061 / LP DCJ0062 (US), 2013. Track listing: "Criminal" / "I Know Better Now" / "Entitled" / "Take My Hand" / "Smash You" / "Better Than Me" / "Someday Girl" / "Into the Fire" / "I'm Not Jesus" / "Humankind" / "Vulnerable" / "Forgotten Years."

Cellophane. DC-Jam CD DCJ16001 (US) / Rusty Knuckles LP RKM044 (US), 2016. Track listing: "Braggadocio" / "I Fix This" / "Cellophane" / "Your Worst Enemy" / "Pretty Poison" / "Enjoy the Silence" / "Just to Be Clear" / "What?" / "I'm Not Ready."